With love, I dedicate this collection to my big sister,
Linda Marmysz-Macioci, who, when I was a child, brought me to see
many movies that I probably should not have been allowed to watch.

Cinematic Nihilism

Encounters, Confrontations, Overcomings

John Marmysz

EDINBURGH
University Press

Edinburgh University Press is one of the leading university presses in
the UK. We publish academic books and journals in our selected subject
areas across the humanities and social sciences, combining cutting-edge
scholarship with high editorial and production values to produce academic
works of lasting importance. For more information visit our website:
edinburghuniversitypress.com

Edinburgh University Press Ltd
The Tun – Holyrood Road
12 (2f) Jackson's Entry
Edinburgh EH8 8PJ

Typeset in 11/13 Monotype Ehrhardt by
Servis Filmsetting Ltd, Stockport, Cheshire,
and printed and bound in Great Britain by
CPI Group (UK) Ltd, Croydon CR0 4YY

A CIP record for this book is available from the British Library

ISBN 978 1 4744 2456 1 (hardback)
ISBN 978 1 4744 2457 8 (webready PDF)
ISBN 978 1 4744 2458 5 (epub)

Contents

Figures

Acknowledgements

Thanks to the many colleagues, editors, peer reviewers, conference participants, friends and family members whose encouragement, support, comments and criticisms have helped to shape this collection.

Chapter 1 originally appeared in *Film International*, issue 68, volume 12, number 2, Spring 2014, edited by Daniel Lindvall (Sweden). A version of Chapter 2 originally appeared in the *International Journal of Scottish Theatre and Screen*, volume 7, number 1, 2014, edited by Simon Brown (Kingston University, UK). Chapter 3 originally appeared in *Screen Bodies*, volume 1, issue 1, 2016, edited by Brian Bergen-Aurand (Nanyang Technological University, Singapore). Chapter 4 is a much reworked and updated version of a paper that originally appeared in *Film and Philosophy*, volume 3, 1996, edited by Kendall D'Andrade (US). Chapter 5 originally appeared in *The Journal of Popular Culture*, volume 46, number 3, 2013, edited by Gary Hoppenstand (Michigan State University, US). A version of Chapter 6 originally appeared in *Film and Philosophy*, volume 8, 2004, edited by Dan Shaw (Lock Haven University, US). A version of Chapter 8 originally appeared in *Film and Philosophy*, volume 16, 2012, also edited by Dan Shaw.

To all of the following, I express my appreciation: The organisers of the *Hawaii International Conference on Arts and Humanities* for the opportunity to present an early version of Chapter 6 at their 2004 meeting and Chapter 5 at their 2005 meeting; David Martin-Jones, David Archibald and Karen Lury for their 2014 invitation to present an early version of Chapter 1 at a session of *Screen Seminars* at the University of Glasgow (UK); The organisers of the 2014 *Film-Philosophy* Conference, also held at the University of Glasgow, for the opportunity to present an early version of Chapter 2; Stuart Hanscomb for his invitation to present a version of Chapter 1 at the Dumfries Campus of the University of Glasgow in 2014.

I am grateful to Stuart Hanscomb and Benjamin Franks of the University of

Glasgow, Dumfries Campus for comments and suggestions on the introduction to this book, as well as for their warm hospitality while I was a visitor at their campus in 2014. I also express tremendous gratitude to Patricia O'Keefe (College of Marin, US), Katie Terezakis (Rochester Institute of Technology, US), Jonathan Weidenbaum (Berkeley College, US), Dr Juneko Robinson, Kent Daniels and Dario Goykovich for helpful comments, criticisms, suggestions and conversations on various aspects of the manuscript.

Thanks to the College of Marin for granting me a sabbatical leave in 2014, during which I completed much of the research and writing involved in this project.

Finally, I offer many thanks to my cousin Amanda McDonald and her husband Andy, my aunt Norah Smith, my late uncle Eddie Smith, my nephew Derek Mallon and his wife Sophie (as well as their two daughters, Lexi and Iona) for putting me up – and putting up with me – at various points during my sabbatical research in Scotland. I couldn't have done it without you.

Introduction: Plato's Nightmare

Figure I.1 Nihilistic abjection in *Trainspotting* (1996).

There is a tradition, the spirit of which begins at least with Plato, that judges media images as 'nihilistic' – and therefore negative – in the sense that they distract attention away from true reality, redirecting it toward representations that are merely *replicas* of reality. In contemporary times, this particular criticism has been levelled most vigorously against the movies, which arguably exercise a wider influence on worldwide popular culture than any other media form. Authors such as Thomas Hibbs and Darren Ambrose, for example, contend that the saturation of world culture by filmic illusions has led to the perpetuation of nihilism in a number of ways; none of them good.

First of all, the content of many popular films, it is claimed, promotes a nihilistic world view by encouraging widespread popular despair, passivity and/or immorality (Hibbs 2012: xiii, xiv, 4–5, 41–2, 61, 73–5, 76, 100–1, 121, 158–9). Second, in depicting idealised images of men and women that are unattainable, many popular films encourage vain aspiration on the part of gullible audiences and the exploitation of artificially created desires by those seeking to make a profit (Ambrose 2013: 147–9). Third, film imagery can often serve to anesthetise the public by engrossing audiences in illusory worlds, thus encouraging them to neglect the 'real' world of personal relationships, politics and creative change (Hibbs 2012: 100–1, 136–7, 158–9, 239; Ambrose 2013: 2–7, 147–9). There are other related complaints, but they all tend to centre on the idea that we live in an age of nihilism, and popular film too frequently serves to deepen our entanglement in this negative situation by keeping audiences focused on debasing illusions while reality passes them by. In a secular age, popular film may have replaced religion as the opiate of the masses.

Because of this generally negative assessment, the literature tends to be dominated by calls for the overcoming of nihilism (Hibbs 2012: xiv; Ambrose 2013: 5, 147–50; Stoehr 2006: 1). In this collection of essays, however, I take a different stance. Starting from the position that nihilism is not an essentially negative phenomenon, I shall suggest that the separation standing between film 'illusions' and the 'real' world is a potentially positive circumstance that actually contributes to the value and philosophical appeal of motion pictures. While it is true that film images may serve to distract audiences from the 'real' world, it is also the case that this sort of distraction inevitably calls attention to itself, thus helping to create an awareness of our separation from the full comprehension of objective reality. This is an opportunity rather than a curse in that it may encourage audiences actively to reflect on their place within the world and upon their own separation from absolute Being. This nihilistic awareness is a kind of revelation reminding us of what it means to be human. We are neither gods nor beasts, but incomplete beings vainly striving to apprehend a Truth that ultimately slips through our grasp. Such a condition is not to be overcome, but rather understood and embraced as the only one appropriate to us. Thus, far from constituting a weakness, nihilism constitutes one of the cinema's great strengths. With cinematic nihilism objective Truth is lost, but at the same time a space is opened within which the distinctively human activity of ceaseless, creative interpretation might be pursued.

WHAT IS NIHILISM?

Nihilism has a bad name. In both popular and academic circles it is, however, a concept often used with little precision or understanding. Commonly, the term 'nihilism' is deployed as an insult; a label intended to discredit any vaguely negative philosophy, movement or condition. Sometimes the charge is used in a more focused manner, being equated with some specific evil, such as the undermining of morality, the claim that Truth is non-existent, or with the general perspective that life is somehow meaningless. Typically, nihilism is characterised as harmful and dangerous, thus being portrayed as a phenomenon calling for resistance and overcoming so that it can be left behind. The term 'nihilism', then, tends to be deployed most commonly as an evaluative designation, referring to things that possess no redeeming qualities whatsoever.

However, the negativity frequently associated with the term 'nihilism' is not, in fact, an essential aspect of the philosophy itself. Rather, it stems from the negative judgments of *critics* who, in one way or another, object to the ideas endorsed by those that they accuse of being nihilists. The philosophy of nihilism holds that the highest human ideals – like Truth, Goodness, Being or Beauty – are mere projections of the human mind, and as such they can never be made objectively real. Humans are, thus, forever separated from the concretisation of these most valued objects of aspiration. As a result, to the nihilist, the real, concrete world comes to appear as substandard, always falling short of the highest ideals at the same time that the ideal world itself comes to appear like a hollow, ghostly illusion incapable of being made 'real'. But unlike the cynic who dismissively mocks empty ideals, or the sceptic who stops believing in them, or pragmatists and postmodernists in whom the desire for ideals evaporates altogether, in the nihilist, a tragic attachment remains to the very ideals that are also experienced as barren. Nihilism, thus, is a phenomenon emerging when we desire the actualisation of absolutes, but no longer have faith in the reality of those very same absolutes. In nihilism, an unbridgeable separation, or gap, intervenes between human consciousness and the 'objective' fulfilment of ideals; a gap that spurs a vain but passionate longing for resolution. Elsewhere I have used the phrase 'nihilistic incongruity' in order to describe this gap (Marmysz 2003: 61–87), and have suggested that it occurs when three conditions are present: (1) When one is separated from an object of aspiration; (2) When one feels that this separation is other than it ought to be; (3) When there is nothing that can be done to change this condition (Marmysz 2003: 71). The phenomenon of nihilistic incongruity may occur when the mind is cut off from objective Truth, producing a sort of epistemological nihilism; when actions fall short of ideal standards of Goodness, producing a form of moral nihilism; when human experience fails to encompass the fullness of Being itself, producing a kind of existential nihilism; or when objects fail to embody ideals of Beauty, producing a kind of aesthetic nihilism. While this list is not exhaustive, it does highlight some of the more common types of nihilistic detachment that are often condemned by critics as paradigms of pessimism and negativity.

Immanuel Kant (1724–1804)

This understanding of nihilism stretches back to its first use as a term of criticism levelled against Immanuel Kant and his philosophy of Transcendental Idealism. According to Kant, we can never know objective reality precisely because our understanding of the world is always filtered through, and structured by, the conceptual categories of the mind. When we perceive our world, what we perceive are the *phenomena* of reality, and never things-in-themselves. We are never in direct contact with objective reality, but with a subjective representation of reality that takes place through the mediation of our own thinking processes. Thus, the noumenal, or objective, world must always remain a mystery to us, since knowing anything requires that it first be filtered through mental concepts. For Kant, we really do have knowledge, but this knowledge is only of phenomena, and as such it is separate and distinct from whatever lies outside of our subjectively constituted conceptions (Kant 1965: 24).

Kant himself was untroubled by this conclusion, but a whole host of critics were not so content. Authors such as Jacob Hermann Obereit, Daniel Jenish and Friedrich Heinrich Jacobi saw something negative and destructive in the world view initiated by Kant's Transcendental Idealism, and it is here that the first polemical uses of the term 'nihilism' started to gain currency (Carr 1992: 13; Cho 1995: 205; Gillespie 1995: 65; Slocombe 2006: 9). These critics protested that Kantian philosophy (and German Idealism generally) had reduced the 'real', objective world to nothing by placing it beyond the grasp of human understanding. This was nihilism according to the critics, and it was an intolerable situation. If Kant was right, then there was no such thing as real knowledge. All knowledge was reduced to a subjective interpretation of the world and the real Truth was lost. Heinrich von Kleist sums up this feeling of nihilistic despair when he writes:

> I recently became acquainted with Kantian philosophy – and now I must quote you a thought from it, though I do not imagine that it will shake you as deeply or as painfully as it did me. We cannot decide whether that which we call truth is real truth or whether it only seems so . . . My sole, my highest goal has foundered and I no longer have an aim. (Goudsblom 1980: 36–7)

Anti-Kantian criticisms were among the first uses of the term 'nihilism', designating what was held to be Kant's debasing perspective on the relationship between the human mind and the world it aspired to comprehend. Traditionally, thinkers had presumed that with the proper training and discipline, the mind could grasp the nature of ultimate reality. Now, pessimism crept into the picture, making it appear that a final comprehension of Being was an idealised pipe dream; an impossibility blocked by the very structures of thought itself. If Kant is correct, the conceptual make-up of human thought inevitably intervenes between the world and us, creating a gap of nothingness, separating us from the real Truth. It is important to emphasise that Kant himself did not consider this to be such a terrible situation, since, as he suggests in *Critique of Pure Reason*, such a gap opens up the path toward progress and forward movement. Even if the target of ultimate Truth is in fact an illusion, it is a useful and desirable illusion that provides a goal toward which humans may strive, thus concentrating and focusing their efforts within the world (Kant 1965: 533). But this was of little solace to those who still harboured hope for the final reconciliation of human thought with Being itself.

Friedrich Nietzsche (1844–1900)

Today, the philosopher most commonly associated with the idea of nihilism is Friedrich Nietzsche. While it is true that Nietzsche devoted much of his writing to analysing the evils of nihilism and determining how to overcome it, his treatment of the topic also highlights certain positive aspects of the phenomenon. For Nietzsche, nihilism is not an unequivocal evil at all, but a phenomenon that is 'ambiguous' (Nietzsche 1968a: §22). Operating on ontological, epistemological, political, aesthetic, spiritual and moral levels, Nietzsche suggests that nihilism permeates all aspects of the world. It is a process at work in the heart of reality that possesses both negative *and* positive potential.

Following on the path already established by Kant, Nietzschean nihilism emphasises an inevitable separation between actual human existence and the ideals by which we orient ourselves in the world. Yet Nietzsche goes further than Kant, calling into question more than merely our ability to *know* the objective world, but also our ability successfully to live by and embody absolute principles of morality, politics, religion and aesthetics. Nihilistic distress is a result of the fact that our actual world appears to us as deficient when we compare it to our internally generated standards of Truth, Beauty, Goodness and so forth. Nietzsche blames much of our tendency toward nihilistic idealisation on the influences of Plato and of Christianity; however he also at times seems to suggest that nihilism is part of an eternally recurring cycle inscribed in the very patterns of the universe. In this sense, it is a structure of our Being; an ontological fact about the nature of our world.

Nietzsche's treatment of nihilism has consequences for all areas of human existence. 'We must accept the possibility that the world consists of an infinite number of interpretations', (Nietzsche 1974: §374) Nietzsche tells us. Whereas Kant's final stance toward the objective existence of things-in-themselves remains unclear (Nenon 2010: 30–1), and while he claims that there is an objective, common set of categorical structures governing human thought,

Nietzsche unequivocally dispenses with both the unseen thing-in-itself and Kant's framework of the Categories of the Understanding, replacing them with the notion of the will to power. The universe, in-itself, is a churning, meaningless chaos of power struggles, according to Nietzsche, and each of us is like an artist who constructs and sustains our own unique picture of reality out of this chaos through the powers of individual will. While, on the one hand, this dooms us to lives in which all objective truths must evaporate into nothingness, it, on the other hand, grants us a sort of freedom in which the very living of life becomes a creative undertaking. We all are, in a sense, artists of life, cobbling together our own unique interpretations of reality. Such is the double-edged nature of Nietzschean nihilism.

Some people are crushed by this situation while others are invigorated by it. Nietzsche makes a distinction in this regard between 'active' and 'passive' forms of nihilism (Nietzsche 1968a: §22). The passive nihilist is a person who – like Obereit, Jacobi, Jenish or Kleist – despairs in the face of the void, becoming paralysed by the absence of objective Truth. Nietzsche seems to have a great deal of disdain for passive nihilists, who he associates with pessimistic withdrawal from the world and a resentful attitude. On the other hand, Nietzsche seems to admire active nihilists, since they regard the absence of objective Truth as an opportunity that opens a path to personal liberation through the exercise of interpretive freedom. The active nihilist is like a lion who, upon encountering the void of nothingness, reacts not with fear and horror but with defiance and self-conscious, wilful vigour. Instead of taking away all purpose from life, an encounter with the void spurs the active nihilist to embrace the nothing. This recognition possesses the virtue of revealing the hollowness of conventional society's deceptive values, which most people accept as a camel-like burden, unthinkingly. This sort of rebellion serves to invigorate, rather than to depress, the active nihilist who takes joy in deflating and exposing the baselessness of 'herd morality'.

Despite his apparent admiration for the active nihilist, Nietzsche still remained committed to nihilism's overcoming. Toward the end of his writing career he began a 'revaluation of all values' (Nietzsche 1976b: §466, Nietzsche 1976c: §568) that he hoped would lay the groundwork for an 'escape' from nihilism altogether (Nietzsche 1968a: §28). For Nietzsche, 'active nihilism' was the means of this escape. It was an instrument of overcoming rather than an end in itself. According to Nietzsche, active nihilism 'reaches its maximum of relative strength as a violent force of destruction' (Nietzsche 1968a: §23), and while this 'violent force' may be useful for toppling old, decaying values, it lacks the capacity to create something new. The creation of new values requires moving beyond nihilism. It requires the innocence and playful naivety of a 'child', (Nietzsche 1976a: §1) who, according to Nietzsche's metaphor, grows out of the lion-like, active nihilism that precedes it. The *Übermensch* ('Overman' or 'Superman') is Nietzsche's vision for this new stage of being:

Man is a rope, tied between beast and overman – a rope over an abyss. A
dangerous across, a dangerous on-the-way, a dangerous looking back, a
dangerous shuddering and stopping. (Nietzsche 1976a: §4)

With the overcoming of nihilism, then, we become something more than
human. We pass from a camel-like acceptance of objective truths, over the
abyss of nihilism, and then move on to become a higher order of being that
accepts responsibility for the legislation of our own values *ex nihilio*. We
become Overmen.

For Nietzsche, nihilism is something ultimately to be overcome, and it is
the active nihilist who is the instrument of this overcoming. The passive nihilist is an object of disdain for Nietzsche precisely because such an individual
wallows in nihilism, changing nothing and leaving the world just as it is. The
active nihilist, on the other hand, is necessary in order to bring nihilism to its
'completion' (Nietzsche 1968a: §28) and thus to leave hollow ideals behind,
transforming reality into something that is no longer lacking or substandard.
So, while Nietzsche does recognise something positive in *active* nihilism, he
still thinks of nihilism itself as a condition best overcome and left behind.

Martin Heidegger (1889–1976)

Martin Heidegger is one of the great thinkers of the twentieth entury who
was inspired by Nietzsche's analysis of nihilism, but who also objected to
Nietzsche's call for the active defeat of the condition. Building on, and criti-
quing, Nietzsche's insights, Heidegger emphasises that nihilism is a part of our
very Being, and thus actively to attempt its overcoming is to fight against an
aspect of our own nature. The attempt to defeat nihilism is a mistake according
to Heidegger precisely because it fails to recognise that in the will to overcome
nihilism, we strive to cover over a part of who we are in order, vainly, to make
ourselves into something that we are not. In so doing we ironically become
ever more deeply entangled within the very condition we hoped to escape in
the first place by becoming increasingly self-alienated and inauthentic. The
solution to nihilism, according to Heidegger, is not to fight against it actively,
but passively to allow it to be what it is and to learn its lessons.

Nihilism is not separate from Being, but an integral part of the rhythms by
which the universe simultaneously reveals itself to, and conceals itself from,
human consciousness. According to Heidegger, reality is more like a process of
unfolding than it is a Kantian 'thing-in-itself'. Nonetheless, there is a parallel
to Kant in Heidegger's claim that our human world comes into existence
through the participation of human consciousness. Instead of the Categories of
Understanding, however, Heidegger outlines a variety of ontological structures
that are a part of human existence and through which the mysteries of reality

are simultaneously revealed and concealed. As humans, we find ourselves existing 'there' (*Dasein*), thrown into a world that requires us to project outside of
ourselves in pursuit of goals. Because of our finitude, the worlds we inhabit and
the projects we pursue are incapable of fully encompassing the infinite Truth of
Being, and so an essential aspect of the human condition is our 'fallenness', or
alienation from the totality of Being itself. This is nihilism. It is, in Heidegger's
words 'the default of Being' (Heidegger 1991: 214–28). Humans are sites for
the revelation of Being, and just as a pebble dropped into a pond both distorts
and exposes the nature of the water's surface, so too do the activities of human
existence both reveal and conceal the potentialities of Being. It is in the process
of Being's concealment that nihilism becomes manifest.

Heidegger concurs with the observation that nihilism consists in the alienation of human consciousness from ultimate reality, but he also cautions 'there
is nothing negative in the essence of nihilism' (Heidegger 1991: 221). In this
Heidegger characterises nihilism as a necessary component of human being-
in-the-world, consisting as it does of our inevitable and essential separation
from the totality of Being's fullness. Part of what it means to be human is to
be caught in the grips of nihilism, to be finite rather than infinite, and so the
attempt to overcome or actively do battle against nihilism in fact does a kind of
violence to the kinds of beings that we are.

Heidegger conceives the pursuit of wisdom as a *process* in the uncovering
of Being – not as an *end point* in which the Truth is grasped once and for all
– and so nihilism, or the concealment of Being, becomes an integral part of
the aspiration toward Truth. In order to engage in the *process* of uncovering
something, it must already be covered over. Thus, human aspiration towards
communion with Being necessarily involves, simultaneously, both revelation
and concealment. As we strive toward the Truth of reality, we also always
find ourselves falling away from the full realisation of that Truth. But this
is nothing to overcome, according to Heidegger. It is simply part of what it
means to be human. We are creatures of finite capacity, thrown into a world
grander and more mysterious than we can ever fully comprehend. Nihilism
is not such an awful condition if we come to embrace and cherish this situation as a necessary part of the ceaseless and potentially productive process by
which humans participate in their worlds. To overcome nihilism would be to
transcend the human condition once and for all, becoming gods or overmen.
And perhaps this is not as good as it sounds.

THE POSITIVE POTENTIAL OF NIHIILISM

The history of thought from Kant to Heidegger charts a trajectory in which we
find a developing acknowledgement of the positive potential of nihilism. If it

is part of the very Being of humans to remain cut off from the infinite mysteries of the universe while still aspiring toward the ideal of absolute Truth, then one of the benefits of embracing nihilism is that it aids us in understanding the human condition. It helps us to acknowledge who we are. Furthermore, in reminding us of our finite, imperfect nature, nihilism may encourage a sense of humility, undermining the all too common tendency we have toward various sorts of intellectual, moral or spiritual arrogance. If nihilism describes our condition, then we must always remain separated from our highest ideals, and we cannot, in the end, successfully achieve what we most passionately desire. Depressing as this might sound, it is also the case, as Kant originally suggested, that this sort of separation nevertheless opens the way to ongoing progress and discovery, since if we never achieve perfection then there always remains something more toward which to strive. After all, if we were capable of finally grasping the absolute, there would be nothing left for us to do.

It is important to emphasise that these benefits are not restricted only to what Nietzsche called 'active' nihilism. In much contemporary scholarship it is assumed that if there is a positive aspect to nihilism, it must consist only in the active undermining of false values and corrupt ideals. But this is to overlook the fact that, as Heidegger suggests, passive acceptance also at times has a constructive role to play in our world. Actively raging against circumstances that cannot be changed very often leads to the perpetuation of unnecessary suffering, destruction and cruelty while passive acquiescence to these same unchangeable circumstances can sometimes result in the dignified acceptance of the limits of human power. Nihilistic rage within a meaningless universe may at times be admirable in terms of its liveliness and energy, but it is also the case that there is, at times, a certain nobility that results from submission to the world's irresolvable absurdities. Cycles of activity followed by passivity are, in fact, common among religious and philosophical sages who find it necessary periodically to withdraw from the world before once again doing battle with the conventions and ideals of corrupt societies. This is due, no doubt, to the fact that human life exists on a continuum between activity and passivity and it is impossible – and undesirable – to occupy one extreme end of this continuum for too long. Too much activity leads to burnout; too little leads to boredom. It is within the gap between these extremes that constructive human projects unfold.

CINEMATIC NIHILISM

There has, in recent times, been a small avalanche of scholarship focusing on the issue of nihilism's relationship to film. Given what has been explored so far, this should not be surprising. Filmic representations operate by way of a separation between visual images and the things that those images are intended to represent, repeating the sort of disconnection between phenomena and noumena that is at the heart of the traditional 'problem' of nihilism. If we think of film images as akin to phenomena and the things that they are intended to represent as akin to noumena, then the problematic that originally led critics to level charges of nihilism against the philosophy of Transcendental Idealism is repeated in the very operations of movie making. As we sit in darkened cinemas, or in front of television or computer screens, our attention is directed toward pictures that entertain and amuse us while we remain disconnected and alienated from their true sources. We live in Plato's cave, watching shadows and reflections cast by a reality that we never actually experience in-itself. And like Plato, who thousands of years ago sought a way finally to overcome this form of alienated existence, many of today's media critics also desire to discover how modern audiences might be rescued from the contemporary 'cave' of cinematic nihilism in order to be reunited with some higher ideal form of Truth.

As Nietzsche observed about the concept of 'nihilism' in general, the concept of 'cinematic nihilism' is itself ambiguous. On the one hand, it suggests a nihilism *of* film, characterised by the hopeless separation between audiences, filmic representations and the things that those representations are meant to depict. On the other hand, 'cinematic nihilism' also suggests nihilism *in* film, which has its source internally, and is to be found in the plots of movies that depict characters experiencing alienation from their own cherished ideals. Since not all movies are *about* nihilism, not all movies are nihilistic in the latter sense. However, I want to argue, all movies, regardless of content, are nihilistic in the former sense. The passionate desire to be transported into a film world is an essential part of the cinematic experience, and yet, in fact, audiences always (1) must remain separated from film worlds by the operations of their own minds, while (2) film worlds, in turn, are also always separated from the realities they purport to depict. In this way, audiences always find themselves in a state of, at least, double separation when at the movies. This is not necessarily a negative thing, however. In fact, as I shall argue in what follows, it is precisely the nihilism *of* film that encourages us to linger in the presence of nihilism *in* film, thus giving us an opportunity to reap the potentially positive lessons found in films about nihilism.

In its essence cinema is nihilistic insofar at it necessarily operates by way of a gap between projected representations and the 'objective' reality that those representations are intended to mirror. Many commentators characterise this nihilism *of* film as especially harmful when the illusions created *within* the plots of films are such that they celebrate bad behaviour or promote negative values. In these cases, the separation between image and reality generates a world of moral nihilism, created by film-makers who glamorise evil rather than good. Such is a major complaint of Thomas Hibbs, who bemoans the destructive, nihilistic influences of films such as *Natural Born Killers* (1994) and *Basketball Diaries* (1995), both of which he blames for influencing real-life murders (Hibbs 2012: 4) and for 'coarsening our public life, desensitizing us to violence, and making us more cynical' (Hibbs 2012: 5). Following in the tradition of Plato's critique of media, Hibbs suggests that in cases like these, the illusions have taken over, and as a result our own culture becomes 'debased' (Hibbs 2012: 5). The nihilistic imagery of films like *Natural Born Killers* and *Basketball Diaries* thus, not only serves to promote destructive values, but by glamorising immoral characters, these movies also inspire viewers to emulate bad behaviours, which in turn has a damaging effect on real-life relationships and society as a whole, thus broadening rather than narrowing the gap between human behaviour and the ideal of Goodness.

The most commonly articulated solution to this sort of nihilism is inspired by Nietzsche's advice, and advocates the active harnessing of the power of filmic illusion for the purposes of value creation rather than value destruction. So it is that Hibbs praises films such as *Star Wars* (1977), *Flight 93* (2006), *Harry Potter and the Sorcerer's Stone* (2001), and *The Lord of the Rings* (2001) for their successes in offering imagery that, while often highly fantastic and disconnected from reality, still promote positive values like community, love and justice. Likewise, Darren Ambrose praises *Star Wars*, as well as avant-garde films in general, which he interprets as promoting the refusal of 'the nihilism of the simulacra and of rediscovering the world' (Ambrose 2013: 7). Additionally, Kevin Stoehr – who goes further than most others in celebrating 'active' Nietzschean nihilism – argues that in films like *The Crying Game* (1992) and *Eyes Wide Shut* (1999) we find laudatory depictions of the defeat of nihilism, which show the way toward the overcoming of our 'detached existence' (Stoehr 2006: 180, 181–94) through positive values like love, connection with others and self-creation. It seems that everyone has favourite movies they believe show the way toward nihilism's defeat.

But even if we grant that any film, in a sense, might be thought of as overcoming moral nihilism *internally* insofar as it depicts characters who are successful in *their own* embodiment of positive values, this leaves untouched the ontological separation between the image and the audience itself; the nihilism *of* film. By focusing on the positive or negative moral content *in* films, critics often seem to ignore the presence of this deeper, ontological form of nihilism, which appears still to separate audiences from the imaginary characters on the screen. Isn't this deeper form of nihilism incapable of being overcome when we are talking about film? Aren't morally positive characters still just characters; illusory projections of some absent reality from which we, as audiences, are all necessarily alienated and disconnected?

There are authors, such as Noël Carroll and Darren Ambrose, who answer these last questions with a clear 'No', claiming that film really does possess a capacity even to mend the ontological gap between image and audience. Carroll and Ambrose both suggest that there is, in fact, a harmony that exists between the cinema and human thinking in that what occurs in the movies is something like a concretised and materialised form of thought. In the flow of images that appear on a movie screen, we find something like an outward projection of the internal processes occurring in human consciousness. Techniques like editing and camera movement, they claim, mimic the ways that human concentration selects, highlights and filters particular images, stitching them together into narratives that hold our attention, and which engross us in artificial worlds of unfolding events. In the movies, we see captured images that are altered, filtered and interpreted in a manner analogous to the ways that the human mind itself constructs its own subjective reflection of reality. The lens of a movie camera is something like a human eye, these authors claim, and the scene transitions, jumpcuts, fades and so on used by film-makers to construct narratives are something like the mental processes by which we make sense of our own everyday empirical observations.

A film, then, might be thought of as resembling the interior dramas that unfold inside actual human minds. Both Carroll and Ambrose see in this a way of bridging the gap between the mind and reality, thus allowing for a 'reconnection with the world in a much deeper and profound way' (Ambrose 2013: 14). Since 'the basic elements of film engage common features of human nature', (Carroll 2003: 54) film, according to this view, has the potential to reach out and directly touch the human mind, influencing thought and holding out the promise of bridging the nihilistic gap between subject and object.

But the separation between the human mind and filmic images is only one of the gaps contributing to cinema's inherent nihilism. Even if this separation is capable of being overcome in the manner that Carroll and Ambrose contend is possible, there still remains a gap between the film images themselves and the non-mental reality that those images purport to reflect. For instance, even if the scene transitions and jumpcuts in the movie *Trainspotting* (1996) – a film Hibbs criticises for being nihilistic because it is unrealistic and 'prodrug' (Hibbs 2012: 24) – do resemble the processes of human thought, there still remains the fact that the movie purports to be about Scottish junkies, which themselves exist independent of both the film's images and the thought processes of the audience members. At the same time that there is a gap between the audience and the film, there is always also another gap between the film images and the absent reality that they purport to represent. Even if the first gap is capable of being narrowed by virtue of the close resemblance between cinematic techniques and the structures of human thought, this still leaves open the question as to whether, and how, the other gap possibly could be closed. If the camera lens is like an eye and the various forms of editing are like patterns of thinking, then the Transcendental Idealist's problematic re-emerges: but in amplified form, as now it is (1) the camera, (2) the cinematic editing techniques, *as well as* (3) the concepts of human thought that intervene between the experience of the audience and the objective, non-film world. Audiences, thus, remain at least doubly, if not triply separated from reality.

It was Plato who first famously objected that all artistic artefacts are 'three times removed from the Truth' (Plato 1997b: 597e). Because artistic imagery reflects the physical world, which in turn is a mere reflection of a higher ideal realm of pure Forms, Plato concluded that artistic representations are mere illusions. In the realm of literature, a similar complaint has more recently been articulated by Yukio Mishima; an author whose work will be examined in Chapter 9 of this collection. Mishima complained about the destructive 'corrosive function' (Mishima 1982: 8) of words. Words, Mishima claimed, separate us from lived experience (just as images do) thus promoting detachment from the world. This initial detachment of the word from reality is bad enough, he asserts, but it is magnified when others, using further words, comment on the initial words (as occurs in literary criticism), thus increasingly corroding the connection between language and life. For Mishima, the only possible solution to this alienation from reality is to abandon words altogether, and to act resolutely within the world, thus eliminating the distorting screen standing between humans and Being itself. Similarly, we might also say that the visual imagery of cinema necessarily corrodes our connection to Being as it mimics an absent reality and then itself becomes the object of reflection when regarded by viewers, who reflect upon the reflections. Consequently, if one seeks to overcome cinematic nihilism altogether, perhaps the only solution is to abandon film in the same way that Mishima recommended abandoning words.

In fact, among the critics and philosophers who bemoan the nihilistic effects of film, one does get the sense that what they are looking for is something that the cinema is fundamentally incapable of accomplishing: a mystical transformation of consciousness that reconnects viewers with the infinite Truth of Being. Both Hibbs and Ambrose point to *Star Wars* in particular as an example of a film that shows a way beyond nihilism, transforming consciousness in such a manner that viewers are reintegrated with 'another larger self' (Ambrose 2013: 2). And while I agree that *Star Wars* is an extraordinary piece of art that certainly has had a deep impact on an enormous number of people, the fact of the matter is that, like all movies, it consists of imagery that can serve only temporarily to engross viewers in a world that remains separate from the reality beyond the movie screen. Because films have limited duration and occur in a realm that is separated from the rest of our lives by a comfortable buffer zone, they can never have the same sort of transformative effect as something like religion. Whereas religion aims to modify our individual being precisely by becoming integrated into our way of life, thus improving us spiritually, cinema operates nihilistically by setting us apart from life, potentially giving us distance and perspective, but never offering a final path toward transcendence once and for all. We must always emerge from the cinematic illusion once a particular film ends, and when we do so we become starkly aware that movies and reality are not the same thing.

But this, I contend, is precisely where the power of film lies.

THE VIRTUES OF CINEMATIC NIHILISM

If a person were unable to distinguish the boundaries separating film worlds from the 'real' world, that person would be psychotic. Film viewers, when they make the decision to go to the movies, have *already* accepted the illusory nature of filmic imagery. Such spectators have already agreed to cooperate in the venture of nihilistic detachment, sitting still passively to consume images they know are cut loose from their sources. This awareness, in fact, is why it is that so many audiences are passionately disposed to sit still for horrifying, awful and unpleasant sorts of dramas when depicted on a screen. They know that the threat being represented is not actually present. It is only a movie. In this we find the real power of cinematic illusion: it calls attention to itself and in so doing creates a space within which human minds might enthusiastically linger and enjoy the free play of imagination and ongoing interpretation. While in 'real' life we recoil from fearful things and eagerly strive toward things we desire, in our engagement with film, nihilistic separation creates a buffer zone that encourages us passively, yet keenly, to linger safely in the presence of fearful or pleasant representations, giving us the opportunity to let our imaginations run free in the passionate yet always incomplete pursuit of meaning.

The nihilistic separation involved in film viewing, by virtue of being consciously chosen and affirmed, can be enjoyed, meditated upon and experienced in a manner unique from that in which our nihilistic separation in everyday life – let us call it 'single separation' – is normally experienced. Single separation typically conceals itself and is discovered only after the fact, when thought reflects upon its own operations. The separation experienced by film audiences, however, is chosen before the fact. It is a situation that we enter into knowingly, willingly and actively when we pay the price of a movie ticket.

In choosing to entertain the illusions of cinema, audiences actively choose a kind of nihilism that is at the same time a passive acceptance of nihilism. Audiences enter into a relationship with the unfamiliar, the strange and the unreal not in order to become reconciled with the nature of reality or to somehow repair their own connection with the world beyond the screen, but to be reminded of a gap that always must exist between the real and the ideal. The incongruity between what appears on the screen and what actually exists independent of the movies is not only what makes film spectatorship tolerable, it is also what makes it valuable. For instance, when watching the characters in *Trainspotting* use heroin and engage in disgusting antics, audiences are doing something different from what they would be doing if they really were interacting with Scottish junkies. They actively and consciously are choosing to engage in a process of make-believe; a process that is intimately connected with thinking about, and meditating on, the meaning of the drama before them. The ability of audiences to remain enthusiastically engrossed in, but ultimately detached from, the plight of the characters in a film such as *Trainspotting* is a consequence of the fact that the characters in the movie are mere reflections of the Scottish drug addict's real world. While Hibbs complains that this falsifies and makes a joke of the true horrors of heroin (Hibbs 2012: 132–3), I would insist that the point of going to the movies in the first place is precisely to avoid 'true' horrors in favour of their faint reflections. If the point was only to reproduce reality with unbearable verisimilitude, then audiences could choose instead to watch real people shooting up rather than actors merely pretending to engage in such behaviour. What is gained by watching a film like *Trainspotting* is not a true and accurate understanding of the life of heroin junkies, but an opportunity to think about, reflect upon and creatively interpret the various meanings and implications of what has been seen. The *process* is the point, and the power of film lies precisely in the fact that it gives us the leisure to enjoy this process by distancing us from the real world. The power of film, in other words, lies precisely in its nihilistic nature.

The attraction of audiences to images is something that philosophers such as Plato and Hegel thought to be an indication of the immature and childlike nature of the masses. They thought that the enjoyment people take in such 'picture thinking' (Hegel 1977: §788) points to a lack of spiritual development and an inability to ascend into the purely conceptual realm of thought. A focus on images, they claim, tends to distract from the reality standing behind the images, thus insulating us from the painful truths of the world and the difficult work involved in trying to understand them. This seems to be the tradition within which much of the literature on nihilism and film still works. There is a presumption, inherited from the Platonic (and later Hegelian) tradition, that pictures and images are easy on us. They don't require much effort and they insulate us from the true nature of life. And this is partially true. There is a degree of passive acceptance involved in the viewing of cinematic images. But perhaps by actively choosing this form or passivity, audiences know that they are setting the stage for the creation of a space – a buffer zone – into which actively creative interpretations and imaginings might spill. In embracing this situation might it not be the case that what is experienced is a worthwhile nihilistic exercise precisely because it involves elements both of passivity and activity? Could it be that this is something we need not overcome at all?

If, like Hibbs, we accepted that the long-term struggle with nihilism results in the 'trivialization of all aspiration, the inability to distinguish between higher and lower' (Hibbs 2012: 13), then film's nihilistic nature might be a problem. However, the logic that he and others like him follow rests, I believe, on a faulty assumption: namely that the only worthwhile aspirations are those that have the possibility of successfully reuniting us with objective targets and goals lying outside of, and independent of, human thought. Anything else, their reasoning seems to take for granted, is 'trivial' or not 'real' because too subjective and thus lacking independent stability. But if we think of our existence as one forever involved in a process of world building and creation requiring both activity and passivity, then perhaps filmic illusions are not such a threat. Perhaps we should embrace the illusions of film, using them as opportunities to engage in the process of ongoing interpretation and active thought, not for the purpose of mending the rift between our own existence and Being itself, but in order to fill our lives with interesting amusement and productive distraction, leading nowhere in particular.

By virtue of the fact that audiences have made a prior choice to be spectators, they have already actively and consciously entered into a situation that calls attention to the separation between images and reality. Audiences know as they watch cinematic representations that they are not actually in the presence of the real thing. They know that they are separated from the source of the screen imagery, and that this separation insulates them from any permanent effects that might result from an encounter with the thing-in-itself, encouraging them passively to linger with the spectacle before them. Audiences have agreed, by paying the price of a ticket, to take part in an unfolding illusion that necessarily acts as a temporary distraction from the complicated reality existing outside of the film world. While this is a circumstance of nihilism, it is not one that is merely passive and despairing, but one that is also active and affirmative insofar as it creates conditions that allow for entertainment, education, creative interpretation and the exercise of the mind's imaginative powers. As Aristotle wrote:

> Imitation is natural to man from childhood, one of his advantages over the lower animals being this, that he is the most imitative creature in the world, and learns at first by imitation. And it is also natural for all to delight in works of imitation. (Aristotle 1941: 1448b5)

CINEMATIC NIHILISM: ENCOUNTERS, CONFRONTATIONS, OVERCOMINGS

The nine essays collected together in *Cinematic Nihilism*, explore an international variety of popular films in order to expose and illustrate the ways in which an ongoing engagement with both passive and active nihilism may ultimately result in affirmative consequences that contribute to, rather than detract from, the value of life. These essays both challenge and build upon much of the scholarship that has focused on nihilism in the media, but which has generally overemphasised the negative and destructive aspects of the phenomenon. In this collection I attempt to present a corrective, re-emphasising the constructive, delightful potential of cinematic nihilism, casting it as an expression of the dynamic rhythms involved in being human.

These essays illustrate ways in which ongoing, creative reflection and interpretation are encouraged by the nihilistic separation that is part of the cinematic experience. Starting from the position that it is precisely because of this separation that audiences are willing to linger in the presence of disturbing, but illusory, themes and images, this collection scrutinises a variety of works whose very contents raise unsettling, nihilistic issues. In this way, the book addresses both the nihilistic ontology of media imagery, as well as the nihilistic content of particular films. My intention is to consider how the nihilism *of* film opens up a space to talk about nihilism *in* film. Like a series of thematically related philosophical thought experiments, my readings of particular movies trace out the logic of nihilistic thinking itself, starting with films illustrating initial encounters with nihilism, then examining films that depict confrontations with nihilism, and finally ending with films that raise issues about the overcoming of nihilism. Contrary to Kevin Stoehr, who contends that 'genuine' nihilism logically culminates either in hypocrisy or suicide (Stoehr 2006: 3), I conclude that it is actually the *overcoming* of nihilism that implies literal or metaphorical suicide (as well as totalitarian intolerance). Genuine nihilism, I find, actually promotes unending interpretation, open-mindedness and a sense of humility.

Many of the movies selected for analysis in this book are notorious for containing imagery that has been criticised as obscene, horrifying or upsetting. Films such as *Night of the Living Dead* (1968), *The Human Centipede* (2009) and *Nymphomaniac* (2013) for example, have been denounced at one time or another as morally suspect or even perverse; but this points to their suitability for a collection such as this. By demonstrating that films such as these reveal something important and surprising about the vicissitudes of nihilism, the idea is reinforced that even the most shocking cinematic illusions harbour a positive philosophical potential when approached from a sympathetic and charitable perspective. Contrary to Thomas Hibbs, who asserts that there is 'little point to watching the most toxic shows', (Hibbs 2012: xiv) I contend that by challenging ourselves to confront difficult and distressing themes and imagery, we cultivate our ability better to understand all aspects of the human condition.

Perhaps because film is one of the most far-reaching and widely consumed of contemporary art forms, previous critics and thinkers have been inordinately eager to solve the 'problem' of cinematic nihilism, precisely because they fear its potentially deleterious and damaging effects on passive minds. However, it is my position that the call to overcome cinematic nihilism ignores its potential to open up a path of unending and productive interpretation, even when the moral contents of particular films are deemed horrendously nihilistic in the worst of ways. By engaging with film illusions both actively and passively – as I attempt to do in this book – we strengthen the capacity of our minds to reason, imagine and think through ideas in a way unrestrained by some static conception of objective Truth. In so doing, the nihilistic gap existing between the real world and the whole variety of film worlds perhaps widens, but it also serves to offer a free, open space into which our interpretations may spill, mingle and propagate in uninhibited, nihilistic liberty.

PART I

Encounters

Introduction: Encounters

The initial encounter with nihilism is commonly experienced as dreadful and debasing. It announces itself as a threat to our highest ideals, evaporating our confidence in the valued and cherished 'truths' upon which we previously grounded our sense of self, world and purpose. With this crisis we find ourselves suddenly at sea, adrift in the blackness of an unfamiliar, threatening and mysterious domain where nothing is certain, nothing possesses meaning, and the world seems unreal. The guideposts that we previously relied upon and had faith in can no longer be trusted, and we are lost.

This crisis is often met with a whimper of despair. Our grandest aspirations – those hopes, desires and ambitions that we thought differentiated us from beasts – turn out to be unattainable abstractions; impossible targets that have lured us into a farcical game of chasing after illusions. Our highest objectives are revealed as mere mental projections, emanating from our own dissatisfaction with what we actually are. Whereas before the crisis of nihilism we were fortified by dreams of Truth, Being and the possibility of progress toward some form of lofty perfection, afterwards we question the point of vainly chasing after what have turned out to be unreal fabrications. Our ultimate ideals can never be made real, and with the ridiculous and pitiful pathos of a mule chasing hopelessly after a carrot on a stick, human aspirations appear absurd. It turns out that we are no better than beasts; we are, in fact, worse off because unlike other animals we unfortunately find it impossible to remain content and happy with our finite, incomplete state of being. The revelation of nihilism leaves us without aim, purpose, or meaning and we fall into despair.

But this despair is an opportunity, as it discloses to us that our previous haughtiness was rooted in a false sense of superiority, that we overestimated our powers, and that we are now in a position to abandon our past arrogance. Nihilism brings us down to earth by forcing us to confront our puniness, our failures and our finitude. It reminds us that we are not gods, and thus helps to put us back into our appropriate place.

The essays in Part I of this collection reflect on these seemingly bleak themes. In this section I consider a number of films that draw our minds to the initially disturbing, but potentially liberating, idea of the 'nothing' that stands between human consciousness and the world outside of consciousness. The essays here examine, meditate upon and scrutinise initial encounters with nihilism as depicted in the movies.

In Chapter 1, 'Scotland as a Site of Nihilistic Sacrifice', the films *The Wicker Man* (1973), *Breaking the Waves* (1996) and *NEDs* (2010) are examined in terms of how they help to illustrate Nietzsche's discussion, from *Beyond Good and Evil*, about the progressive stages of sacrifice leading toward total nihilism. Here, the question is raised, 'What would a completely nihilistic sacrifice look like?' In this chapter the question is imperfectly answered, but it nonetheless helps to open the way toward a deeper understanding of just what an encounter with the abyss must entail.

The country of Scotland returns in Chapter 2, 'The Myth of Scotland as Nowhere in Particular'. In this chapter, a peculiar phenomenon is examined involving a crop of movies – including *Prometheus* (2012), *The Dark Knight Rises* (2012), *Perfect Sense* (2011), *Under the Skin* (2013), *World War Z* (2013), and *Cloud Atlas* (2013) – set or filmed in Scotland. In these movies, Scottish settings, which in the past have commonly been mythologised as unique and deeply meaningful, instead recede into the background, becoming nothing more than empty, meaningless spaces for the unfolding of generic dramas. While this serves nihilistically to undermine the mythos of the nation's distinctive, traditional character, it also reveals the potential for Scotland to be a place like any other, granting it status as part of the wider, world community.

Chapter 3, 'Monstrous Masses: The Human Body as Raw Material', moves from films that depict the reduction of an entire nation to nothingness to looking at films in which individual humans are reduced to nothing more than physical objects. In movies such as *The Human Centipede* (2009), *Nymphomaniac* (2013), and *Videodrome* (1983), human characters are debased and relegated to the status of mere things. This debasement, however, is here shown to have ambiguous, moral implications. Though the objectification of key characters, on the one hand, promotes the nihilistic reduction of humans to meaningless bodies in motion, on the other hand, this same reduction potentially provokes a sense of sympathy in viewers who are also embodied, and thus can see their own condition reflected in the experiences of the suffering characters. Depictions of others as meaningless matter remind us of our own corporeal nature, disgusting us, titillating us, amusing us, but also moving us to empathise with the consciousnesses that we presume, by analogy with ourselves, must exist within the bodies depicted on screen.

Taken together, the chapters in Part I help us to linger in contemplation of what it is like initially to encounter nihilism without too eagerly trying to overcome or move beyond the experience itself. This lays the groundwork for Part II, in which I will examine a number of films that take things a step further, showing how, once encountered, nihilism and its implications are confronted, wrestled with and resisted.

CHAPTER I

Scotland as a Site of Nihilistic Sacrifice

Figure 1.1 Lord Summerisle (Christopher Lee) offers a sacrifice to the nature gods in *The Wicker Man* (1973).

INTRODUCTION

Friedrich Nietzsche delineates three stages in the development of sacrificial behaviour. The first stage consists of the sacrifice of particular human beings to a god. The second stage involves the sacrifice of one's own 'instincts' to a god, and the third stage culminates in the sacrifice of God Himself (Nietzsche 1968b: §55). This last stage describes the death of God and signals the 'final cruelty' of our present times. Ours is an age of nihilism, the point in history during which humans 'sacrifice God for the nothing', fulfilling a kind of nihilistic sacrifice.

The idea of nihilistic sacrifice may seem oxymoronic since, after all, sacrifices are normally thought to be for *something* rather than for *nothing* at all. Sacrifices are offered in order to sanctify and to make holy the earthly realm, and thus there seems always to be a benefit derived from such acts. If no positive consequence was anticipated in the offering of a sacrifice, then why would it be made in the first place? At the very least, must not a sacrifice be *intended* to yield some positive outcome; some sort of valuable result that outweighs the loss incurred by the sacrifice itself? Socrates, in sacrificing his own life perhaps lost everything, but he anticipated transforming the Greek world. Jesus, in dying on the cross, anticipated saving the entire human race from damnation. Even in cases like these where human beings have surrendered their own corporeal existence, they did so for some form of greater, long-lasting benefit, and not simply for nothing. What could it even mean to describe as 'sacrificial' an act that neither accomplishes anything nor that was intended to accomplish anything?

This is a complicated question, and it is one that I will attempt to think through by examining three different cinematic depictions of sacrifice, two of which clearly illustrate the possibility of Nietzsche's first two stages, and the last of which suggests the possibility of the third, nihilistic, stage. The films I have selected share a common thread insofar as they are all set in the country of Scotland. The first two films, *The Wicker Man* (1973) and *Breaking the Waves* (1996), take place in rural, northern Scotland, and both capitalise on what scholars have called the myths of Tartantry and the Kailyard (McArthur 1982: 40–69, Petrie 2000: 3) in order to depict the act of sacrifice as something disengaged from the modern world; something that, if it happens at all today, only occurs in far-flung, isolated, and 'primitive' communities. The third film, *NEDs* (2010), takes place in modern Glasgow and draws on a myth that scholars call 'Clydesideism' (Petrie 2000: 4). This myth highlights the post-industrial, gritty, urban face of Scottish cities like Glasgow that lie on the river Clyde. In *NEDs*, the sacrifice made by the main character is of a sort thinkable only in modern times and in an urban setting, and it comes very close to what may be a kind of nihilistic sacrifice.

NIHILISTIC SACRIFICE

The idea of sacrifice has long been entangled with the idea of exchange value. In this sense, the offering of a sacrifice requires that a person give up something (or someone) that is valuable in exchange for something that is even more valuable. As stated by Henri Hubert and Marcel Mauss, a sacrificial offering acts as an instrument through which some *benefit* accrues to the person or community making the sacrifice (Hubert and Mauss 1981: 9–11). The

benefit, furthermore, is normally thought to be religious in nature. In sacrificing something (or someone), an object (or person) becomes 'consecrated', and
thus acts as an 'intermediary' between the realms of the earthly and the divine
(Hubert and Mauss 1981: 11). Thus, sacrificial acts serve to create connections
between humans and God, or between the profane and the sacred. These sorts
of connections, it seems obvious to observe, are considered valuable insofar as
they reinvigorate the world with a divine presence. Humans in this way benefit
by obtaining access to the holy here on earth. They get something in return
for their sacrifice.

    However, sacrifice has also always been associated with the ideas of self-
lessness and surrender. In this sense, a true sacrifice is made when a person
or a community gives up something out of devotion to their God or for some
principle, regardless of the outcome. Here I suppose we could say that there
is still some benefit that accrues to those offering the sacrifice insofar as they
gain a renewed sense of integrity, moral worthiness or divine favour. The
sacrifices made by Socrates, Jesus, Martin Luther King Jr, (perhaps even
The Buddha?)[1] could be understood in this way. In sacrificing themselves,
these individuals achieved a moral high ground, and although they lost
their lives, they gained a kind of immortality as symbols for human aspiration. Nonetheless, it was because of their very willingness to die and to give
up everything that they achieved this status. The respect we have for these
figures is rooted in our perception that they wanted nothing for themselves in
exchange for their sacrifices.

    So, on the one hand, sacrifice involves some sort of divine benefit, but on
the other it involves devotion without the expectation of benefit. Philosophers
such as Jacques Derrida and Dennis King Keenan have noted this ambiguity,
calling the first aspect – that which is bound up with some sort of reward –
'economical' sacrifice and the second aspect – that which is completely selfless
– 'aneconomical' sacrifice. But this clearly poses a riddle, as sacrifice cannot
possibly be both economical and aneconomical at the same time. If a sacrifice is
selfless, then those who carry it out could never actually anticipate contact with
the holy, since that would be a form of personal benefit. And if sacrifice does
involve the anticipation of contact with the holy, which is a form of personal
benefit, then it cannot be selfless.

    Both Derrida and Keenan claim that this 'aporia', or paradox, rests in the
very heart of the concept of sacrifice. It is the 'question that is the essence of
sacrifice' (Keenan 2005: 3). According to Derrida, the Judeo-Christian tradition has attempted to resolve this paradox by positing a God who is hidden and
yet all-knowing. This God 'sees' and knows everything that human beings do
and think, but He operates in secrecy so that humans are cut off from His calculations and judgments. Humans, thus, must act and live their lives without
ever knowing how things are going with God's calculations at the same time

that they know God is watching. In this way, humans, from their own perspective, become dissociated from the watchful 'gaze' of God, requiring that when they act, they must do so, for all practical purposes, *as if* no one is watching, and thus *as if* there is no reward for their actions. Derrida tells us that this is the true 'inauguration' of sacrifice:

> One must be just without being noticed for it. To want to be noticed means wanting recognition and payment in terms of a calculable salary, in terms of thanks [*remerciement*] or recompense. On the contrary, one must give, alms for example, without knowing, or at least by giving with one hand without the other knowing, that is, without having it known, without having it known by other men, in secret, without counting on recognition, reward, or remuneration. Without even having it known to oneself. (Derrida 1996: 107)

Sacrifice, in this Judeo-Christian sense, involves the renunciation of one's own will to the will of God, who is wholly 'other' and thus unknown. Since God is unknown, humans cannot anticipate God's calculations, and so all that remains is to submit to His mysterious and (from the human perspective) incalculable judgment. The individual human being is expected to renounce his or her finite calculations as the condition under which God makes His own infinite calculations. This allows the economic aspect of sacrifice to be pushed aside by the aneconomic aspect of sacrifice insofar as one must be motivated purely by devotion to God and not by the anticipation of any particular kind of reward.

Derrida draws on Nietzsche[2] to explain how this resolution to the paradox of sacrifice is perfected in the death of Jesus. In becoming flesh, God comes out of hiding, takes on the debts of mankind and obliterates them, thus wiping the slate clean and paying Himself back for the injustices of humans. In this way, the economy of creditor and debtor is eliminated in a single, unique event: the Crucifixion. Christ (God) sacrifices Himself to Himself for the selfless purpose of paying Himself back for the sins of mankind, thus saving all humanity from damnation. Here is an act that is both calculating and selfless, and neither calculating nor selfless. It is a true sacrifice, accomplishing what Derrida calls 'the sacrifice of sacrifice' (Derrida 1996: 114). In it we find a 'calculation that goes beyond calculation', absorbing both the economic and the aneconomic aspects into one mysterious act that is both impossible and yet which pushes the logic of sacrifice forward.

Derrida suggests that a further step may be taken past this Christian notion of sacrifice in order further to universalise the concept, making true sacrifice a real possibility for all of us. He recommends that we should internalise the idea of God, so that God is not thought of as something outside of ourselves, but as something that exists within us, as a part of our own hidden, secret, inner consciousness (Derrida 1996: 108–9). We should become our own secret witnesses and constantly sacrifice ourselves to ourselves, rather than relying on a saviour like Christ, who exists outside and apart from us. If we are able to do this, then every action we take would be an act of consecration in which our own spirits flow into the world to make it 'holy'. This would mean that the need for a transcendent realm beyond here-and-now reality would become superfluous. We would, it seems, be constantly wiping the slate clean, just as Christ's crucifixion wiped the slate clean according to Christians.

This step toward the internalisation of God constitutes the death of God as an objective presence in the world. It corresponds to the third stage of sacrifice described by Nietzsche in *Beyond Good and Evil*, and it reverses the direction of what Hegel described as the 'Unhappy Consciousness' of Christianity in his *Phenomenology of Spirit* (Hegel 1977: §207–230). Instead of the mind projecting outwards, and reifying consciousness, as God, 'into a *Thing*, into an *objective* existence', (Hegel 1977: §229) now God becomes de-reified, and reintegrated into consciousness as a facet of the mind that is hidden to us, but which still 'calls' to us, serving as the secret, internal voice of personal responsibility. Now, as Nietzsche writes, the ideas of God and sin 'seem no more important to us than a child's toy and a child's pain seem to an old man' (Nietzsche 1968b: §57). In sacrificing God, we become our own gods, and so there is no one left to whom we can offer sacrifices except ourselves. We have truly sacrificed sacrifice. This is a nihilistic sacrifice.

Nihilistic sacrifice is a sort of sacrifice accomplishing 'very little, almost nothing', (Keenan 2005: 8) and it is for this reason that Keenan thinks of it as the purest form of sacrifice. In nihilistic sacrifice, we strive to give up on sacrifice itself, and in the course of so doing, we also give up the hope for any divine reward as a result of our efforts. If God is dead, as Nietzsche proclaims, sacrifice, in the traditional, economical sense, is no longer feasible. Since consecration involves the presence of an intermediary through which divinity may flow into our world, then both humans and God, or the profane and the sacred, must be believed to exist. But if God is dead, the bridge leading from humans to the holy ceases to function. Instead of leading to God, the bridge leads to nowhere, and thus sacrifice is transformed into vain forfeiture. Nothing is gained by giving up something (or someone) valuable in an age of nihilism, and yet understood in its aneconomic sense, this sort of vain forfeiture may, strangely, appear as the purest form of sacrifice. If God is dead, then there can be no possible expectation of a benefit or a return for any sacrifices that we offer. Any 'sacrifice', then, would involve giving up something valuable in the expectation of receiving nothing whatsoever as reward. It would, thus, be an act representing the epitome of selflessness and surrender, and thus of utter self-sacrifice in the aneconomic sense. For Keenan this is precisely what true sacrifice must be:

Sacrifice must necessarily be a sacrifice for nothing, a sacrifice for no reason, no goal. It must necessarily be a nonsensical aneconomical sacrifice. (Keenan 2005: 1)

THREE SCOTTISH MYTHS: TARTANTRY, THE KAILYARD AND CLYDESIDEISM

The theme of sacrifice is one that recurs often in films utilising the country of Scotland as a backdrop. Existing on the far northern boundaries of Britain, Scotland is steeped in a history that continues to involve struggle with, and rebellion against, English domination. It is, for these reasons, a country both familiar and exotic to audiences in the West. At the same time that it is a part of British civilisation, Scotland strains against English influence. Films set in Scotland have long drawn on this ambiguity in the country's spirit, using it as a stage upon which encounters between civilisation and savagery are played out (Goode 2007, Martin-Jones 2010: 214–35). Both the rural and the urban landscapes of Scotland have served as settings for such dramas for many years, but it is only in recent times, and particularly beginning in the 1990s, that something like a indigenous Scottish film industry, which engages with authentically native issues, has begun to emerge. The motivations behind the push for a distinctively Scottish national cinema are manifold, but one of the primary, overarching reasons is a growing eagerness among Scottish film-makers to produce movies that break with some of the stereotypes and myths that have traditionally been used to characterise Scotland and its culture.

When one thinks of Scotland, no doubt images of kilted Highlanders wielding broadswords come to mind; or perhaps thoughts of the Loch Ness Monster. This typifies one of the routine forms of Scotland's depiction in cinema: as a premodern wilderness where mystery, magic and monsters still exist. In a negative sense, Scotland is often shown as a backwards, superstitious and savage place on the periphery of an otherwise civilised British Empire. In a more positive sense, Scotland has also been portrayed as a location where, because of its resistance to modern influences, communities continue to be tight knit and men remain principled and courageous. The myths of Tartantry and the Kailyard are names given by scholars to two interrelated stereotypes describing these sorts of portrayals.

The myth of Tartantry is illustrated by films like *Braveheart* (1995) and *Rob Roy* (1995), which focus on the struggles of noble Highland warriors as they battle against the corrupt and modernising influences of invading (normally English) forces. In a more negative manner, this same myth is exploited in those films that depict Scotsmen as drunken, hard-edged, backward brutes out of step with the modern world (think of Groundskeeper Willie from the television show *The Simpsons*). Whether deployed in a positive or a negative way, the myth of Tartantry depicts the land of Scotland as an insular, primal, primitive and clannish place. The myth of the Kailyard (Cabbage Patch) is an associated stereotype, which focuses on the idea of Scotland as a place where small, tight-knit communities are populated by shrewd, canny characters who, upon encountering individuals from big cities, demonstrate that the life of the small Scottish community is preferable to the hectic, fast-paced life of the modern world. *Brigadoon* (1954) is perhaps the most famous example illustrating this myth, but the film *Local Hero* (1983) is another more recent case in point. As Duncan Petrie observes, 'What unites Tartantry and Kailyard is the abdication of any engagement with the realities of the modern world. Rather than being directed towards transformation or transcendence of material conditions, the popular imagination seeks shelter in the retreat into a nostalgic mythic past' (Petrie 2000: 3).

In contrast to the myths of Tartantry and the Kailyard there is the myth of Clydesideism. This stereotype departs from Scottish rural settings instead to focus on urban life in Scottish cities along the river Clyde. These films, despite their focus on urban life, have been criticised as no less steeped in myth than either of the other categories already discussed (McArthur 1982: 40–69). Instead of tartan-draped Highland warriors and close-knit communities, here Scotland is depicted as a place populated by working class 'hard men' who toil away in coal mines or shipyards. In more recent times, since the post-World War II decline of industry in Scotland, the focus of these sorts of films has become more 'miserablist' (Martin-Jones 2010: 222) in character, dwelling especially on the lives of young men existing in poverty and who are involved with alcohol, drugs, violence and gang life. Films such as *Small Faces* (1996) and *Ratcatcher,* (1999) typify this genre.

The myths of Tartantry and the Kailyard, on one hand, and Clydesideism, on the other, represent two different ways that the landscape of Scotland has been utilised in order to evoke the distinction between the premodern and the modern worlds. Sacrifice has been a consistent and common theme in many of these movies, and so it is not surprising that the sacrificial act has taken on differing features depending upon which of these stereotypes has been emphasised. Typically, in those films exhibiting characteristics of Tartantry or the Kailyard, sacrifice is dramatised in a manner that resonates with the first two stages of sacrificial behaviour delineated by Nietzsche; namely, the sacrifice of particular human beings to a god, or the sacrifice of one's instincts to a god. In contrast, when the mythic lens shifts to a modern perspective and Clydesideism becomes the focus, the form of sacrificial behaviour depicted becomes more nihilistic, with the protagonists discovering a void in the place of God.

The Wicker Man, *Breaking the Waves* and *NEDs* offer striking illustrations of this change from the premodern to the modern form of sacrifice in films set in Scotland. In each case, the theme of sacrifice is central, but the purpose of the sacrifices depicted shifts from something intended to satisfy the gods (or God) to something directed toward no spiritual or supernatural audience whatsoever. In the case of *The Wicker Man* and *Breaking the Waves*, the myths of Tartantry and the Kailyard are deployed. Both films take place in remote Scottish locations, evoking the premodern mystique of the rural landscape and, as in the first two stages of Nietzsche's typology, the sacrifice of a particular human being, or of a particular human being's instincts, serve the purpose of supernatural appeasement. On the other hand, in *NEDs*, a film taking place in the modern, urban setting of 1970s Glasgow, individual sacrifice is depicted through the lens of Clydesideism and, as in the third stage of Nietzsche's typology, the main character's sacrifice appears absurd and nihilistic, being offered in service of nothing lasting, transcendent or holy at all. While in *The Wicker Man* and *Breaking the Waves*, the existence of the gods (or of God) remains a palpable reality, in *NEDs*, God has died and has been replaced by nothing. In what follows, I shall scrutinise the depiction of sacrifice in these three films, highlighting the manner in which the aneconomic aspect of the phenomenon becomes increasingly pronounced as we move from the earlier stages of sacrifice, as depicted in *The Wicker Man* and *Breaking the Waves*, toward the later stage, as depicted in *NEDs*.

THE WICKER MAN

The Wicker Man opens with a 'thank you' to the fictitious Lord Summerisle and the inhabitants of his island for allowing the film-makers to make a record of their native religious practices. This opening message, appearing on screen before any other images, is intended to give the story that follows a sense of documentary reality, but it also sets up a contrast between life in the isolated, insular, premodern community of Summerisle and life in the outside, modern world. This contrast erupts into discord during the opening scene of the film when an aeroplane, flown from the mainland of Scotland by police officer and lay minister Sergeant Neil Howie (Edward Woodward), makes a sea landing in the island's harbour. As a police officer, he has come to Summerisle to enforce the law. As a Christian, he brings with him a set of moral and social standards that soon prove to be completely at odds with the culture of the island. The men who greet Howie tell him that the island is private property and that he needs the permission of Lord Summerisle (Christopher Lee) in order to set foot on land. It is only after forcefully insisting on his own wider and more rightful legal authority to investigate the disappearance of a child that Howie is finally ferried from his plane by the harbour master. This initial confrontation sets the stage for a conflict that will continue throughout the film between the Christian-legal authority of modern, mainstream British culture and the Pagan-mystical authority of Lord Summerisle.

Led by their authoritarian leader, the people of the island practise a form of nature worship that is a throwback to ancient times. The life of the island is saturated with pagan practices: couples have sex openly in the fields, children are instructed in the life-giving symbolism of the phallus, locals sing bawdy songs celebrating sex, and young women dance naked and jump through bonfires. In order to reinvigorate the harvest, which the islanders rely upon for their livelihood, worship of, and sacrifice to, the gods of the earth has been re-established on this island. Lord Summerisle tells Howie that while the Christian God has died, 'Here the old gods aren't dead'. It is interesting to note that this island culture is depicted as having lived through the death of God, but instead of resting with the nihilism of modernity, its people have made the decision to look backwards in order to embrace a form of worship and faith that historically preceded the advent of the Judeo-Christian tradition. In this sense, the people of Summerisle have engaged in what Nietzsche would call 'antiquarianism', a viewpoint that looks to the past for guidance on how to live in the present (Nietzsche 1988: §3). This antiquarian perspective rejects the modern, liberal form of government for one that is rooted in ancient tradition and premodern forms of organisation. As observed by Benjamin Franks, 'The conflict between Howie and the islanders is thus apparently between two different forms of authority, one associated with liberalism, modernity and democracy and the other with tradition, pre-modernity and authoritarianism' (Franks 2005: 70).

The flourishing of this ancient type of religious practice and political organisation on Summerisle is only possible because of its remoteness from the mainland of the UK. Away from the watchful eyes of mainstream culture, the inhabitants of this land are free to practise what would otherwise be thought of as a depraved anachronism. But this is the attraction of the myths of Tartantry and the Kailyard. They promote the idea that there are still places on the periphery of civilisation where small, tight-knit communities can thrive by rejecting outside, modernising influences. In *The Wicker Man*, however, these myths take on a dark, rather than a nostalgic, perspective insofar as the backward look toward traditional Scottish pagan practices, and the community solidarity that results, are possible only on the condition that sacrifices be offered to the nature gods. As it turns out, this is precisely why Sergeant Howie has been allowed to come to the island. He has been lured in order to serve as a human sacrifice. He is to be burned to death inside a giant wicker man as part of the island's upcoming May Day festival.

'Once one sacrificed human beings to one's god' (Nietzsche 1968b: §55). This, according to Nietzsche, is the first rung of 'religious cruelty', and in the concluding scenes of *The Wicker Man*, this form of cruelty is played out with exceptional enthusiasm and gleefulness. Because the previous year's harvest was a failure, Lord Summerisle has decreed the need to offer appeasement to the gods of the sun and the orchards in return for more successful future harvests. The sort of reasoning that he engages in here is economical in character, presuming that the sacrificial act will be paid back in agricultural benefit to the community. Howie warns Lord Summerisle that this logic is faulty, and rationalises that if it is carried through, then when the harvest again fails, the only sacrifice that will suffice in the minds of the villagers will be that of the Lord himself. Lord Summerisle, however, turns the economical logic of sacrifice back upon Howie. He points out that by virtue of his own beliefs Howie should actually be happy about being sacrificed. As a Christian, he professes belief in an afterlife where he will spend eternity in God's heaven. Lord Summerisle observes that this is, thus, a rare opportunity for him. The sergeant is being granted the chance for martyrdom. He is being given the chance to die for his faith, to triumph in the end and to sit with his God. What greater reward could there be? He will get to die like Jesus!

The sergeant appears to be conflicted about this logic, and as the film draws to a close, he wavers back and forth between begging for his life, casting curses and singing hymns. On the one hand, Howie is terrified to die. As a member of the modern world, he fears that death brings sheer nothingness. On the other, his Christian beliefs tell him that there is something on the 'other side'. Like Lord Summerisle and the islanders, Howie harbours a conviction at some level that there will be a return on this investment. His own sacrifice could not be for nothing at all. It should yield some reward in heaven. But there is no way of being sure until the deed is done. So it is that as Howie is dragged toward the terrifying, looming figure of the wicker man, and as he is locked inside its massive thatched torso, his screams of 'Jesus Christ!' are ambiguous. We are not sure if he is invoking his God as a sign of faith or if he is using his God's name in vain.

This final sacrificial scene concludes with Howie being burned to death. As the flames and the smoke overcome him, his screams of 'Jesus Christ!' are mixed together with the sickening, terrified shrieks of the other animals – a cow, chickens, sheep – that are also burned to death in the wicker man. These sounds of raw fear and pain are in contrast to the sounds of the villagers who joyously dance and sing as their sacrifice is consumed in flames against the backdrop of a setting sun.

So it is that *The Wicker Man* illustrates Nietzsche's first stage of sacrifice. Taking place in a remote, Scottish location, and drawing on the myths of Tartantry and the Kailyard, the sacrificial act portrayed in the film is plausible only because it occurs in a community disconnected from the nihilism of modern culture. As audience members living in the contemporary world, we regard with horror the economical return that Lord Summerisle promises for the sacrifice of Howie, but part of what is interesting about this film is that it also encourages us to entertain these same feelings about the death of Jesus. Christianity, although still practised in the modern world, has its roots in the premodern world. Part of its sensibility is drawn from a time when the literal sacrifice of a human being to a god in return for some holy benefit still made sense. Today, however, our sensibilities have changed and such a sacrifice is more likely to be viewed as a horrifying act of cruelty.

BREAKING THE WAVES

In Lars von Trier's *Breaking the Waves*, the Christian God is still palpably alive, and the transition has been made to Nietzsche's second stage of sacrifice:

> Then, during the moral epoch of mankind, one sacrificed to one's god one's own strongest instincts, one's 'nature': this festive joy lights up the cruel eyes of the ascetic, the 'anti-natural' enthusiast. (Nietzsche 1968b: §55)

The setting for *Breaking the Waves* shares an affinity with the setting for *The Wicker Man* insofar as both films take place in isolated Scottish villages. Both films depict communities cut off, by matters of degree, from the modern world, allowing for the existence of beliefs and practices that appear to be from another time. However, there is a distinctive difference between the communities depicted in these films. While in *The Wicker Man*, the villagers appear gleeful and joyous in their pagan practices, in *Breaking the Waves*, the Christian villagers are depicted as repressed, anxious and gloomy. Asceticism is the norm, and this attitude is mirrored in the bleak harshness of the Scottish rural landscape. There are no orchards or May Day festivals here; only the ocean, oil rigs and severe, bearded elders who are disdainful of everyone and everything. The churches do not even have bells since, as the local minister says, 'We do not need bells in our church to worship God.'

This austere backdrop is the setting for the story of Bess (Emily Watson), a psychologically damaged young woman who falls in love with and marries Jan (Stellan Skarsgård), a Norwegian oil rig worker. Bess suffered a nervous breakdown after the death of her brother, and since then she has devoted herself to the Church and her relationship with God. She regularly speaks with God, seeking strength and guidance in His directives. When her new husband leaves to go back to the oil rig shortly after their marriage, Beth falls apart and pleads for God to return him to her. Her prayers are answered when Jan is paralysed in an accident and he comes back to the village an invalid. In this ironic fulfilment of her prayers, Bess sees evidence of her own powers. She feels both guilty and hopeful: guilty that she has brought this misfortune to her husband, but hopeful that she will be able, through self-sacrifice, to restore him to health.

Jan suggests that Bess have sex with strangers and then come back to tell him about it all as a replacement for their own lost physical intimacy. The reasons why Jan makes this suggestion may be ambiguous, but they are, as Roger Ebert correctly states, beside the point (Ebert 1996). What is important to the story is that Bess is convinced, despite her own disgust at the thought of giving herself to other men, that such self-sacrifice will heal Jan's paralysis. As she engages in progressively more and more dangerous and self-debasing behaviour, Jan's physical condition does improve. Finally, Bess knowingly subjects herself to brutalisation at the hands of a ship of sailors, faithful that in so doing, Jan's life will be saved and he will be made able to walk again. Jan is indeed made whole, but Bess also dies as a result of her injuries. In the film's final, emotionally stunning scene, the bells of Heaven ring as Bess is accepted into paradise.

God is alive and well throughout *Breaking the Waves*, but no one except Bess is truly able to hear Him. Bess at one point tells another character that her God-given skill is her ability to believe; and it is this skill that allows her to deny every instinct she has against fornicating with strangers. The first time she does so, in fact, she becomes physically ill, vomiting before going to tell Jan about the experience. It is here that Bess's bizarre form of asceticism becomes apparent. Whereas those in the community around her embrace the denial of sensual delight as their sacrifice to God, Bess interprets the repulsion she feels toward her own engagement in loveless promiscuity as a form of self-sacrifice for love of her husband. In fact, her sacrifice is the most extreme in her community, since no one else can even understand it. Everyone in the village who comes to know about Bess's behaviour condemns her or thinks she has lost her mind. She is hounded by local children who throw rocks and call her a 'tart'. Her mother won't allow her in the house and the local minister bans her from the church that she so loved. In this way, Bess's sacrifice leans toward the aneconomic side of the spectrum. She gives up her own happiness and place in the community, getting nothing in return for herself.

Yet, there is still an economic side to Bess's sacrifice insofar as she still anticipates a reward from God in the form of Jan's recovery. It is not out of sexual lust that she engages in infidelities, but out of a conviction that doing so will heal Jan, allowing him to live, even when this implies her own destruction. This is the economical logic at work in her mind. After all, it was because of her own selfishness that her husband became paralysed in the first place. God answered Bess's prayers, giving her what she wanted at Jan's expense. In order to set this straight, she must pay God back and sacrifice her own body in order to balance the scales. Like Jesus, Bess must suffer, taking on the sins of the world, forsaking her selfish desires in order to heal Jan.

In *Breaking the Waves*, Nietzsche's second stage of sacrifice is dramatised as Bess internalises the same sort of cruelty that, in *The Wicker Man*, was directed outward toward Sergeant Howie. Bess turns this viciousness inward, transforming herself into a sacrifice to God. Her strongest 'instincts' against infidelity are disobeyed, and she surrenders to the will of God in order to demonstrate her unselfish commitment and love to her husband. She lets go of her own desires in order to heal the one she most loves, and in this way moves close to the aneconomic form of sacrifice. Nonetheless, in forfeiting her own instincts, Bess does so in anticipation of a reward from God. The one she loves, Jan, will be healed, and thus there remains an economic reward in the end. Though she will die, Jan will live. Furthermore, in the film's finale, we see that Bess herself has, in fact, been rewarded with a place in Heaven for her sufferings. In terms of an economical calculation, then, it seems that Bess's sacrifice made perfect sense. Though she was willing to suffer through an incredible amount of pain, ultimately it all pays off with infinite profit to spare.

NEDS

In the films discussed so far, the myths of Tartantry and the Kailyard have been drawn upon to depict sacrifices that take place in communities exhibiting aspects of premodernity. Under these circumstances, the gods (or God) are still alive and present, watching, judging and calculating rewards and punishments. Before their watchful eyes, sacrifice remains, to a large degree, economical in nature. In the film *NEDs*, however, sacrifice becomes an almost completely aneconomical phenomenon. Unlike *The Wicker Man* and *Breaking the Waves*, both of which are set in far-flung, rural locations, *NEDs* is set in the heart of 1970s Glasgow, drawing on the myth of Clydesideism in order to depict a modern, urban, post-industrial community where God has died. In grappling with this reality, the main character engages in the 'final cruelty' of nihilistic sacrifice.

The title *NEDs* stands for 'Non-Educated Delinquents'. It tells the story of John McGill (Greg Forrest/Conor McCarron), a bright young man growing up in a violent working-class Scottish neighbourhood. His father (played by the director Peter Mullan) is an abusive drunk, his brother Benny (Joe Szula) is a petty criminal and gangster, and his mother (Louise Goodall) and aunt (Marianna Palka) are ineffectual bystanders, helplessly observing the dysfunction that unfolds around them. The film throws us into John's world as he is being promoted from grade school to middle school. After the completion of the ceremony, and unnoticed by the adults who are busy in celebration, John is accosted by an older boy who threatens to 'do him in' when he arrives at 'the big school'. John is stunned and terrified, and as the summer begins, he spends his time indoors with the curtains drawn, too scared to leave the house. When he tells his brother Benny about what happened, Benny and one of his gang mates hunt down the boy, beat him up and humiliate him in front of John.

With this incident, John starts to understand how street justice works and how this 'justice' is actually a reflection of the more accepted and visible structure of mainstream society. In the schools, teachers humiliate and beat students to keep them in line; in the home, fathers humiliate and assault their wives and children to maintain dominance; the police humiliate, beat and threaten suspects to keep order. The entire urban culture of Glasgow, it seems, is premised on the logic of dominance and submission. Humans are like caged animals, packed into the city to become factionalised into tribes and mobs that are pitted against one another in a battle for dominance. Even in church, as he assists the priest in administering communion, John is menaced by the very boy who threatened his life at school. The 'house of God', thus, is not a safe haven from urban savagery. Unlike in *The Wicker Man* and *Breaking the Waves*, in *NEDs*, there is no sacred ground or holy sanctuary. The church is a place just like any other, and John can find no refuge anywhere. Every character, including John, is left to fend for him or herself, and there is never any indication of God's comforting or protective presence.

Nietzsche writes:

> Finally – what remains to be sacrificed? At long last, did one not have to sacrifice for once whatever is comforting, holy, healing; all hope, all faith in hidden harmony, in future blisses and justices? Didn't one have to sacrifice God himself and, from cruelty against oneself, worship the stone, stupidity, gravity, fate, the nothing? To sacrifice God for the nothing – this paradoxical mystery of the final cruelty was reserved for the generation that is now coming up: all of us already know something of this. (Nietzsche 1968b: §55)

This is the point of nihilistic sacrifice, sacrifice for the nothing, and it is a step that is taken by the main character in *NEDs*. John is bright enough to excel in school, but because he sees through the hypocrisy of his teachers and of the educational and class system itself, he becomes cynical, turning toward gang life. He chooses to become a member of 'Young Car-D', spending his time drinking, using drugs and fighting with rival gangs. John's sacrifice of his educational future for life in the gang is depicted as really netting him no true benefit. Certainly he seems, at times, to enjoy the company of others, but his choice appears to be motivated more out of seething anger and fear than it is out of love for his fellow gangsters. His choice to join the gang is something

Figure 1.2 John McGill (Conor McCarron) and his former enemy walk among the lions in
NEDs (2010).

done almost on a whim, for no good reason whatsoever. It is irrational and
prompted by an overwhelming rage against the world rather than by a calculation of costs and benefits. In forfeiting his educational future, John engages
in an almost completely aneconomical sort of sacrifice made with virtually no
expectation of return or benefit. He has simply turned his anger inward, and
made a self-destructive, nihilistic leap into the abyss, sacrificing himself for
nothing at all. Later in the film, he even rejects his own gang's attempts to save
him from being beaten to death by a rival gang. This signals the juncture at
which John decides that there really is nothing to be gained from living his life.
His sacrifice has resulted in nothing.

John's nihilism is unequivocally dramatised at one point as a literal battle
with God. After beating both his father and the boy who initially threatened him early in the film almost to death, John wanders into The Glasgow
Necropolis, collapsing in a drug-induced stupor beneath a grave marker on
which a crucified Jesus hangs. John begins to talk to the figure of Christ,
telling him to come down off the cross so that the two of them can take on the
world. Jesus descends, the two of them embrace, and then they begin to fight.
They struggle with one another for a long time, and just as it looks as if Jesus
will win, John pulls a knife and stabs him to death. John has now unequivocally killed God. Of course, God was already dead in this urban, Glaswegian
setting, but now John is consciously aware of this fact. His battle with God,
significantly, takes place in a graveyard, clearly calling to mind the grim alternative to God's existence. If God dies, then the hope for an afterlife in heaven
likewise evaporates. This world can no longer be judged or justified in comparison to some other higher form of supernatural reality. This is all there is.
There is no otherworldly payoff and any sacrifices made must be understood
as valuable in themselves, and not in terms of holy rewards.

In an interview with *The Guardian*, director Peter Mullan says, 'I remember the day I killed God. It scared the fuck out of me because where do I go now?' (Clarke 2011). Later in the interview, he answers his own question, saying that one can only go 'back to humanity'. In *NEDs*, this seems to be the final message. John goes back to school and is placed in the most remedial of programmes along with the boy who initially threatened his life, but who is now brain-damaged after being beaten in the graveyard. The two of them are abandoned by their teacher in an outdoor wild animal park where, as the film concludes, the two of them walk hand-in-hand through a pride of lions that watch peacefully as they pass. The image of the two boys hesitantly making their way across this dangerous terrain seems intended to call to mind their own lives in urban Glasgow. Yet whereas in the city they regarded one another with hostility, here in the nature park they are fellow travellers through the 'wilderness'. Of course, the irony is that this is no more a wilderness than is Glasgow itself. It has been manufactured as a place where wild animals are penned up and controlled. Like the urban dwellers in modern Glasgow, the lions in this park inhabit an artificially manufactured environment that exists due to a system of control and domination. In the modern world, even the wild animals have been civilised, and for them, just as for John and his classmate, all higher authorities are absent.

CONCLUSION

By using a Nietzschean lens to scrutinise the depictions of sacrifice in *The Wicker Man*, *Breaking the Waves* and *NEDs*, we have taken some firm steps toward clarifying at least three issues. Nonetheless, one issue still remains unresolved:

1. It appears that the logic of sacrifice most often operates on a continuum between economical and aneconomical extremes. Especially in those cases where sacrifice is intended to appease the gods (or God), the expectation of holy reward is present. This expectation is strongest in Nietzsche's first two stages of sacrifice (as depicted in *The Wicker Man* and *Breaking the Waves*) and it weakens the closer that a person or culture moves toward the third stage (as depicted in *NEDs*).

2. Although the sacrifice of something (or someone) is often accompanied by the expectation of some sort of holy return, in the wake of God's death, the presupposition standing behind economical forms of sacrifice becomes eroded. This is why purely aneconomical sacrifice, if it is possible, could only occur in an atheistic world. In times when the gods (or God) are still a reality, offering economical sacrifices in anticipation of holy reward still makes sense. Only with the advent of the death of God does nihilistic sacrifice become a possibility.

3. Given that nihilistic sacrifice is a possibility only in an atheistic world, there is still the issue of how this kind of sacrifice could manifest itself concretely. Since nihilistic sacrifice occurs when a person moves to the farthest of aneconomic extremes, no reward, no benefit and no redemption is anticipated in return for the sacrificial act. There is no calculation and no anticipation of costs and benefits on the part of the one who makes such an offering. There is only a welcoming gesture toward nothingness. In the film *NEDs*, we have encountered a plausibly realistic depiction of what this sort of sacrifice could look like. Here we have a character, thrown into a world without God, who out of utter frustration and despair sacrifices any hope for success in mainstream society by rebelling against authority, embracing gang life and ultimately courting oblivion. This film does, in its concluding scenes, however, back away from complete nihilism in suggesting that the main character has experienced some redemption by 'turning back toward humanity', which leaves one final issue unresolved.

The question still remains as to what a *completely* nihilistic sacrifice would look like. Even Keenan seems to be unable to imagine that a nihilistic sacrifice could be completely aneconomic, as he writes that it accomplishes 'very little, almost nothing'. In claiming this, he seems to be suggesting that even nihilistic sacrifice contains an economical aspect, though it is an aspect that is pushed as far to the sidelines as possible. But in accomplishing 'very little', it seems that a nihilistic sacrifice still accomplishes something, leaving open the question of whether or not such a sacrifice is, in the end, truly nihilistic.

NOTES

1. Karen Armstrong suggests that The Buddha's last meal may have been intentionally poisoned, and that he knew this but ate it in order to keep others from being harmed (Armstrong 2001: 178–80).
2. Derrida's thoughts here are addressed toward Nietzsche's comments in the Second Essay of *Genealogy of Morals*, §21.

CHAPTER 2

The Myth of Scotland as Nowhere in Particular

Figure 2.1 An alien (Scarlett Johansson) wanders through Scotland, a backdrop of nothingness, in *Under the Skin* (2013).

INTRODUCTION

Chapter 1 introduced us to Tartantry, Kailyard and Clydesideism, three familiar, mythic stereotypes consistently deployed in television shows and films depicting Scots or using Scotland as a setting. Critics have very often noted that these myths offer portrayals of Scotland that are, in many ways, false idealisations (Craig 1982, McArthur 1982, Hardy 1990: 1–8, Petrie 2000, Oria Gomez 2008, Martin-Jones 2010, Balkind 2013: 5). At the same time, however, these myths have also served an important purpose in helping to shape and form an image of Scotland as a unique place with its own special essence.

In recent times a cinematic countermovement has appeared that de-emphasises Scottish uniqueness, depicting Scotland as a place largely indistinct from, or indeed interchangeable with, other locations around the globe. Authors such as Duncan Petrie, Ian Goode, David Martin-Jones, Sarah Neely, Simon Brown, Sarah Street and Nicola Balkind have previously commented on this emerging phenomenon in Scottish Cinema in which, as Brown writes, we find, 'Scotland itself literally receding into the background', so as to act as a 'mere location for a universal story' (Brown 2011: 6). While on the one hand serving to undermine some of the old, familiar and at times cherished ideals associated with Scotland, this countermovement has also helped to create a new way of thinking about the nation, emphasising it as a place much like any other, and thus highlighting it as part of a larger, world community. In this chapter I examine the nihilistic dynamics of this new cinematic countermovement, which I shall call 'the myth of Scotland as nowhere in particular'.

This new myth takes the countryside and cities of Scotland as raw material for the telling of stories having transcultural and transnational interest. In this, Scotland becomes a kind of space or clearing with no particular defining characteristics of its own that might distract from the dramas themselves, thus allowing for the unfolding of narratives that, while they use Scotland as a location, have little if anything to do with things uniquely Scottish. In trying to understand this phenomenon I shall draw upon the insights of Martin Heidegger, in particular his discussion of Being as a 'nothing' that underlies and supports the emergence of worlds. I shall argue that while Scotland has, in many contemporary films, lost a great deal of its exotic appeal by becoming a 'nothing', or a 'clearing' that lacks any intrinsic meaning of its own, this effacement of Scottish distinctiveness has also allowed for increasing attention to issues of universal – rather than just regional – significance. I conclude this chapter with an examination of a number of recent films that embody the myth of Scotland as nowhere in particular.

TRADITIONAL SCOTTISH MYTHS

Myths are meaningful stories that help to give shape and context to our understanding of reality. Unlike historical narratives, mythic stories tend to rely heavily on allegory and do not function primarily as instruments for the expression of literal facts. Instead, they operate by means of a symbolic 'pantheon' of characters and images that help us to picture in our minds the overarching nature and significance of the universe as well as our place within it (Schorer 1968: 355). Joseph Campbell calls myths 'depersonalised dreams', (Campbell 2008: 14) emphasising their reliance on symbolism that, while sometimes manifestly false or absurd, is nonetheless expressive of latent truths concerning real patterns and structures that operate in collective human thinking. In the West, with the rise of science in ancient Greece, friction developed between mythmakers and those demanding that symbolism, metaphor and storytelling be set aside in favour of the careful observation of nature and its systematic, logical explanation. Nevertheless, mythic storytelling has continued to thrive, and today exists in fields like religion, literature, theatre, television and – most importantly for our purposes – the cinema.

The most common, traditional myths concerning Scotland have characterised it as a place that is primal, mysterious and earthy; a setting rooted in unique geography, people and legends. Medieval castles, bagpipes, whisky, haggis, kilted Highland warriors and the Loch Ness Monster are the sorts of images that immediately come to mind in this regard. In numerous motion pictures released up through the present time, traces of these mythic images still remain, and thus we find a Scotland that is imagined as a location set apart from the rest of the world by a distinctive collection of people, artefacts, practices and ways of life. In film, this characterisation has commonly been idealised as a place inhabited by 'hard men' steeped in a history tying them to their soil, their families and their past. These hard Scotsmen are independent, passionate, sentimental and resistant to the encroachment of the modern 'civilised' world. The myths of Tartantry (emphasising the noble and heroic image of the Highland warrior), Kailyard (emphasising the ideal of Scotland as a place made up of tight-knit, traditional communities), and Clydesideism (emphasising the urban, often violent, face of Scotland) are three related aspects of this general mythic vision that are repeatedly drawn upon in the cinema.

Ever since Plato, thinkers have been concerned with the ways in which media images influence public perceptions of the world and of other people. Plato recognised that such images potentially can act as conduits for the Truth, but due to his commitment to a mimetic theory of art he also remained very critical of works produced by artists that were unrealistic, worrying that they could act as nihilistic distractions from the 'real' world (Plato 1997b: 514a–518e). Many contemporary critics of Scottish cinematic myths seem to carry this Platonic perspective into the present when they express indignation at films offering what they see as inaccurate and illusory depictions of Scotland, its people and their ways of life. But if the purpose of mythic stories is to express symbolic or allegorical truths rather than literal ones, then it may be productive to distance ourselves from Plato's mimetic perspective on art, keeping in mind that media imagery accomplishes something more complicated than merely imitating the world around us. If we do this, we can then raise the question of what the *very idea* of Scotland means to the people who are involved in mythmaking rather than searching for an objective collection of things 'out there' – such as premodern communities, kilts or 'hard men' – that somehow correspond, or fail to correspond, to cinematic representations. We can then use the gap opened up between reality and fantasy as a space in which to linger while examining the meaning and significance of the images themselves.

THE MYTH OF SCOTLAND AS NOWHERE IN PARTICULAR

Cinematic representations drawing on Kailyard, Tartantry and Clydesideism have tended to convey a sense of Scotland as a place that is different from the rest of the world; a unique location, where regional 'truths' not indicative of humanity as a whole are played out. I agree with David Martin-Jones's observation that such traditional Scottish myths need not be completely condemned, but 'may be productively considered as being both [positive and negative] at the same time' (Martin-Jones 2010: 223). An emphasis on Scottish uniqueness, for instance, may be helpful to develop and solidify a national identity, fostering a sense of shared community, culture and tradition. And yet, this same focus can also serve to alienate and separate Scots from non-Scots, making them think of others as fundamentally different and foreign. Traditional Scottish myths, thus, can serve both to unite and to divide people insofar as they reify 'Scottishness' into an essence that imagines Scots as inherently unlike those who originate from outside of their nation.

A new form of cinematic depiction has recently emerged, however, that, on the contrary, emphasises the ways Scotland is the same as other places in the world. In this new depiction, we find that particular, exotic things about Scotland are no longer so insistently foregrounded as fixations for audience entertainment. Rather, Scotland is offered as a more or less blank canvas against which film-makers and audiences are invited to project their own aspirations, fears, concerns and interests. This portrayal of Scotland as 'nowhere in particular' serves to solidify a new idea of Scotland as a place much like any other where human beings are born, live, struggle, suffer and die. It is a depiction of Scotland increasingly stripped of its exoticism and uniqueness, making it at times appear indistinguishable from anywhere else.

This has occurred in two related ways: First, there are films such as *Prometheus* (2012), *Perfect Sense* (2011), and *Under the Skin* (2013). These films involve storylines that, while they do take place in Scotland, do not require the country as a setting. Second, there are films such as *The Dark Knight Rises* (2012), *Cloud Atlas* (2013), and *World War Z* (2013). These movies, while being filmed (at least partly) in Scotland, nevertheless have plots that do not involve Scotland. Scottish locations, in this second group of movies, act as stand-ins for locations in other cities and places.

The first group of films – which I shall refer to as *incomplete* examples of the myth of Scotland as nowhere in particular – represent an initial step in the direction of the full obliteration of Scottish distinctiveness. These movies, while they tell stories not tied to Scotland, still make a point of identifying their Scottish settings, retaining traces of past mythology. In this regard, they are not as successful in perfectly evoking the myth as is the second group of films. This second group – which I shall refer to as *completed* examples of the myth of Scotland as nowhere in particular – take the final step in the direction of showing Scotland as nothing more than a blank backdrop containing no peculiar or unique characteristics of its own at all. Here we find 'Scotland' receding almost completely into the background and becoming indistinguishable from other locations such as Philadelphia, San Francisco, or the airspace above some anonymous, rural location.

We can see the differences between the incomplete and the completed versions of this myth clearly by comparing the opening sequences from *Prometheus* and *The Dark Knight Rises*, both major Hollywood movies released in 2012. Neither of these films have plots that involve Scotland or Scottish culture in any essential way. *Prometheus* is a science fiction tale that, while mostly set on a distant planet, begins on the Isle of Skye, while *The Dark Knight Rises* is an installment in the Batman franchise that mostly takes place in 'Gotham City', but which begins on a plane in the skies north of Inverness, Scotland.

The opening scenes from *Prometheus* are an example of the incomplete depiction of Scotland as nowhere in particular. Here, the Scottish location is explicitly announced with titles printed across the screen reading 'Isle of Skye – Scotland 2089'. A rock formation called the Old Man of Storr is prominently on display, marking this location as both picturesque and awe-inspiring. Two archaeologists (Noomi Rapace and Logan Marshall-Green) scamper across the green, rugged and exotic landscape, and proceed into a cave to investigate a painting that shows a humanoid figure pointing to the stars. The significance of this painting is later revealed when the two explorers explain to the crew of the spaceship Prometheus that the same sorts of images have been discovered in various ancient locations around the globe. They take this as an indication that the picture is in fact a map showing the way to some mysterious, far-off planet that holds the promise of revealing humankind's origin.

Nothing about this story requires that the opening should take place in a specifically Scottish setting. All that it requires is some sort of exotic, mysterious location with an ancient feel; and this is precisely the purpose served by situating this opening scene in the Scottish countryside. It is indicative of the *general sort* of place where archaeological discoveries are made, and so the exotic and premodern mythos of Scotland is purposefully evoked. The date stamp '2089', however, places the action in the far future, serving further to accentuate how removed the scene is from our own present-day experience. The landscape is thus presented as ambiguously exotic: it is both ancient and futuristic all at once. By existing in both the ancient past and the far future, it evokes a sense of timelessness. Later in the film, the Scottish cave painting is placed within the context of similar discoveries from other world locations, all of which are likewise ancient and exotic. We see artefacts from ancient Egyptian, Mayan, Sumerian, Babylonian, Hittite and Hawaiian cultures. These are all civilisations to which we look for our origins, and yet they have declined and been replaced by modern societies. Scotland is one among many locations in the world where ancient cultures and peoples once existed; a place where the cycles of history have played out and where modern humans can still discover the traces of these cycles. This is how we find in *Prometheus* an incomplete manifestation of the myth of Scotland as nowhere in particular. In this film the Scottish landscape is identified, but only insofar as it is generally symbolic of many places where ancient peoples lived and died and where their artefacts continue to be found undisturbed and intact. In this way, while Scotland is still somewhere, it is not somewhere unique.

Compare this to the opening scenes of *The Dark Knight Rises*, a film that begins aboard an American aeroplane in which CIA agents are interrogating suspected terrorists. As the plane flies over an anonymous landscape of green hills and lakes, the plane is hijacked and destroyed by Batman's (Christian Bale) arch-enemy Bane (Tom Hardy) and his henchmen, who then proceed to try and take over Gotham City. In this opening scene, there is no indication that the landscape above which the drama plays out is the highlands of Scotland. As in *Prometheus*, the opening of this film could have transpired in any number of places, but unlike in *Prometheus*, there are no attempts by the film-makers to establish by means of screen titles or dialogue where in the world the action really is occurring. This is because in *The Dark Knight Rises* there is no need to draw upon the mythos of any particular place. The drama that is the focus of the film is absolutely divorced from time and location in a way that the drama in *Prometheus* is not. Batman and his adversaries live in a fantasy world that truly is nowhere at no time. The effect produced is made possible by the fact that in the absence of any indicators concerning its real identity, the rural landscape of Scotland appears devoid of iconic or easily recognisable landmarks that could distract audiences from the timeless and placeless nature of the fantasy world in which the characters operate. If Mount Fuji, Mount Kilimanjaro or Niagara Falls were to pop into view during the course of Bane's battle with the CIA agents, audiences would be yanked out of their illusion and thrust into a distracting setting of familiar, real world markers. The action would cease to be the only point of focus, and this is not what is called for. Rather, the action requires a geography that does not call attention to itself. In the world of Batman, the landscape acts as raw material against which epic, fantasy battles play out. It is nowhere in particular, and here we see the countryside of Scotland utilised in order to evoke this mythos.

By receding completely into the background, Scotland ceases to call attention to itself at all, perfecting its purpose as a clearing, a space that is nowhere and nothing but a location for action.

THE PHILOSOPHICAL SIGNIFICANCE OF THE MYTH

So what is the philosophical significance of the myth of Scotland as nowhere in particular and what does it tell us about how the idea of Scotland has evolved in present times? In order to explore this question, we need to understand the ways in which a work of art may evoke, rather than simply imitate, a world. We can find guidance in this direction from Martin Heidegger, in particular his essay 'The Origin of the Work of Art', which focuses on how works of art provide sites within which Being itself is revealed. This will further illuminate the meaning of Scotland as a location in such films as *Perfect Sense, Under the Skin, World War Z* and *Cloud Atlas*.

According to Heidegger, 'All [artworks] have this thingly character', however, 'the artwork is something else over and above the thingly element' (Heidegger 1993a: 145). In this, he highlights the symbolic, rather than the imitative, nature of art. Artworks certainly must exist as objects, yet the function of an artistic object is to 'manifest something other; it is an allegory' (Heidegger 1993a: 145). When viewing an artwork, the minds of an audience are drawn to something beyond the visible, tangible artefact and toward the meanings that the artifact makes present. In this sense, the work itself acts as a point of focus that gathers together and embodies some sort of significance. This significance, according to Heidegger, does not consist of the mimicry of objectively present things, but is best understood as an upsurge of Truth that constitutes the evocation of a 'world'. He uses the example of a pair of peasant shoes painted by Van Gogh to illustrate the point (Van Gogh 1886). The artistry of Van Gogh's painting does not consist in the materials or the colour or the structure of the shoes themselves, but rather in 'the dark opening of the worn insides of the shoes' (Heidegger 1993a: 159), which reveal the whole world of the peasant's toil and labour; something which itself is not present to our senses. The image of the shoes only offers a site or a location within which we can find suggestions of the cycles and regularities that constituted the peasant's daily existence. What matters here is not how accurately the shoes are depicted in an objective, technical sense. What matters is how well the image of the shoes reveals and makes way for the peasant's unseen world of labour. Ultimately, any work of art 'holds open the open region of the world' in order to 'set forth the earth' (Heidegger 1993a: 170). By this Heidegger means that the purpose of art is to offer a space within which particular manifestations of Being (things) can be displayed. But as an artwork opens up a space, it also at the same time must close it down by means of the depiction of particular objects. This 'closing down' is what Heidegger elsewhere refers to as nihilism, or the 'default of Being' (Heidegger 1991: 214–28). Art, thus, operates both by revealing and by nihilistically concealing possibilities simultaneously. The space opened up by art reveals how particular objects may become manifest, and yet in their manifestation, particular objects crowd out the possibility for the appearance of other objects. According to Heidegger, this is the same sort of dynamic that we see at work in the world as a whole, and thus through art we are given the opportunity to behold an aspect of the rhythms of reality itself.

This Heideggerian perspective offers insight into what is significant about the myth of Scotland as nowhere in particular. We could say that movies evoking this myth strive to clear away, more or less completely, distracting 'things' (like kilts, haggises, 'hard men' and whisky) in order to evoke the pure opening of Being. The conundrum of course is that in striving toward this openness, film-makers have to use *something* in order to coax this *nothingness* out of hiding, and yet the moment that something makes an appearance, the pure openness of Being itself is once again nihilistically concealed. In trying to clear away distinctively Scottish symbols, then, something else must inevitably rush in to fill the space.

INCOMPLETE EVOCATIONS OF THE MYTH IN *PERFECT SENSE* AND *UNDER THE SKIN*

We can see this conundrum enacted in *Perfect Sense*, one of a crop of Scottish films evoking the (incomplete) myth of Scotland as nowhere in particular. Set in Glasgow, this film tells the story of a love affair between Michael (Ewan McGregor), a chef at a trendy restaurant, and Susan (Eva Green), a scientist who is tracking the expansion of a worldwide epidemic that robs people of their senses one by one. The twin themes of love and disease work to place the subject matter on a universal, human level that transcends any particular time or place. All people, regardless of national origin, are concerned with such experiences, of course, and the Glaswegian setting, though it is alluded to, is not a necessary component of the film's message. In fact, throughout the film we are reminded that the drama playing out within this particular city is merely part of a worldwide pandemic afflicting all of humanity. As in *Prometheus*, Scotland is simply treated as one place among many others. The story is not really about Scotland, but something universal to the human condition.

Perfect Sense goes further, however, in suggesting that the loss of attachment to particular senses may actually grant humans access to the infinity of Being itself. Preceding the loss of each sense, the film's characters experience

Figure 2.2 Glasgow: a city that could be anywhere, in *Perfect Sense* (2011).

emotional outbursts, which soon evaporate to be replaced with peaceful acquiescence. First smell is lost, then taste, then hearing and finally sight. At each step of the process, it seems initially that civilisation might collapse. Nonetheless, as the narrator informs us, 'Life goes on'. People adapt to living with decreasing sensory input, testing the boundaries of how many things can be subtracted before the world disintegrates altogether. In the final moments of the film the two lovers embrace and everything goes black as they lose their ability to see. With the evaporation of all sensible 'things', the movie ends, but we are left to consider that the most important and enduring human reality still remains. This fundamental reality is not a thing or an object at all, but the bonding power of love, which was previously obscured by all of the world's particular entanglements and distractions. In this film, it is the emptiness of the blank screen that finally evokes the true message. Take away all things, and Being still remains, which is finally revealed as pure, sublime, loving and all embracing nothingness.

Perfect Sense strives to demonstrate that we should not equate reality with the sum total of 'things' that appear in our environment. As Heidegger suggests, Being is not a thing, but the condition that allows for the emergence of things, and while the evocation of a world is made possible through the presence of tangible sensory objects, the world thus evoked is not reducible to those objects. Objects are merely conduits through which the nothingness of Being 'speaks'. In this way, we can see that the Glaswegian setting of *Perfect Sense* acts merely as a site that allows this more universal, philosophical message to be conveyed. The irony, of course, is that in order to make any film, some sort of imagery is necessary, and yet the imagery itself is not the most important focus. What is most important is to understand that as sensory objects progressively disappear, the underlying reality of Being remains. And while the ultimate point of the film is actually realised at the end when everything goes black, this point could not be made without the previous unfolding of sensory events. We need the unfolding events to appear in contrast with the nothingness of the film's conclusion in order to even have a drama in the first place. If the film consisted of nothing but blackness and void, its message would fail. The void would have no objects through which to 'speak'. It would remain mute. In this way, *Perfect Sense* does offer a completed evocation of the myth of Scotland as nowhere in particular; but only in its final moments before the roll of the credits when everything fades into nothingness. It is then that the city of Glasgow fully recedes, making way for the clearing that is pure Being itself.

Glasgow reappears to offer an incomplete evocation of the myth of Scotland as nowhere in particular in *Under the Skin*, a film focusing on a space alien (Scarlett Johansson) who trolls the streets of Glasgow in search of human victims. In this film, the specific choice of Glasgow as a location for the action is, once again, unimportant to the film's narrative.[1] As in *Perfect Sense*, we know that this is Glasgow, partly because of the broad accents of the people encountered by the main character during her journey through the streets. These accents, however, don't really serve to set the story in a particular time and place so much as to highlight the generally strange, vaguely threatening and exotic nature of the location as experienced from the perspective of the main character. As with the Scottish imagery at the beginning of *Prometheus*, the specific identity of these accents is not really what is significant; rather they act as a particular kind of marker – a 'thing' – highlighting this as a place foreign and unusual. This is a feeling reinforced by the disorienting and surreal nature of some of the film's imagery, such as the scenes where characters are lured toward, and suspended in, a weird pool of black ooze whose place and location remain puzzling. Traces of the mysterious and exotic mythos of Scotland, thus, are still present, but here they are used in order to channel a more general mood of dislocation and 'alien'ation.

In *Under the Skin*, the streets of Glasgow could be anywhere that people are difficult to understand and the territory is unfamiliar. What is evoked is not uniquely Scottish, but a universal sense of displacement, or what Heidegger terms 'homelessness' (Heidegger 1993b: 363). Part of this universal, human condition consists of being 'thrown' into a world not of our own making (Heidegger 1996: 127). In *Under the Skin*, this condition is evoked by depicting a character who has been uprooted and thrust into a city – and a skin – that is not her own. She is an alien among aliens. What is symbolised through the film's imagery is the experience of an unsettling estrangement from Being itself; an absence of any sense of belonging or connection. This is clearly articulated at one point by a Czech tourist who tells the main character that the reason he came to Scotland was precisely, 'Because it's nowhere'. He didn't come to hear bagpipes, eat haggis or to see castles. He came to lose himself in a strange, unfamiliar and foreign land. This landscape acts merely as a backdrop against which a universal drama of existential loneliness and dislocation plays out.

When the action in *Under the Skin* moves to the Scottish countryside, the backdrop becomes even more nondescript than were the dark, shadowy and disorienting streets of Glasgow. Here, the alien character makes her way along trails and through woods that give no indication of their location. The people, buildings and streets of the city are cleared away to make room for unremarkable trees, bushes and trails. Now the main character really is lost, wandering in the middle of nowhere, headed no place in particular. She ultimately meets her doom in a snow-covered field, a clearing in the woods that serves to suggest the openness of Being itself. It is here where she is exposed for what she really is: an imposter, an interloper upon this landscape who has been pretending to be human. This character, who previously was portrayed as an aggressive, otherworldly predator, is transformed into a vulnerable victim for whom we now feel sympathy. Her skin is torn away and she is exposed as a mortal, death-bound creature existing beneath the open skies and grovelling upon the surface of the earth. Here we find a powerful evocation of the universal existential condition of all mortal creatures. The closing scene of the film, which focuses on snowflakes filling an empty sky, parallels the final blackness of *Perfect Sense*. Each flake, unique and fragile, passes by, eventually to melt away, while the open sky, the backdrop of Being, remains.

COMPLETED EVOCATIONS OF THE MYTH IN *CLOUD ATLAS* AND *WORLD WAR Z*

The effacement of identifiably Scottish objects, landmarks and locations is carried out in an even more complete but less philosophically self-conscious manner in two Hollywood films: *Cloud Atlas* and *World War Z*. Like *Perfect Sense* and the first part of *Under the Skin*, and in contrast to *Prometheus* and *The Dark Knight Rises*, in these films it is urban, rather than rural, locations that act as backdrops to the storytelling. Both films are notable in their use of Glasgow as a set, which in both cases acts as a stand-in for other, US cities. In the case of *Cloud Atlas*, Glasgow's financial district is used to depict the streets of 1970s San Francisco, while in *World War Z*, Glasgow's George Square acts as a backdrop to a zombie invasion that is supposed to be taking place in Philadelphia. In neither film are Glaswegian locations ever identified. Instead, they fade into the background, providing only the space within which the action unfolds. As in *The Dark Knight Rises*, where the nondescript nature of the rural backdrop allowed for the emergence of a fantasy world, so too in *Cloud Atlas* and *World War Z*, the fantasy worlds that are evoked are made possible by the nondescript urban backdrop of Glasgow. What is brought into existence are generic, urban spaces, neither uniquely Scottish nor American, that exist nowhere in reality, and so serve perfectly to support fantastic narratives that, likewise, share no connection to real-life events.

By clearing away any distinctive Scottish markers, these completed examples of the myth succeed in evoking fantasy worlds by using a collection of buildings, streets and other 'things' as raw material. It is interesting to note that in these two films, the city of Glasgow serves as a stand-in for otherwise very different sorts of US cities: one from the East Coast and the other from the West Coast. It is significant that both Philadelphia and San Francisco themselves are capable of being evoked in this way. This may suggest that like Glasgow, these two cities could be anywhere, and that what is most important about them is not necessarily found in their locations or cultures. What is important is that they are sites in which any type of *human* action might take place. They are world cities, like New York City (which Glasgow also stood in for in *The House of Mirth* (2000)), embodying something more than simply a collection of 'things'. They embody the ideal of the metropolis within which many different sorts of *human*, not just *American* or *Scottish*, dramas unfold. Insofar as the specifically Scottish locations in *Cloud Atlas* and *World War Z* fade into the background, then, we seem to find an almost perfect evocation of the myth of Scotland as nowhere in particular. And yet, insofar as the stories told in these films still require some sort of city as a setting, the pure openness of Being remains covered over, even as it strains to 'speak' through images of buildings, roads, cars and sidewalks.

CONCLUSION

Traditionally, Scotland has been used as a setting that evokes worlds through displays of meaningful but stereotyped imagery. In films such as *Prometheus, The Dark Knight Rises, Perfect Sense, Under the Skin, Cloud Atlas* and *World War Z*, however, we have encountered something new. In these films, the rural and urban landscapes of Scotland are used in order to undermine past mythic idealisations and to provide a space within which dramas having very little (if anything) to do with Scotland unfold. In *Prometheus, Perfect Sense* and *Under the Skin* we see the incomplete effacement of Scottish 'things', while in *The Dark Knight Rises, Cloud Atlas* and *World War Z* there is a more complete accomplishment of this removal, which then makes way for non-Scottish fantasy worlds of superheroes, supervillains, foreign cities and zombies. The resulting images, by becoming disconnected from their objective sources, appeal to a cinematic experience that is more than just regionally significant. It is an experience that is transnational, transcultural and, insofar as Being itself is evoked, perhaps even transhuman in scope.

The nihilistic dynamic described in this chapter is not restricted to Scotland alone. Canadian cities like Toronto and Vancouver, the countryside of Iceland, the deserts of Jordan and the wilds of New Zealand are among some of the many other world locations commonly used as backdrops in films whose plots involve stories taking place nowhere in particular. What we find in all of these cases are landscapes stripped of their unique histories, traditions and heritages and then used as raw material in the evocation of cinematic worlds that are themselves disconnected from objective reality. This disconnection, while sometimes criticised as deceptively propagating illusion, nonetheless makes possible filmic worlds that would not otherwise exist. These fantasy worlds certainly conceal various features of reality, but they do so as part of a process that also reveals other, deeper features we might not have otherwise noticed.

NOTE

1. The book by Michel Faber upon which the movie is based, in fact, takes place in the highlands of Scotland, not in Glasgow itself (Faber 2000).

CHAPTER 3

Monstrous Masses:
The Human Body as Raw Material

Figure 3.1 Dr Heiter (Dieter Laser) explains the use of human bodies as raw material in *The Human Centipede* (2009).

> This veneer had melted, leaving soft, monstrous masses, all in disorder –
> naked, in a frightful, obscene nakedness.
>
> Jean-Paul Sartre, *Nausea*

INTRODUCTION

Depictions of the human body as raw material are common in the cinema, stimulating a wide variety of disparate responses in audiences. To portray the human body as raw material is to show it as a 'thing', as an object susceptible to the impersonal, natural forces of cause and effect. Purely physical objects may be modified, manipulated, stimulated, torn asunder and sewn back together according to any logic consistent with the laws of physics, and when the human body is depicted in this way, it becomes a potential object of fascination, disgust, horror, and sometimes even sexual titillation. Portrayals of this kind are reminders of our brute, corporeal nature, which is not governed by intellect or free will, but by the push and pull of physical impact; of violent forces having nothing at all to do with our own personal hopes or desires. Such imagery provokes us to consider the implications of embodiment and to reflect on the latent vulnerabilities – as well as the potentialities – of flesh and blood.

In this chapter I shall investigate the varied, and sometimes incongruous, reactions that audiences experience when viewing cinematic depictions of the human body as raw material. My investigation will proceed, first, by explicating an ontological distinction between *being-in-itself* and *being-for-itself*, which will allow for a clarification of the processes involved in the objectification of other human beings, both men and women. Following this, I shall then argue that in films such as *The Human Centipede*, *Nymphomaniac* and *Videodrome*, where the boundaries of bodily objectification are pushed to a nihilistic extreme, a strange thing occurs. Rather than simply resulting in the debasement of the bodies of men and women, the extremity of objectification in these films opens an empathetic potential in audiences that is related to, but not distinct from, other horrific, humorous and erotic sorts of feelings. I conclude that the objectification of human bodies in film is not only unavoidable, but also a potentially positive and productive moral exercise for audiences.

THE BODY AS AN OBJECT

Over the years, much scholarly attention has been (and continues to be) brought to bear on the objectification of human bodies – in particular the bodies of women – in the popular media (Bordo 1993, Brunner 2003, Kaplan 1983, Mulvey 2009, Tasker 1993, Williams 1999). This concern with the body and its manner of visual representation is often tied to worries about the destructive effects of objectification, centering on issues related to domination, control and human degradation. Thus, for instance, feminists like Laura Mulvey argue that cinematic depictions of the 'image of woman as (passive) raw material for the (active) gaze of man' works to reveal and to reinforce structures of patriarchy and phallocentrism in our culture (Mulvey 2009: 843). Susan Bordo develops a similar point when she argues that in the media, representations of black women's bodies in particular are often accorded the status of 'mere matter, thing-hood', thus perpetuating the historical legacy of slavery (Bordo 1993: 11). Women, it is often argued, are commonly depicted as if their whole being is encapsulated in their bodily appearance, and a recurring complaint is that this serves to propagate the idea that women are merely objects whose inner lives are of no concern to those who gain pleasure by possessing them with a look. In this, women are thus turned into 'things', less than fully human and so disposed toward being dominated, subjugated, controlled and oppressed. Simone de Beauvoir uses the term 'immanence' to refer to that quality, commonly applied to women, which classifies them principally as bodies, continuous with the natural, non-human world of other physical things. Indeed, it is the acceptance of women's relegation to the status of immanence that is the key to the whole history of women's subjugation by men according to Beauvoir (Beauvoir 1989: 61–5).

And yet this susceptibility to objectification is not unique to women. It is also a process that occurs with men. As Bordo writes, today 'women are indeed objectified more than ever, but, in this image-dominated culture, men increasingly are too' (Bordo 1993: 118). While the objectification of female bodies in the media has traditionally drawn complaints related to their perceived reification as passive and vulnerable things, depictions of the male body, it is complained, tend, on the contrary, to emphasise and reify men's supposedly active and threatening nature. Bordo observes, 'Mostly, men's bodies are presented like action-hero toys' (Bordo 1999: 191). Likewise, Thomas Schatz, developing themes in Mulvey's work, argues that Hollywood films tend to highlight male 'aggression, power and control' (Schatz 2004: 129). As with the female stereotype, such depictions are criticised for encouraging audiences to look at the male body as something with no inner life. In its 'hardness' it is solid – like an inert 'thing' – and even though depicted as active, aggressive and powerful, male characters in the media also commonly appear as shallow, with no unseen, inner vulnerabilities. They are all surface: soulless. George Yancy has observed that this sort of objectification appears in an even more extreme form when race is injected into the picture. From the perspective of the 'white gaze', black male bodies become threatening 'things', menacing in their darkness and symbolic of filth, danger and animality. They are not truly human, he argues, but something like what Heidegger calls 'standing reserve', things 'merely present-to-hand', that are 'usable and [that] can be manipulated' (Yancy 2008: 219n14). In these depictions, the black male body primarily becomes something to subdue and to master.

As we can see, much scholarship has been devoted to highlighting the ways in which the aggressive gaze of an audience can be harnessed in order to belittle and denigrate the full dignity of both women and men. However, what has not been made clear is that such denigration is always, or must *necessarily* be, the case. In what follows, I shall argue that while the objectification of both men and women is in fact an inevitability for us, this process is not always objectionable. I shall argue that it only becomes objectionable when pleasure is had at the *expense* of the full humanity of the one who is being gazed at.

Objectification, I shall claim, is not always disagreeable, but may become so when the human body is regarded as *nothing but* raw material for the pleasure of another. When regarded in this way, it becomes easy to forget that human beings are not merely 'things'. It becomes easier, as Bordo points out, to act as if their 'moral and emotional sensibilities need not be treated with consideration', (Bordo 1993: 11) thus potentially paving the way toward atrocity.[1]

BEING-IN-ITSELF VS BEING-FOR-ITSELF

Ultimately, there is no way completely to avoid making ourselves and others into objects. In order even to form a consciousness of one's 'self', a person must solidify, and thus objectify, an identity that acts as a focus of awareness. As a self, I am both one and multiple at the same time. To have a sense of 'myself' I must recognise an inner part of 'me' as it is mirrored in another inner part of 'me'. This implies a self-regarding 'turn' involving a break between differing regions of the mind, which we might call the inner *observer* and the inner *observed*.[2] The inner observer, in reflecting, makes the inner observed into an object of reflection. Without such a 'turn', no self-recognition would be possible, and thus there could be no awareness of a distinct and unique 'I'. My 'self' is, thus, split between an in-itself and a for-itself: a reflected and a reflecting. I am both subject and object. This is Hegel's point in the *Phenomenology of Spirit* when he writes, 'A self-consciousness, in being an object, is just as much "I" as "object"' (Hegel 1977: §177). When thinking about ourselves, we become objects of our own thought, in a way analogous to how our own bodies become objects when we gaze into a mirror. In this sense, self-consciousness and self-identity require objectification. Without it, 'I' would not even exist as a unique and separate being. 'I' would dissolve away into the undifferentiated mass of Being that is the universe. 'I' would become nothing at all.

Just as self-reflection requires that we encounter *ourselves* from a kind of 'inner-outside' perspective as objects, when we experience *others*, we must also encounter them from the outside, as objects that are present to, and yet outside of, our own consciousness. In this encounter, the outer other is analogous to our inner observed self. It is a thing that we reflect upon and thus that is reflected back into us. It is like our body image in the mirror; an object that stands apart and away from us. Unlike the inner self that I take as the object of my self-consciousness, however, this outer other is foreign and strange to me insofar as it is separate from both my inner observer and my inner observed. It is not me in any sense. It is merely an outer object present to my gaze. In this way, it is even more removed from me than is my own body image, which is, after all, still 'my' body image. I still retain some understanding of what is going on 'inside' that body. The true other, however, is in no way 'mine'. It is independent of my will and mysterious insofar as I lack an understanding of it from the inside. I know it purely as an external appearance. It is a mere object to me: a thing-in-itself.

When a mind takes in outer appearances, it sees them as stable and complete entities that are 'in-themselves'. Jean-Paul Sartre defines the 'in-itself' as that which 'is what it is'. It has no inside. It 'has nothing secret; it is solid' (Sartre 1992: 28). An object in-itself is purely a thing with no hidden life, no freedom and no capacity to avoid the contingencies of cause and effect. Insofar as we encounter the outer world from our own inner perspective, we are always seeing it as composed of objects; of beings in-themselves. By analogy with our own inner consciousness, however, we may infer that some of the objects 'out there' that we interact with may actually have an inner world like our own. When I look in a mirror at my own body and I have a sense that my consciousness resides inside of that reflected mass, so too I may have the sense that there exist objects in my world that possess inner minds like my own, and thus that the world outside of me is populated by other beings-for-themselves; or self-reflective consciousnesses.

Sartre defines a being-for-itself as 'being what it is not and not being what it is' (Sartre 1992: 28). Thus, if I regard others in my world as beings-for-themselves, I suppose that they are unstable and unpredictable because they possess inner, secret lives from which I am cut off. They have consciousness and the freedom to make choices. A being-for-itself possesses an inner mind that undergoes transformation and change by initiating projects; it flees from its current, present state of being in the pursuit of goals. A being-for-itself, in other words, is the kind of freely choosing and aspiring consciousness that incessantly projects away and ahead of itself, moving forward into an uncertain future. It never rests satisfied with what it is, and always pursues what it is not. As such, recalling Bordo's remarks, it has hidden, inner 'moral and emotional sensibilities' that need to be treated with consideration.

While objectification is a seemingly necessary part of the process by which human beings recognise themselves, interact with one another and by which they build their worlds, a troubling issue is apparent. If I always encounter the beings in my world from the outside, then they always appear objectified to me as beings-in-themselves. Likewise, if another being-for-itself is to encounter me, I will become objectified in his or her eyes as a foreign thing; a being-in-itself. Hegel noted this issue and saw it as the initiating confrontation that leads to a 'life-and-death struggle' (Hegel 1977: §187) between human consciousnesses. In confronting one another, two consciousnesses engage in mutual objectification, trying to solidify and fix the essence of the other and to deny the other's autonomy. We cast the other as a thing that is outside of us, which we contemplate and thus make into an object of our own reflective consciousness. This 'trial by death' (Hegel 1977: §187) kills the dynamic and lively inner nature of the other, and consequently we must, it seems, always come to treat others as things-in-themselves, since we must always come to know them from the outside and never from the inner perspective of their own conscious awareness.

In the world of cinema, this process is especially pronounced. By its very nature, the cinema is a visual medium, displaying images (usually accompanied by sounds) that are intended to be looked at and reflected upon by audiences. While some of the finest and most moving films are those that attempt to convey the inner emotions and sensibilities of the characters depicted, by virtue of the fact that audiences are spectators who approach films from the 'outside', the objectification of characters seems to be an inevitability. And while it may be the case that the actual human beings who portray characters in film are beings-for-themselves – after all, they are always more than just the characters that they play – it does seem that once performances are completed and recorded in a final form, they become fixed and stable, and so pass over into the realm of the in-itself. If this is so, what sense can it possibly make to complain about the objectification of women, men or anyone else portrayed in the media? Furthermore, if objectification is a mechanism implicated in the very way that we situate ourselves in the world, why should we even be concerned with overcoming it?

Some interesting insights into these last questions can be gained by examining a sample of motion pictures that have attempted to push the boundaries of human objectification. In so doing, we can study the effects they produce in audiences, and explore what these effects reveal to us about the nature of human empathy. I have chosen three notorious films for this task: *The Human Centipede*, *Nymphomaniac* and *Videodrome*. These are films that, in differing ways, draw attention to the human body in terms of its physical vulnerabilities and potentialities. In the case of *The Human Centipede*, both male and female bodies are laid bare as objects of surgical manipulation. In the case of *Nymphomaniac*, a female body appears as an object driven by sexual inertia, but that is finally changed into something more than just a thing. In the case of *Videodrome*, a male body is depicted as an object seized by inexorable, disease-like influences transforming it from within. In each case, the focus is on how human bodies respond when impersonal forces beyond individual control exert themselves. I shall argue that in the process of objectifying human bodies, not only do these films encourage audiences to experience feelings of disgust, arousal and various kinds of curiosity, but that they also encourage feelings of empathy by showing what may potentially happen to *any* body, male or female, put into similar circumstances. If *any* body is subject to such abuse, then we as audience members can imagine what it would be like for *our own* bodies to be put into similar circumstances. Since we know how we ourselves react, mentally, from the inside, we can thus come to feel sympathy for the characters on the screen who we know only from outside appearances. In this way, films such as *The Human Centipede*, *Nymphomaniac* and *Videodrome* evoke the ambiguous nature of human existence as something encompassing both the in-itself of physicality and the for-itself of conscious awareness. Through the objectification of others, we are reminded of the vulnerabilities of our own bodies, and thus these films, while starting in nihilism, also end up carrying a common positive, moral message concerning our capacity to feel compassion for others.

THE HUMAN CENTIPEDE

The Human Centipede provides a startling example of the ambiguous implications of human objectification, demonstrating its capacity at once to nauseate, fascinate, titillate, amuse and provoke sympathy in audiences. Without exception, critics were simultaneously repulsed and impressed with this piece of film-making. Roger Ebert, while refusing even to award the film a star rating, nonetheless admitted to its nauseating originality, claiming that 'the soul of a dark artist' (Ebert 2010) stirs within the director, Tom Six. Peter Bradshaw, reviewing for *The Guardian*, called the film 'deplorable and revolting, but sort of brilliant' (Bradshaw 2010). These reactions attest to something powerful about *The Human Centipede*. This power lies in the film's unflinching depiction of human bodies as raw material in a mad scientist's creative project. Tom Six, in dramatising the in-itself nature of human embodiment, pushes the logic of human objectification to its utmost extreme, forcing audiences to confront a host of uncomfortable issues related to the cold logic of biology and science as applied to the human organism. And yet, in the end, the movie successfully triggers the audiences' sense of inner humanity insofar as it demonstrates a real truth about our shared vulnerability as embodied creatures.

The premise of *The Human Centipede* is simple and atrocious: a mad scientist, Dr Heiter (Dieter Laser), has abducted three people and plans to sew their bodies together, mouth to anus, in order to create a living 'human centipede'. As the film progresses, his project inexorably takes shape. He first describes the procedure to his test subjects in full medical detail and then successfully carries out the operation. The consequence is a pathetic monstrosity of three human bodies connected as one. Soon after completion of the surgery, the various implications of this new physical state of affairs are explored. The creation crawls across the floor like a gigantic insect. With the connection of the victims' various gastrointestinal tracts, food eaten by the first person in the chain passes as faeces into the mouth of the second person in the chain, which in turn passes through to the last person. Infections result, and the first and the third segments of the 'centipede' eventually die. In the bleak and sickening conclusion to the film, the main character remains alive but helpless, sandwiched between two corpses.

The poster for *The Human Centipede* proclaims the surgical procedure depicted in the film is '100% medically accurate'. The details of the operation were worked out by the director in consultation with a surgeon from Holland, (Indie London 2010) and this attention to medical realism is one of the keys to the film's success, capitalising as it does on our curiosity about other people's bodies, how they function, and how they respond when manipulated. We already know that the human body, as a physical object, may in reality be altered surgically, and that parts from differing bodies can successfully be sewn together. The operation carried out in *The Human Centipede* does not depart radically from what we know is possible, and thus it builds on our scientific understanding of the human body as a mechanism, a thing-in-itself, capable of being cut up, reassembled and mechanically altered according to basic laws of nature. In this film, graphic close-ups of a scalpel cutting into skin and peeling flesh illustrate the concrete, technical steps for creating a monster out of the raw material of human body parts, and although less than three minutes of screen time are actually devoted to the operation, this is sufficient to provoke powerful feelings of both disgust and technical fascination in the audience.[3]

However, there are other interests, like sexual curiosity, also catered to by this movie. It is not accidental that two of the segments in the centipede are women. Lindsay (Ashley C. Williams) and Jenny (Ashlynn Yennie) are stripped nude for most of the film, and as with sexual pornography, audiences are at times led to ignore that they have inner lives, instead becoming fascinated by their physical exploitation. Early in the film the women are depicted as 'party girls', concerned with their appearance and sexual attractiveness as they prepare to go out to a nightclub. On their way to the club, and before their abduction by Dr Heiter, these women are intimidated by a lone male traveller who menaces them with sexual taunts, setting the scene for them to be treated as objects whose purpose lies in being used and exploited physically for the pleasure of others.

The sexualisation of Lindsay and Jenny continues once they are abducted. After the completion of the operation to turn them into a human centipede there is a dramatic change in the film's lighting – from dark grey to bright yellow tones – that serves to highlight and better display the softness and vulnerability of the newly created composite body of which they are a part. The camera plays over the thighs, bellies and faces of each body (especially the female bodies) as Dr Heiter caresses them, rejoicing in his success. The mouths of the two female characters have been sewn to the buttocks of other bodies, and so the only sounds they can make are moans and groans that could (absent the visual imagery) be mistaken for sounds of sexual arousal. It is only the male 'segment', Katsuro (Akihiro Kitamura), whose mouth remains functional, and he hurls insults, curses and even bites the leg of Dr Heiter, actively rebelling and fighting against his objectification in a way that the female characters do not. While he remains active, the females remain passive and sexualised.[4]

But there is also a great deal of humour in *The Human Centipede*. From the moment that Dr Heiter mourns the death of his beloved 'Drei Hund' – the 'three-hound' or dog-centipede that was his preliminary project – to when he unveils his own cartoon-like drawing of the proposed human centipede, there is something both sinister and humorous about what he is up to. Our amusement is no doubt related to the fact that, as mentioned above, we know this medical procedure is a plausible one. The simple, cartoon outline of the three figures depicted in the doctor's drawing, with their single, shared alimentary tract highlighted in red, provokes a feeling of revulsion, but also an uncomfortable laugh. It calls to mind the sort of sketch a child might make, depicting a conceivable but absurd situation. Humour often functions by means of incongruity (Marmysz 2003, Moreall 1983), and there is certainly something incongruous about a difficult medical procedure with extreme and awful implications being depicted in such a simple, childlike way. Indeed, the doctor's matter-of-fact treatment of other humans as mere objects throughout the film also produces a vaguely humorous incongruity that permeates the entire movie. Dr Heiter is depicted as if he is a child who has never matured, who has never learned to treat others as full human beings, and to this extent there is something comical about him.

The 'lead' segment of the human centipede is a man, Katsuro, and like Dr Heiter, but unlike the female victims, he is depicted in a somewhat comical manner at points. The humour in his situation seems to focus on his inability to control his own anger or his bodily functions. First of all, he is Japanese and so is unable to communicate with the other, English speakers in the film. When he gets angry, his vocalisations are unintelligible to everyone else, sounding like battle cries from an old samurai movie, and this impotence comes across as both frustrating and funny all at once. Then there is his inability to control his bodily cravings and functions. After the operation has taken place, Katsuro hungrily gobbles down a bowl of food offered to him by the doctor. Shortly afterwards, he has a bowel movement, which travels into the mouth of the woman now attached to his rectum. Katsuro apologises, expressing embarrassment and regret, and as he does so the effect is both disgusting and humorous. These twin feelings of disgust and humour are related to Katsuro's reduction to a passive object in the grip of biological forces. Unlike the women, Katsuro is never sexualised; rather his situation serves as an incongruous contrast to his masculinity. A male human being who can neither make himself understood nor control his bodily functions is more like a baby than a man, and so for most of the film, he is depicted as an infantile, disgusting and ridiculous character.

Despite its technical, sexual and humorous aspects, *The Human Centipede* is advertised primarily as a horror film, and it builds its atmosphere through some familiar techniques. Authors such as Julia Kristeva (Kristeva 1982) and Noël Carroll (Carroll 1990) have observed that horror operates by provoking feelings of disgust in audiences through the depiction of objects and creatures that transgress natural boundaries. These unnatural transgressions provoke fears of contamination and infection, and thus our horrified response is to recoil from what is perceived as a disgusting, dangerous threat. The horror response on this account consists of a mixture of fear and disgust. Monsters, according to Carroll, are an especially common element in this regard, and in *The Human Centipede*, the titular creation, consisting of three human bodies sewn together as one, certainly represents a disgusting, monstrous, unnatural abomination. But while we are shocked by this monstrosity, it is really the human mad scientist who horrifies us most. The 'centipede' itself is disgusting in obvious ways – it displays stitched wounds, it drips blood and pus, and faeces are passed between its anuses and mouths – but we nonetheless retain sympathy for the victims who have been subjected to this ghastly operation. While they are harmless, the mad scientist is terrifying in his treatment of human beings as mere raw material. Thus he is the one toward whom we primarily direct our fear, not his creation. We realise that our own bodies could be abused in the same way, and so we sympathise with the humans who have been victimised. Our feelings about the 'monster', then, are likely mixed with a dose of pity, thus bringing us close to an experience that is tragic in the Aristotelian sense. For Aristotle, tragedy occurs when characters for whom we feel sympathy suffer (Aristotle 1941: 1452a). Because we care about them, we fear what will happen as they face danger. We pity their situation and dread the harm that will come to them. *The Human Centipede* horrifies us at times by provoking feelings of fear and disgust, but it also evokes a sense of tragedy by stirring feelings of pity and fear within us. Ultimately, we are horrified by Dr Heiter, but we feel compassion for his victims who we think of as more than just things-in-themselves, but as beings-for-themselves with inner feelings and emotions like our own. It is for this reason that while their plight is at times fascinating, titillating and humorous, in the end we identify with their suffering and have sympathy for their pain.

The Human Centipede contains elements that provoke a whole range of affective responses in audiences. All of these disparate reactions, however, are related to the film's depiction of human beings, both men and women, as things-in-themselves. When we elevate ourselves 'above' the victimised characters, we detach ourselves from their suffering so that it is not something we ourselves feel. At these moments we are able to exercise our sense of technical or erotic curiosity, or to laugh at the absurdity of the scenario. However, once we find ourselves sympathising with the for-itself nature of these same individuals, our perspective takes a shift, with curiosity and amusement being pushed to the side by pity, fear and indignation. As in the story of Frankenstein, we ultimately do experience a sense of sadness for the monster that is brought into existence when we realise that within these bodies exist minds capable of comprehending their plight and suffering as a result of being degraded to the status of mere objects. Especially in the concluding scene of *The Human Centipede*, when the camera lingers on the two female characters clutching onto one another's hands for emotional comfort, we cannot help but sympathise with the inner humanity of the victims. The sight of their two clasped hands displays their fear and pain even more dramatically than do their muffled moans, provoking us to understand that by virtue of our own corporeal natures, we also could be subject to the same sort of abuse. What is both brilliant and yet repulsive about this film is that it unflinchingly displays the in-itself nature of the human body while also reminding us that as humans, we are always more than just the in-itself. We suffer and become degraded when our aspirations are taken from us and we become mere raw material for the projects of others.

NYMPHOMANIC

In the concluding pages of *Being and Nothingness*, Jean-Paul Sartre offers a strange yet fascinating analysis of 'slime', which he characterises as a substance symbolising the horrifying qualities of the in-itself. 'Slime is the revenge of the In-itself', (Sartre 1992: 777) he writes, suggesting that its stickiness and lack of distinct boundaries make slime an awful reminder of how precarious and shaky our personal identities really are. We exist by negating the undifferentiated mass that is the in-itself, raw material of the universe, solidifying and building a world around us by carving out regions of Being and artificially sustaining their borders. Without the imposition of human consciousness, all that would exist would be raw 'stuff' possessing no meaning, value or margins. Slime is a reminder of this unstable state of affairs. We are always in danger of being reabsorbed into the slimy meaninglessness of the universe, and it is only by the negating powers of the for-itself that we fend off this horrifying possibility. In *The Human Centipede*, Tom Six explored the slimy nature of the human body's boundaries, showing that as a thing-in-itself, the body is subject to any number of interpretations and reconfigurations. In Lars Von Trier's four-hour sexual epic *Nymphomaniac*, we find yet another exploration of this idea. However, whereas in *The Human Centipede* we are introduced to people whose bodies are used against their wills, in *Nymphomaniac*, we find a main character who willingly consents to her own objectification.

Nymphomaniac focuses on the life of a female character Joe (Stacy Martin/ Charlotte Gainsbourg), who in her own words, 'wanted to be treated like a *thing*'. In a manner reminiscent of the Marquis de Sade, Joe makes a seemingly philosophical choice to live as if she was no more than a body among other bodies, immersing herself in sexual excess. The irony in this film is that the more that Joe loses herself in sex, the less her body responds in the expected manner. The automatic pleasure she assumed was part of the physical manipulation of her body evaporates, and halfway through the four-hour-long film, she is distraught to find that she no longer feels anything.

Images of sliminess abound in this film as bodies merge sexually, one into another. The young Joe is penetrated vaginally and anally; her mouth graphically drips with slimy semen[5] after performing oral sex on a resistant train passenger; her own vagina is licked in close-up by one of her many partners. The older Joe is depicted in an act of double penetration by two African brothers; her own slimy, vaginal lubrication is shown to flow as she is tied and whipped by an emotionless, domineering partner. Sex, throughout the film, is represented as a slimy, messy and disgusting activity. Rather than being simply arousing for the audience, here sexual acts are also depicted as filthy and sometimes humorous attempts by the main character to disappear into oblivion; to become a thing-in-itself. 'I want to have all my holes filled', Joe states, expressing a sentiment that Sartre also articulates: 'A good part of our life is passed in plugging up holes, in filling empty places' (Sartre 1992: 781). The filling of holes is a way to lose one's conscious self and to become a part of other things. When bodies interpenetrate, the boundaries between them become blurred. They merge into each other, and so become unified and one. The sliminess of sex is, in *Nymphomaniac*, an unsettling reminder of how our identities as unique for-itself consciousnesses slip away in the act of mechanical copulation.

Like *The Human Centipede*, *Nymphomaniac* utilises the depiction of human bodies as things-in-themselves in order to provoke a number of differing emotional responses in audiences. The primary ones are sexual curiosity, disgust and humour. Strangely, unlike many of Von Trier's other films, *Nymphomaniac* avoids a despairing, depressing tone, instead opting for one that is more absurd, surreal and amusing. Joe never seems traumatised in the way that the victims in *The Human Centipede* have been traumatised by their objectification at the hands of Dr Heiter. Instead, she is eager and curious to pursue her own objectification further and further, merely following the amoral logic of cause and effect by allowing her body to be pushed this way and that by its own desires and inclinations. Once her body loses the ability to feel sexual pleasure, however, her for-itself nature takes over, and she must start to makes choices for which she is fully responsible. In the absence of sexual inertia, she can no longer blame her own body for propelling her toward impersonal acts. Instead, she must start to make conscious decisions about what she *wills* her body to do.

The transition between the depiction of Joe as a mere 'thing' to her depiction as a fully formed human being is flagged by the director's visual choice to use two different actors to portray the younger and the older characters.

This might seem like a nod to realism except for the fact that none of the other characters in the film are played by more than one person. While Joe's body ages, no other body in the film does. The result is a sense that everyone except Joe is static and unchanging; they are mere backdrops for the story of the main character who we see transformed from youth to middle age, from sexual object to full personhood. The feelings provoked in the audience, as they watch these two different bodies on screen, also change. The young Joe's body seems calculated to excite sexual curiosity and arousal in the audience while the older Joe's body seems more often associated with feelings of abjection, or sometimes humour. For instance, in the scene where the older Joe organises a threesome with two African brothers, the brothers end up being more concerned with how they will be positioned in relation to one another than they are with consummating the sexual act with Joe. Joe's middle-aged body is of very little interest to them, and amused, she quietly withdraws from the room as the brothers continue their argument. It is worth noting that the black bodies of the African brothers in this scene are not depicted as especially threatening, but rather as comical in their overwhelming concern with sexual technicalities and details. Joe's own amused response to their indifference suggests not that they are sexual threats, but objects of laughter.

In the second volume of the film, Joe becomes less concerned with her own body and more focused on the manipulation of other people's bodies. She begins work as a shake-down artist, pursuing people who have defaulted on loans. Instead of beating them up, however, she uses the skills she has developed to understand people's inner hidden, shameful, repressed sexual desires in order to coerce her victims into paying their debts under the threat of exposure. In one key scene, an especially difficult client resists her efforts. He sits tied to a chair with his pants pulled down as Joe recites various sexual scenarios, trying to find one that will have an arousing effect on him. Finally, she tells a story about a little boy in a playground, and the man's penis begins to become erect. The man himself is surprised and upset by this response; it is one that he neither anticipated nor enjoys. He begins to cry as he realises that his bodily mechanism has reacted to a stimulus that his mind finds reprehensible. Here we see Joe's skill at work. She is adept at provoking the raw material that is the body, making it move and act in ways that the mind inhabiting that same body refuses to welcome. There is something quite abject and disgusting about what she accomplishes by unearthing something deep within her victim's body and making it visible on the outside. It is like showing someone his own intestines. Something that was hidden and ugly has become visible, and now the traumatised victim will never be able to forget what lurks inside his own body.

Joe states that she 'ruined his life' by revealing this aspect of his bodily desire. Here was a man who never knew that he harboured paedophilic potential. Had it not been for Joe's efforts, this aspect of his being would not have been revealed. She was the one who pushed his body to betray his will. Joe reduced him to a mere thing-in-itself, and it is now that she becomes a monster, like Dr Heiter in *The Human Centipede*. She has become a dangerous, slimy exploiter of other people's bodies, and in this we come to understand why it is that she is so filled with self-loathing. It is not because she was promiscuous, following her own bodily drives, that she considers herself a bad person, but because she started using her understanding of the body's sexual logic to destroy other people's lives so that she could reap profit from their ruin. She has treated *others* as if they were things, and it is at this point, unlike Dr Heiter, that Joe realises she must accept full moral culpability for her actions. She becomes something more than simply a body among other bodies when she accepts her own responsibility for the manipulation of others, and this is also the point at which the audience is able to sympathise with Joe. Before this point, she was something to ogle, to laugh at, or to feel disgusted by. Now she has become someone that we are horrified by, but whom we also pity and feel sorry for precisely because we now know that she possesses a conscience.

The themes in *Nymphomaniac* help to advance our understanding of the nature of the relationship between the in-itself and the for-itself. Joe embodies the idea of 'slime' as discussed by Sartre. She is initially depicted as a slippery, slimy, sexual being-in-itself whose bodily boundaries are loose and penetrable. In this, she excites a kind of sexual curiosity in the audience; but this sexual curiosity is frequently overtaken by feelings of disgust, revulsion and sometimes humour. The young Joe's body seems to mean nothing at all, and as we watch her engage in all sorts of sexual gymnastics, we feel distanced from her as a conscious, feeling being. She seems to have no inner life. Everything she does is simply a reaction to her body's erotic commands; until the second half of the film when our amusement and disgust at her self-abuse are replaced by sympathy for her own inner feelings of remorse concerning her abuse of others. It is then that we become aware she has solidified her own boundaries and developed an inner consciousness. Visually, the film signals this change with the introduction of an older body, one that no longer exhibits the innocent sexual suppleness of youth. The older Joe wears her experience on her skin for all to see. She is not a mindless child, but a middle-aged woman, and it is at this point that the audience is finally provoked to feel sympathy for her. We realise that she has an inner life, that she feels regret, and that she is more than a mere body in motion.

VIDEODROME

In *The Human Centipede*, we view both male and female bodies manipulated by a monster from the outside. In *Nymphomaniac*, we witness a woman's body compelled to operate by inner sexual forces. In both films, human bodies are treated as things, as beings-in-themselves lacking the dignity due to full human persons. Our reaction as audience members to this sort of exploitation is ambiguous, ranging from curiosity and disgust to amusement. However, when we are reminded that the bodies in these films are much like us, in that they possess inner emotions, feelings and life projects, our response becomes predominately sympathetic, and we feel horrified by the treatment of these bodies, which could just as well be our own. It is then that we come to resonate with the presumed for-itself potential hidden within these physical shells.

Inner and outer bodily manipulation become intermingled to a disturbing degree in David Cronenberg's *Videodrome*, a film that on the one hand depicts the main character's victimisation by others, but on the other hand shows how such victimisation can lead to a transformation in the main character's being that is then embraced and intensified by the force of his own, inner will. Here, the border between inner and outer collapses, problematising the relationship between the in-itself and the for-itself aspects of human existence.

Videodrome tells the story of Max Renn (James Woods), the owner of Civic TV, a cable station specialising in low budget, sexually explicit programming. Max has been looking for a 'breakthrough' programme that is 'tougher' and edgier than the softcore porn he usually airs and he thinks that he has found what he is looking for when a Civic TV technician introduces him to a pirate broadcast called *Videodrome*. *Videodrome* has no plot, no recurrent characters and no apparent message. All it consists of are scenes of sexual violence and torture. The problem is no one seems to know from where this programme originates. Its signal has been scrambled and can only be viewed for short periods of time before it is lost. As Max tries to track down the source of *Videodrome*, he begins to experience disturbing hallucinations, which turn out to be the result of a brain tumour, the growth of which has been triggered by a hidden signal embedded in the *Videodrome* broadcast. The inventor of the technology, Brian O'Blivion (Jack Creley), explains to Max that the tumour is actually a new organ opening his mind to previously unknown dimensions of experience. Max now becomes (or hallucinates that he becomes) a pawn in the struggle between a mega-corporation that wants to use *Videodrome* for political purposes and a revolutionary organisation that sees *Videodrome* as a potential means of liberation for the underclass.

The battle cry of the revolutionary group that Max finally becomes an agent for is 'Long live the new flesh!' In consuming the *Videodrome* signal, Max's body begins to change. He develops a vaginal slit in his stomach and a slimy, 'cancer gun' grows as an extension of his hand. It is unclear to the audience how much of what is happening to Max is a hallucination, but Max himself becomes convinced that with these bodily changes, he is moving closer and closer to an as yet undiscovered reality representing the next phase in human evolution. At the end of the film, he is beckoned by Nicki Brand (Deborah

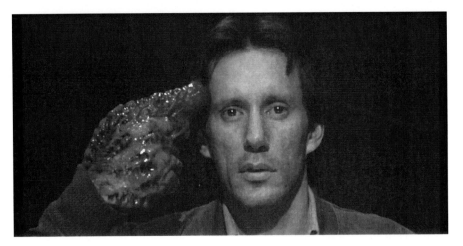

Figure 3.2 'Long live the new flesh!' Max Renn (James Woods) turns his cancer gun on himself in *Videodrome* (1983).

Harry) to commit suicide and take the final step into this next realm. Max shoots himself in the head with his 'cancer gun' after reciting the final words in the film: 'Long live the new flesh!'

In *Videodrome*, it is Max Renn's body, a male body, which primarily serves as raw material for the fascinating and disgusting transformations that take place. As in *The Human Centipede*, one of the reactions we have to these transformations is sheer curiosity about what shape Max's body will take on next. Unlike *The Human Centipede*, however, we do not operate under the assumption that what is going to happen is '100% medically accurate'. The film is filled with quick, abrupt cuts switching between Max's warped perceptions and an apparently 'objective' point of view free of those perceptions, suggesting that what transpires may simply be subjective to the mind of the main character. Nevertheless, there is an intriguing notion that the changes his body undergoes do follow a logic similar to the sorts of transformations that occur over longer periods of time when organisms are subject to evolutionary forces. In this way we are encouraged, at the same time we are disgusted by the grotesque nature of these changes, to consider them in another light as adaptive advances. The make–up artist for this film, Rick Baker, used physical prosthetics to produce these effects, and so they have a sort of tangible, slimy and organic appearance often missing from CGI. This appearance helps to buttress the plausibility that some sort of impersonal, corporeal, causal force is impelling Max's body toward its transmutations. A surreal mood is thus set, somewhere between reality and delirium, by the appearance of the bizarre growths that occur on the main character's body. It is both disgusting and fascinating all at once.

Cronenberg's achievement in this film (and many of his other films) is to get us to think beyond conventional categories of disease and health in order to regard the body as a malleable sort of substance capable of being formed and moulded in any number of unanticipated ways. Max's body takes on the shapes and forms that are necessary in order for him to complete his 'mission' as he navigates through the world of *Videodrome*, becoming more and more receptive to the potential of these new orifices and organs as he goes on. His body becomes like a block of clay, ready to take on any shape imparted to it by his programmers.

As Max becomes increasingly accustomed to his corporeal malleability, he does not, like the characters in *The Human Centipede* or *Nymphomaniac*, reject what is happening or feel victimised by his manipulation. Rather, he comes to embrace it and to willingly harness its potential. He becomes a revolutionary who incorporates an awareness of his in-itself nature into his global for-itself project. As he becomes more and more confident, we see Max willing his body to change, summoning the slit to appear on his stomach so that he can accept the insertion of videos, and willing his cancer gun to materialise so that he can attack his enemies. His own body becomes a tool, a thing that is instrumental to his mission, and which in the final scene becomes the final means, as well as the final impediment, to his transcendence. Though he seems to start off as a victim whose body is abused by others, in the end it is this very abuse that transforms his physicality so that he may then harness a new potential in service of his own, new project. This is the 'new flesh' that he salutes in the closing scene. It is an incorporation of the for-itself into the in-itself so that the body, in being what it is, opens the door to something it is not.

In Max Renn, we find a rare sort of film character. He is someone who undergoes agonising bodily abuse, but who comes to embrace the transformations that this abuse makes possible so that he may evolve into something more than he could ever imagine. His old flesh, which was raw material, passive stuff, being-in-itself that simply reacted to external environmental stimuli, becomes something more. It becomes the 'new flesh', which is active, being-for-itself that can choose to transform itself from the inside depending upon the project that it desires to pursue. His body develops a will of its own, and in identifying with this will, Max overcomes victimhood. He no longer thinks of himself as a slave to his body, or subject to the constraints of his body. Rather, he becomes one with his body, which is a conveyance toward his own revolutionary goals. Because of this, while we feel disgust, fear and horror at what transpires in *Videodrome*, we also have a sense of respect and regard for Max, who emerges as a heroic figure.

CONCLUSION

What our examination of these three films has done is to demonstrate some of the differing reactions that portrayals of human objectification may provoke in audiences. Contrary to the criticisms of many contemporary commentators, the depiction of human bodies as raw material does not necessarily end in the complete debasement of the individuals in question. Rather, there is a whole range of reactions that such depictions may provoke in audiences, some of which actually involve feelings of sympathy. When we see other human bodies being used as if they are simply things, there may sometimes be a tendency emotionally to distance ourselves from the feelings of those who actually inhabit those bodies. In such cases we may remain detached and curious about what is happening, we may find it funny, we may find it arousing, or we may be disgusted. However, none of these feelings necessarily crowds out the possibility that we may also develop an empathetic response to the suffering of victims. By virtue of the fact that we also possess bodies that could be abused and misused, we may become sympathetic toward their plight, as we ourselves could imagine what it would be like to be in their place.

Our sympathy for the victims in films seems to be connected to the fact that human beings exist as both beings-in-themselves and beings-for-themselves. Our bodies, which are physical objects, and so governed by the laws of cause and effect, are things-in-themselves. On this level, they mean nothing. They only take on meaning from the perspective of the for-itself, which is the living, changing and aspiring human consciousness. When we look at others, we objectify them by necessity. However, this objectification may allow us, by analogy, to consider the unseen, for-itself nature residing within the bodies at which we look. When we do this, we come to understand that other humans are more than simply bodies; they are thinking, feeling, conscious minds that, much like ourselves, are subject to suffering and abuse when their projects are taken away from them.

NOTES

1. This is a point made by Hannah Arendt in her classic work *The Origins of Totalitarianism* where she argues that the Holocaust and Stalin's gulags were made possible by the antecedent 'preparation of living corpses' (Arendt 1976: 447). It is also a main thesis in: Giorgio Agamben's *Remnants of Auschwitz: The Witness and the Archive* (Agamben 2002).
2. This is the inward turn first described by Socrates/Plato in *Phaedo*, 66a. (Plato 1997c).
3. The follow up film in this series, *The Human Centipede II*, plays on the fascination with connecting ever more bodies together in chains. *The Human Centipede III* depicts a 500 person-long centipede!

4. One of the tag lines appearing on the poster for *The Human Centipede* is 'Their flesh is his fantasy', evoking a sentiment that might come from the advertising for a porn film.
5. Strangely, Kristeva claims that, despite its sliminess, sperm does not have 'polluting value' (Kristeva 1982: 71).

PART II

Confrontations

Introduction: Confrontations

Once awareness of nihilism has been awakened by an encounter with the abyss, there is a choice to be made. How do we respond? Do we now collapse into passive despair, or do we defiantly push forward, feeling our way through the darkness, striking out on a path leading nowhere? With the death of God, the collapse of objective meaning and the revelation of an absurd void underling human life, it becomes apparent that nothing remains outside of ourselves to compel aspiration. If we are to avoid utter despondency, we must turn attention inward, toward our own powers of creative imagination, making the resolute decision to become self-motivated.

This is not easy. A glimpse into the abyss permanently changes us, making us suspicious forever after of claims to finality. Our faith in the existence of objective and independent standards of worth dissolves. We no longer believe that we can possess the Truth, and now we must either passively accept the absurd nature of the world or actively confront this situation and rebel against it by becoming creators of our own values.

If we choose the former of these two options, we descend into passive nihilism. In this, a sense of resignation and despair dominates. We become convinced that the world has no point, value or purpose and that despite our wishes, there is nothing we can do about this. While passive nihilism has long been condemned as pessimistic and life-denying, it nonetheless has the potential benefit of forcing us to accept reality and the limits of human power. If nihilism is indeed our true condition, then passive resignation may even be preferable to an active orientation that propagates cruelty, pain and suffering by vainly lashing out at a world that, in the end, cannot ultimately be changed. Perhaps we do less damage in passive withdrawal.

If, however, we choose to rebel against the absurdity of the world, we become active nihilists. With this we experience the full burden of responsibility, as we accept that it is up to us to create and establish our own values and goals. The standards that we measure our accomplishments against are self-imposed, and it is only we ourselves who are to blame or praise for the state of things. This responsibility can both be terrifying and exhilarating. If it is too exhilarating, we may become intoxicated by our power, reifying our own self-created ideals, once again mistaking them for something objective. In this way, the enthusiasm of active nihilism may potentially, on the one hand, promote personal autonomy and authenticity, while on the other it may also promote arrogance and a false sense of potency.

Part II of this collection explores themes related to the confrontation with nihilism and the choices made by film characters who either take on the burden of value creation or who passively fall into a state of despair. Whereas the essays in Part I focused on the initial encounter with nihilism, the essays in this section focus on confrontational struggles on the part of characters as they decide what to do in a state of existential crisis.

Chapter 4, 'From *Night* to *Survival*: Nihilism and the Living Dead', scrutinises the structure of George Romero's Living Dead films, starting with the classic 1968 feature *Night of the Living Dead*, and ending with 2009's *Survival of the Dead*. In this series we find a progressively building ambiguity in the film-maker's attitude toward the passive forces of the zombie invasion and the active efforts of the human survivors. Initially, Romero's sympathy seems to be with the humans; especially with those who are ethnic minorities, women and the disabled. Yet as the films progress, sympathy shifts toward the undead, who are increasingly depicted as targets of human cruelty and abuse. What begins as a nightmare of nihilistic passivity eventually ends with an equally nightmarish scenario of nihilistic activity, exposing the awful potential of human power unleashed from all moral constraint.

In Chapter 5, 'The Lure of the Mob: Cinematic Depictions of Skinhead Authenticity', focus falls on a genre of film featuring neo-Nazi skinheads. In *Romper Stomper* (1992), *American History X* (1998), and *The Believer* (2001), we find examples of characters who, despite their racism and violence, are depicted in a sympathetic light, precisely because they are engaged in the struggle to understand and take responsibility for their authentic selves. The backdrop of right-wing ideology serves, in these films, to provide the set of ideals against which these characters come to define themselves and then rebel. In the course of these dramas, the active, nihilistic struggles of the main characters eventually culminate in self-understanding and the acceptance of personal responsibility. In their tragic conclusions, these movies illustrate the consequences of being liberated from ideals that are, in the end, revealed to be hollow.

The third and final chapter in this section, 'Cultural Change and Nihilism in the *Rollerball* Films', picks up on the theme begun in the previous two chapters, and then carries it to a crossroads. In this chapter, I contrast the message of the original, 1975 version of *Rollerball* with that of the 2002 remake. Whereas the original version features an existential hero who dooms himself to a tragic end by nihilistically rebelling against the forces of corporate control, the remake instead gives us a hero who engages in a successful revolution against the powers that be. In so doing, he promises the establishment of a counter-order that will bring Truth and Justice back to a chaotic world, thus accomplishing an overcoming of nihilism.

At the end of this section we are repositioned: from an encounter with the abyss, we have moved to a confrontation with the abyss, and finally to the re-establishment of an artificial order that is taken as the Truth. This sets the stage for Part III, in which we will look more closely at a set of movies illustrating the potentially totalitarian consequences that may follow on the heels of nihilism's overcoming.

CHAPTER 4

From *Night* to *Survival*: Nihilism and the Living Dead

Figure 4.1 Zombies as the embodiment of passive nihilism in *Night of the Living Dead* (1968).

INTRODUCTION

Upon its release in 1968, George Romero's *Night of the Living Dead* was attacked by many critics for being a low budget, exploitative movie of dubious moral value. *Variety* charged that it raised 'doubts about the future of the regional cinema movement and the moral health of filmgoers' (Samuels 1983: 61). An outraged Roger Ebert, in a review describing a screening he attended that was packed with terrified, sobbing youngsters, wrote, 'I suppose the idea was to make a fast buck before movies like this are off-limits to children' (Ebert 2004). This sort of angry response was prompted not simply by the film's graphic depictions of cannibalism and dismemberment, but more importantly by its downbeat tone and pervasively bleak perspective. *Night of the Living Dead* presents a simple, brutal and unsettling story of human beings driven by the desire for survival in a bare, vicious and uncanny world. There is no redemption for the main characters, all of whom end up dead, and so audiences are left uneasy, anxious and without any sense of comfort or reassurance upon the film's conclusion.

For reasons such as these, Stuart Samuels goes so far as to suggest that *Night of the Living Dead* is nihilistic (Samuels 1983: 52); and he is correct. But it is nihilistic in a deeper philosophical sense than I believe most scandalised critics have had in mind. This film and the succeeding installments in the cycle – *Dawn of the Dead* (1978), *Day of the Dead* (1985), *Land of the Dead* (2005), *Diary of the Dead* (2007), and *Survival of the Dead* (2009) – are nihilistic in the sense that they all contribute to a narrative illustrating an inexorable struggle between the impulses of active and passive nihilism. In the first film, Romero throws us into a chaotic and absurd world, establishing a mythos that is carried over through the rest of the cycle. Recurrently, in all of the *Dead* films, active and aggressive humans fight hopelessly to prevent their own extinction, engaging in a battle we know ultimately is doomed to failure. What is especially disquieting about this fictional fight is that it reminds us too clearly of the real-life, human predicament in which we all participate. As humans we all, in the end, are forced passively to submit to death. There is no victory in the war against human mortality, even though we passionately wish there could be. We are mortal, time-bound creatures who vainly, yet actively, fight against the inevitable, inescapable victory of passive nothingness over life. This is the kernel of Romero's nihilistic message.

NIHILISM

As previously discussed in the Introduction, the term 'nihilism' is popularly used as a derogatory label. In this normative sense, it is often meant as nothing more than an exclamation of negative sentiment; a way of expressing distaste for the phenomena or ideas to which it is applied. Taken seriously as a philosophical concept, however, it acquires a deeper, more interesting dimension. Derived from the Latin word *nihil*, meaning 'nothing', nihilism is, literally, a 'doctrine of nothingness'. This doctrine is rooted in the contention that human beings are, by their very nature, forever alienated from the realisation of their highest, most valued aspirations and goals. There exists an unbridgeable gap of nothingness separating concrete human existence from the perfect consummation of absolute ideals such as pure Being, Truth, Justice, Beauty, and so forth. Such objectives never can be made real, and so the highest, most valuable human goals must ultimately slip through our grasp, remaining forever unactualised. In this, nihilism implies that any final state of perfection, whether it be moral, scientific, political or theological, is impossible. We are forever alienated from what is ultimately Real, True or Good by this account.

The loss of faith in the objective existence of ideal truths is associated with a syndrome that Nietzsche has characterised as the 'death of God' (Nietzsche 1974: §108). Without God, all we are left with is a variety of fragmentary, subjective interpretations of the world, and in confronting this situation the nihilist comes to a potentially crippling realisation: I alone must assume responsibility for my interpretations. This insight may, potentially, lead to feelings of despair and negativity. If all human ideals are merely subjectively generated phantoms, and if there is no God to guarantee the worthiness of the standards by which I judge truth from falsehood, or meaning from nonsense, then life might come to be seen as futile, meaningless and absurd. Further, if life is futile, meaningless and absurd, it becomes unclear whether there is any real justification for choosing life over death.

All nihilists must deal with the issue of if and how life has value. This is the very topic that propelled Albert Camus's writing career, and as he observed, the nihilist is not, as it turns out, necessarily committed to life denial or suicide. Instead, the nihilist may elect to suffer through life in uncertainty, struggling each and every day with feelings of negativity as an option against suicide and death. As another option, the nihilist may choose to rebel against this negative propensity and instead of feeling resentment toward his or her situation, embrace nihilism and come to experience the exhilaration of interpretive freedom. The choice of the nihilist is, then, not necessarily the choice between living or dying, but the choice between adopting a passive or an active stance toward the world. We find both Camus and Nietzsche advocating the choice of active over passive nihilism for the very reason that in being active, a human overcomes psychological despair and learns to embrace the creative, vital forces of life (Nietzsche 1968a: §903–8; §1027–31, Nietzsche 1974: §246–347, Camus 1955: 3–48).

Passive nihilism is indicative of a decline in spiritual power. It is characterised by the inability to create, or in the extreme, to react. The passive nihilist is one who, when faced with the world's imperfection and uncertainty, withdraws and refuses to engage. For such a person, uncertainty is a sufficient condition not to proceed through life, and so paralysed by fear of the unknown and unknowable, the passive nihilist does nothing. Nietzsche describes this tendency as 'the weary nihilism that no longer attacks . . . a passive nihilism, a sign of weakness' (Nietzsche 1968a: §23).

Active nihilism, on the other hand, is indicative of a relative increase in spiritual power. The active nihilist sees freedom where the passive nihilist sees only absurdity or meaninglessness. This person chooses action and creation instead of passivity and withdrawal. The lack of objective standards against which to judge what is truly real or good motivates such an individual toward self-created standards and criteria of value. The active nihilist is not active despite the unknown, but because of it, summoning a rush of creative energy and power motivated by a desire to rebel against the void of nothingness, thereby imposing personal meaning onto the world. Never forgetting that it is his or her own subjective wilfulness that is the source and progenitor of meaning, the active nihilist faces the world with defiant courage and purpose.

The struggle between the impulses of active and passive nihilism is a theme played out repeatedly in George Romero's work. In his cycle of *Dead* films, the clearest examples of this theme occur in the ongoing battle between the living dead and the surviving humans, the evolution from weakness to strength on the part of the central female characters, and in the progressive shift of sympathy away from the surviving human characters and toward the living dead zombies. In Romero's films characters are thrust into a world of nihilism, and this forces them to confront the tension between an active drive for survival, on the one hand, and the passive tendency toward capitulation, on the other.

PASSIVE ZOMBIES, ACTIVE HUMANS

A war erupts between zombies and humans in *Night of the Living Dead*, initiating a process that will eventually lead to the extinction of humankind and the triumph of passive nihilism. Romero's zombie invasion is an attack on the foundations upon which all civilised societies rest, and it forces the surviving human population into a confrontation with nihilism. Civilised humans take for granted that order is better than chaos and that due to the natural structure of the world, certain things are simply impossible. An assault by flesh-eating ghouls, however, calls into question this assumption. It is only in an irrational, absurd world that the dead may rise and overthrow the living. This is, in fact, a complete inversion of what humans take to be the natural design of things.

The zombies in these films are a kind of revolutionary force of predators without a revolutionary programme. Their only concern is to satisfy an instinctual drive for predation; a drive that, as is pointed out in *Day of the Dead*, serves no actual biological purpose. They appear and attack without explanation or reason, violating taken-for-granted principles of sufficient cause and rationality. Because of this, they are especially confounding to the surviving human beings. Enemies such as Nazis, Communists or terrorists are comprehensible in terms of their historical backgrounds, economic interests, religious, political or philosophical beliefs. But these zombies are a different breed of enemy insofar as they do not operate according to normal human motivations. They are a nihilistic enemy, which as lifeless, spiritless automatons, exemplify the epitome of passive nihilism. They wander the landscape exhibiting only the bare minimum of power that is required for locomotion and the consumption of living flesh. They must steal life from the strong because they possess such a depressed store of innate energy. They are, literally, the walking dead.

The eruption of the zombie threat forces the protagonists in Romero's films to confront the world in all of its absurdity. As the threat worsens, there is a progressive realisation that the interpretive tools available to the survivors are inadequate for dealing with this situation. Science and religion prove equally impotent in performing their traditional roles of providing frameworks by which to find purpose and meaning in the world's events. Life is reduced to a violent struggle for survival and even the hope of a serene afterlife is destroyed. As the invasion worsens and the outlook for humankind becomes bleaker and bleaker throughout the course of the cycle, it becomes apparent that the struggle for survival is hopeless as well, and that regardless of whether one adopts an active or a passive stance toward this threat, survival is impossible.

The initial reaction of the humans is to turn to the tools of science in search of an explanation for, and a solution to, the problem at hand. In *Night of the Living Dead*, it is hinted that the cause of the zombie phenomenon has something to do with a space probe that has returned from Venus, but this explanation is presented as hypothetical and very peripheral to the plot. The main role that scientists and authorities play in this first film is to warn citizens against the irrational attachments that they may feel toward loved ones who have become zombies. They warn that these irrational feelings of sympathy are dangerous and will only lead to an exacerbation of the problem. In *Dawn of the Dead*, one of the characters from the first film returns as a TV psychiatrist who, in frustration at the panic all around him, repeats over and over, 'We must remain rational', like an eerie mantra that echoes throughout the compound of some survivors who have taken refuge in a shopping mall.

In juxtaposition to appeals to science, another one of the characters in *Dawn of the Dead* invokes a Voodoo warning: 'When there's no more room in Hell, the dead will walk the Earth'. This religious explanation is simply another example of the same tendency that provokes scientific explanations. It is a natural human response to look for causes and solutions to seemingly baffling problems. To live is to have a perspective and to interpret and evaluate the world. In the attempt to impose meaning and order on their environment, all humans are engaged in activity. Even the weakest and most passive character in of all of the films, Barbara (Judith O'Dea), asks repeatedly throughout *Night of the Living Dead*, 'What's happening?', demanding an explanation. Not until *Day of the Dead*, which prominently features a scientist who is engaged in futile experiments to determine the cause of the zombie invasion, is it realised that all rational modes of explanation are useless. There is no explanation. It is then, as passive nihilism triumphs, that the overthrow of humankind is almost complete. Only then do humans realise that, 'the cause doesn't matter because it's beyond the realm of human understanding anyway' (Romero 1979b).

In the films made after *Day of the Dead*, the zombie mythos is firmly in place and the need for explanation largely recedes into the background. No longer do we find attempts to harness the tools of science or logic in order to understand the zombie apocalypse; it now becomes clear that the world has fallen apart and that explanations are unlikely and, in fact, unnecessary. In *Land of the Dead*, a major Hollywood production made twenty years after the release of *Day of the Dead*, it is taken for granted that the audience is familiar with the Romero zombie mythos, and characters are introduced who, it is clear, have adapted to living in a world already hopelessly overrun by the living dead. *Diary of the Dead*, an independent production released two years later, in some ways represents an interruption in the unfolding timeline established between *Night* and *Land*, bringing us back to the start of the plague. As Romero himself suggests, *Diary* is in this way much like *Night*; only transported into a contemporary setting where ubiquitous video technology captures and records the world's horrors moment by moment (Romero 2008). While the characters in this regard are depicted as being unfamiliar with the zombie phenomenon, the audience is nonetheless already primed for the action, anticipating the hopelessness of the unfolding situation. Viewers of *Diary* are already familiar (either directly or indirectly) with *Night*, and so there are no surprises about how the action will unfold.

Diary of the Dead is filmed in a hand-held, point-of-view camera style that emphasises the frantic and fragmented perspectives of the main protagonists. Unlike in the previous films, where traces of an objective perspective still remain, *Diary of the Dead* dispenses with objectivity altogether by placing the audience squarely in the midst of the action so that they share the stress and bewilderment of the protagonists. The neutral 'view from nowhere' completely evaporates, and so the very conditions that would make unbiased, detached and unprejudiced explanations possible are wholly absent from this particular film. While, as in *Night*, there are still speculations and suggestions – heard in background radio reports – that there may be some sort of natural cause behind the reanimation of the dead, the chaos of the situation is the pressing concern, and it is very quickly established that the only way to confront the zombie invasion is either to fight or to flee. Indeed, the film ends with the same dilemma faced by the characters in *Night*; is it better to face the walking dead aggressively, or passively retreat into a locked room in order to avoid confronting them? Since the characters in this film never have the chance to understand the structure or scope of the plague from a detached and objective perspective, there is no way to determine for certain what constitutes the best course of action.

Figure 4.2 The remains of a female zombie used for target practice in *Diary of the Dead* (2007).

The compulsion to film everything is presented in *Diary* as one of the ways that the characters attempt to make sense of, and to master, the situation that they find themselves in. Romero seems to suggest that in filming everything, the characters are, on the one hand, admitting to their passive inability to do anything but document the horrors that are unfolding around them. Yet, on the other hand, the camera is also likened to a weapon that separates and actively distances the camera person from the horrific immediacy of the world. Filming is the most passive of activities, and in *Diary of the Dead*, it strikes us as the last means of resistance on the part of characters who have no idea of what else to do.

Lacking the grounds for rational, detached explanation, in *Diary of the Dead* the surviving, active human beings become more terrible and horrifying than the passive zombies who have overrun the world. This is an idea that has been part of the Romero mythos from the start. As Romero himself puts it, 'The real villains in my films have always been the humans. The zombies are just an inconvenience' (Romero 2008). In *Diary of the Dead* this idea is emphasised during the closing scene in which two living humans use incapacitated zombies for target practice. One of these creatures, a female, hangs from a tree by her hair. The human shooters blast away most of its body, leaving only part of its head remaining suspended below the branch. This image – which evokes the uncomfortable memory of lynchings in the US – upsets us not because the undead zombies feel anything, but because it suggests that there are human beings, part of our own species, who take delight in maiming and mutilating other beings unnecessarily. The narrator's voice, speaking in a flat, sombre tone, asks, 'Are we worth saving?' as the film comes to an end. The audience is left to consider that the active, aggressive threat posed to us by other people might be more troubling than the passive 'inconvenience' posed by the walking dead.

This idea – that active humans are more dangerous than passive zombies – was first invoked in *Night of the Living Dead* when a sheriff's (white) posse sweeps across the countryside, indiscriminately shooting and killing anything that moves, including the film's hero, Ben (Duane Jones, a black man). In *Dawn of the Dead*, the point is again made when the main characters fly their helicopter over a field where another posse is at work, and one of the characters comments, 'I bet those rednecks are enjoying this'. The message is repeatedly stressed throughout the cycle: in *Day of the Dead*, where the main villains are a band of stupid and vicious military men; in *Land of the Dead*, where it is a rich, oppressive class of surviving humans who appear as the bad guys; and finally in *Survival of the Dead*, where the main conflict is between a pair of feuding families. In all of these instances, Romero seems to be suggesting to us that there is something worse than the passive, inexorable onslaught of the walking dead themselves. What is worse is the morally unconstrained, active cruelty of living, breathing human beings. We can't blame the dead for what they do, but those survivors who exhibit cold and brutal cruelty can be blamed, since they still have the power of choice and free will. Their decisions actively and joyfully to desecrate dead bodies and to fight with one another is indicative of a frightening tendency in human beings; the tendency to separate into warring factions while taking advantage of the weak and passive. Perhaps the fact that the dead have come back to attack the living is the result of an instinct inherited from the living themselves. After all, in *Dawn of the Dead* we are told that the zombies have come back to the shopping mall as a result of instinct. At the end of *Survival of the Dead*, the two feuding family heads continue to face off against one another even when they themselves have become zombies. Maybe the dead's desire to consume the living is simply indicative of their inability to resist a basic human instinct toward violence, cruelty and the exploitation of others.

This certainly is the theme in the fourth film in the cycle, *Land of the Dead*. In this installment, the dead are equated with a kind of new oppressed class that is exploited and abused by the upper classes who use them for entertainment and diversion. In this film, as in *Day of the Dead*, there even emerges a sympathetic zombie character who leads his zombie army in a revolt against the upper classes. In so doing, the zombies become something like the heroes in this film, overthrowing the rule of those who have actively been seeking to keep them, and other living humans, down. In this movie, the triumph of passive nihilism is greeted with a cheer, since it is the lesser of the two evils. When confronted with the choice between active exploitation and cruelty, on the one hand, and passive, instinctual momentum, on the other, it appears that passivity is sometimes the preferable choice.

ACTIVE MEN AND PASSIVE WOMEN VS ACTIVE WOMEN AND PASSIVE MEN

The contrast between active and passive nihilism is further dramatised in the character development of the main protagonists throughout the film cycle. There is an especially satisfying symmetry over the course of the first three films in the development of the female characters and the development of the male characters. In the first installment of the series, the conflict between activity and passivity is introduced through the characters of Barbara and her brother Johnny. On a yearly trip to the country, where they place flowers on the grave of their grandmother, the two characters bicker about the tradition of honouring the dead. Johnny is cynical and bitter about the whole process, complaining that it is an empty gesture to convention serving no real purpose. Barbara, on the other hand, is committed to paying homage and showing respect for the dead. Johnny's actively rebellious attitude toward convention is contrasted with Barbara's relatively passive attitude toward duty and routine. She becomes very upset when Johnny's irreverence reaches its peak and he begins to tease her as though she were a child again. 'Barbara! They're coming to get you!' he says, impolitely pointing at a figure walking through the grave-yard. It is embarrassment over her brother's behaviour that initiates the first action in *Night of the Living Dead*. Barbara feels compelled to approach the lumbering figure pointed at by Johnny in order to apologise. It turns out that the figure is a zombie, and it attacks. Johnny intervenes and is killed in the fight that ensues. Barbara's respect for the dead and her observance of the tradi-tional rules of politeness betray her, and she withdraws into a state of confused passivity lasting until her death later on in the film. Throughout, she remains crippled by her inability to come to grips with the situation.

The strongest, most active character in *Night of the Living Dead* is Ben. He appears at the farmhouse to which Barbara flees and secures the build-ing against the approaching zombies. Ben is an organiser and a fighter. His strength is directed toward survival, but he must struggle with the character of Harry Cooper (Karl Hardman) as well as with the zombies. Harry Cooper and his family have barricaded themselves in the basement of the farmhouse and Harry is intent upon staying there. He retreats instinctively to the basement, content to abandon the rest of the world to the zombies. Ben, on the other hand, is unwilling to retreat. He reasons that in order to keep their options open, it is best to defend the house and formulate a plan for escape. This clash between the strategies of Mr Cooper and Ben culminates in Mr Cooper's murder. Yet despite this, the thing that distinguishes Ben as admirable and noble in the eyes of the audience is his active stance toward the zombie threat. He epitomises the heroic, active strain of nihilism found in those who choose to engage the world in battle for the sake of affirming and expressing their own life force. However, even though Ben is the strongest, most reasonable and admirable character in the film, ultimately he is doomed to die just like everyone else. Regardless of their activity or passivity, all humans must eventually submit to death.

In *Dawn of the Dead*, the female lead, Fran (Gaylen Ross), at first appears to be doomed to the same sort of passivity exhibited by Barbara in the first film. Fran's boyfriend is a helicopter pilot named Steven (David Emge) who rescues her from the television studio where she works, and then picks up Peter (Ken Foree) and Roger (Scott Reiniger), two SWAT team deserters. The group eventually lands at, and secures, a suburban shopping mall, setting up home at a place that George Romero calls a 'temple to consumerism' (Romero 1979a: 18). Fran, as the only female character, is expected to perform the duties of housewife and maid. She is excluded from all decision-making and is not allowed to participate in the exploration of the shopping mall. When she becomes pregnant, her passive role seems sealed. But unlike Barbara in *NOTLD*, Fran is not committed to tradition and convention. She demands to be given a gun, to be taught how to fly the helicopter, and to be given a voice in the decision-making process. Fran's character develops from passivity toward activity and she is, in the end, responsible for the rescue of the only other surviving character in the film. Whereas at the beginning she is one of three passengers in a helicopter, at the end she is the pilot, flying the craft into the sunset and oblivion.

Dawn of the Dead dramatises a transition between the worlds represented in *Night of the Living Dead* and *Day of the Dead*. In *NOTLD*, even though the zombie threat exposes the nihilistic character of the world, the structures of social convention temporarily survive. Certainly, humans have been given a disturbing peek at the 'abyss', but they are still able to reassert the conventional order. In *Dawn of the Dead*, the zombies have come to dominate the living by virtue of their superior numbers (and not, it should be noted, because of superior knowledge, moral correctness or reasoning). Society has crumbled, and it becomes apparent that individual activity or passivity will be what determines the quality and character of human life. Fran's development from a passive to an active nihilist is in response to this fact. She must take responsibility upon herself to impart meaning to life. Her pregnancy may be just the thing that gives her an orientation toward the future, providing her with the strength to take survival, and life, seriously.

Progress toward the domination of the world by zombie forces is complete in *Day of the Dead*, but it is in this film that the assertion of power and strength by the female lead reaches its peak. Sarah (Lori Cardille) is a doctor doing research into the zombie threat at a military installation. Civilisation has crumbled, and it may be that the individuals at this installation are the last surviving humans on earth. Sarah finds herself trying to act as a mediator between three conflicting groups; the doctors who are still trying to find a rational explanation for the zombie phenomenon, the soldiers who simply want to fight the zombies, and the technicians who want to fly away to find an island where they may live and die in peace. Sarah continues her development where Fran left off, becoming the strongest and most active character in the film; a reverse image of Barbara from *NOTLD*. Her boyfriend, on the other hand, becomes the weakest, most dependent character who eventually sacrifices himself passively to the zombies. Sarah's active orientation is exhibited in her attempt to mediate between the three warring groups. Whereas in the previous films the female leads played little or no part in plan-making or the organisation of the group, in *Day of the Dead* Sarah is the sole organiser and plan-maker. The doctors are isolated and out of touch with the severity of their situation, the soldiers are panicky and hysterical, unable to trust each other, and the technicians simply want passively to retreat. In Sarah, we find all of the attributes exhibited by Ben in *NOTLD*. She is a plan-maker, an organiser and a leader. Like Ben, she also is doomed to die, despite her strength. But in her rebellion against the world, and in her struggle to survive, she exhibits the nobility that is expected of any hero.

In the films following the initial trilogy, female characters participate more equally alongside men in the active fight against the zombie threat. Perhaps because of changes in social attitudes during the two-decade gap between the release of *Day* and *Land*, the female characters in the last three films are integrated into the action more seamlessly, and rather than being depicted as essentially weaker than their male companions, they are depicted as their peers. While this may represent a positive social development, it also, unfortunately, results in the perpetuation of a different set of stale stereotypes. Thus, in *Land of the Dead*, the main female character is Slack (Asia Argento), a sexy, tough, smart-talking woman who fights with the skill of any soldier. In *Diary of the Dead*, the female leads are college students who rise to the challenge, fighting just as aggressively as the male leads. One of them, Tracy (Amy Lalonde), is from Texas, and this fact is exploited throughout in order to portray her as a tough gal who you just don't 'mess with'. Finally, in *Survival of the Dead*, one of the National Guardsmen is a tough-talking lesbian by the name of Tomboy (Athena Karkanis) who is just as skilled at fighting as the other members of her unit. It is notable that in each of these cases, while the female characters are depicted as strong and capable, they are also inevitably sexualised in ways that women in the previous films never were. When Slack is first introduced, she is wearing fishnet stockings and a revealing, latex top; Tracy's breasts are exposed at one point when she is attacked by a zombie; and in one scene Tomboy masturbates in a jeep as her fellow soldiers stand nearby. So while the main female characters in these films are certainly depicted as active, their sexuality is nonetheless exploited, and this continues to set them apart as different from their male companions.

Unfortunately, despite their growing active roles, most of the female characters in the last three of Romero's films are clichéd and thus psychologically uninteresting. The exceptions to this are the characters Janet and Jane (both played by Kathleen Munroe), twin sisters who appear in *Survival of the Dead*. What makes these two characters intriguing are the roles they play in introducing an unusually positive element of hope into the complicated dynamic of human activity and passivity. Both Janet and Jane are the daughters of Patrick O'Flynn (Kenneth Welsh), the patriarch of one of the feuding families locked in a struggle for control of Plum Island. Jane is dead, but continues to ride about the island on her horse, driven by the same sort of instinct that drives other zombies mindlessly and passively to continue carrying out predatory activities. Janet, on the other hand, is still alive, and she actively defies her father by refusing to leave the island with him once he is exiled by his nemesis, Seamus Muldoon (Richard Fitzpatrick).

The recurrent image of Jane on her horse is perhaps the most evocative and memorable image from *Survival of the Dead*. Her gaunt, shrivelled face and hollow eyes are signs that she is one of the undead, and yet the fact that she still rides a living horse gives her character a sublimely mysterious presence. She is not like the other zombies that are only concerned with predation. She does not consume her horse's flesh, but rather retains a special bond with it, as is demonstrated when the horse defends her from being attacked by one of the living characters. The fact that Jane is the twin sister of Janet leads us to suspect that the two of them, in life, were very similar to one another. Janet, who is strong-willed, active and concerned with ending the feud between her father and Muldoon, is depicted as one of the most sensible and sympathetic characters in the film, and so we are led to suspect that her sister, by implication, probably shared these qualities in life. This helps to explain why it is that as a zombie she stands apart as somehow uniquely noble among the rest of the characters on the island. Recall that Romero suggests repeatedly throughout his cycle of films that what drives the undead is instinctual inertia. They are driven to engage in the same activities and routines that they were inclined to engage in during their lives. Normally in Romero's world these activities and routines are far from laudatory. His films display a consistent cynicism about humans and their enthusiasm for empty consumerism, violence and aggression. In the case of Jane (and Janet) however, this cynicism is absent. They appear to be two of the few pure and good characters in Romero's world, and so in death, Jane's instinctual drives are not, as is usually the case, toward cruelty and violence, but toward the promotion of harmony and personal freedom. She is, like her twin, an especially active and well-balanced human being, and so once she falls prey to the undead plague, the momentum of her basic positive instincts carries on; at least until the final moment when she ultimately does bite and infect her twin sister. It is here, in the last of the *Dead* films, that we see something like a flawed glimmer of hope. Good people do exist, although even they retain the potential for aggression and cruelty. Like bad people, they must also die. From this there is no escape.

UNSYMPATHETIC HUMANS VS SYMPATHETIC ZOMBIES

Over the course of Romero's zombie films, it becomes increasingly apparent that the director's sympathy shifts from the surviving human protagonists toward the living dead zombies. This shift is linked to an increasing emphasis on the active, yet shameful, capacity of humans to engage in acts of excessive cruelty. With each successive film in the cycle, Romero seems less intent on horrifying his audiences with the gruesome nature of the living dead zombies, and more concerned with revealing to his audiences the horrific potential of living, breathing human beings.

In *Night of the Living Dead*, the zombies are more threatening and frightening than they are in any of the succeeding films; at least in part because it is our first introduction to them. It has been noted frequently that Romero invented the modern zombie, and in the first film of his cycle these undead creatures appear with all of their terrifying force. When they are introduced in this film, we are not sure what to make of them. They are uncanny, unfamiliar and unexplainable. As already noted, they are thrust upon us so that it seems as if the world has suddenly fallen apart, and that the normal rules of rationality no longer apply. Their appearance announces the reign of nihilism.

Additionally, in this first film the zombies are relatively nondescript and lacking in personality. Although we can see their faces and recognise them as representatives of various social types, overall they are not particularly unique or distinct from one another. They shamble along, appearing especially shadowy (because the film is made in black and white), blending into a mass. In this way, they make us fearful in the same way that any large, faceless, advancing group would. We don't understand what they want as they keep pursuing the living with inexorable and unstoppable persistence.

Dawn of the Dead possesses an entirely different look than *Night of the Living Dead*. First of all, it is made in colour, and so the shadowy mystery that is part of the first film is, to a great degree, absent. In *Dawn*, the zombies appear in full light for most of the film, and thus we are able to get a good look at them, seeing that each of them has a different face and personality. Throughout the movie, the same zombie characters reappear – the fat, shirtless man; the nun; the mechanic – all of whom we get to know in a way that we never got to know the zombies in *Night*. This makes the creatures more familiar and unique, and thus more sympathetic to us. Instead of shocking and horrifying us for the entire picture, in *Dawn* the zombies also amuse us

Figure 4.3 Bub (Sherman Howard), a likeable zombie from *Day of the Dead* (1985).

and make us laugh. There is something comical about their bewilderment on the escalator, as well as their attraction to the consumer goods displayed in the shopping mall windows.

In *Dawn of the Dead*, the real villains are the marauding bikers who attack the mall that has been secured by the heroes of the story. These aggressive survivors are depicted as being more frightening than the undead. They are organised, determined and capable not only of taking away what the main characters have fought to secure, but we imagine that they are also cruel and vicious in ways that the zombies are not. These bikers would not be content simply with killing their enemies; they would no doubt enjoy torturing and raping them as well. So it is that in this film, the audience's fear starts to be directed away from the zombie threat, and toward the threat posed by surviving humans who seek to exploit other surviving humans.

Day of the Dead introduces us to the first zombie that has a full personality and who is presented as a kind of good guy. This is Bub (Sherman Howard), a domesticated zombie who used to be a soldier, but who now 'lives' in the laboratory of a scientist trying to understand the causes of the undead plague. Bub is chained to the wall with a collar around his neck, resembling a pet dog who remains content because he is fed and cared for by his master. At one point when his chain comes loose from the wall, he is confused and concerned, seeking for his master to reattach it. He salutes those who are his superiors in rank, exhibiting the sort of respect for authority that he showed in life. We might be tempted to think that this is all a matter of reflex, as we have seen with the other zombies in Romero's films, except that when Bub's master is killed, he wails in despair, and seeks revenge by shooting the murderer, another military man. Bub, in these ways, is more than a shambling corpse. He is a human being with feelings and a thirst for revenge. He becomes the first truly likeable zombie in Romero's films.

Continuing this theme in the next film, *Land of the Dead*, 'Big Daddy' (Eugene Clark) is introduced as another likeable zombie who is the leader of his own undead army. Unlike Bub, Big Daddy is not friendly toward humans, but he is a character who exhibits emotions and who cares about his group, which he leads in an attack upon those who threaten their dominion. Like Bub, he knows how to use a gun and he is calculating in his approach to threats. There are a number of characters who accompany him in his forward march toward the enemy, and as they overthrow the rich, upper-class oppressors who occupy an opulent luxury tower in downtown Pittsburg, the audience is led to identify with them and to cheer their triumph. In this film, the zombies appear as the underdogs, and we are happy to see them win.

As mentioned above, *Diary of the Dead* in many ways is a throwback to *Night of the Living Dead*, and as such the zombie threat is reintroduced in a shadowy, terrifying fashion. But while most of the creatures are nondescript and frightening, the same sort of depiction is also granted to many of the still living humans. The college students who are the central protagonists in this film soon realise that navigating their way around rogue National Guard units and violent rednecks who want to rob and abuse them is of just as much concern as avoiding being bitten by zombies. In the closing scene of this movie, we are left with images of cruelty that the surviving humans are capable of inflicting, drawing directly from imagery reminiscent of lynchings.

In *Survival of the Dead*, there are no heroes left, except perhaps for a pair of twins, one of which is alive and one of which is dead. In this film, the main protagonists are a band of thieving, rogue National Guardsmen. Their main struggles are with other survivors, including a group of racist rednecks who have decapitated a number of black zombies and displayed their still writhing heads on stakes; and, most centrally, with two bands of warring families on an island off of the coast of Maryland. As in *Day* and *Land*, a sympathetic zombie appears, this time astride a living horse. The survivors periodically see her riding across the landscape, and they express a kind of enchantment and admiration for her. One of the National Guardsmen even exclaims that she, a rotting corpse, is 'beautiful'. In this, the final film in Romero's cycle, living characters actually seem to experience a sense of fascinated delight, rather than disgust or horror, upon seeing one of the undead. How did this happen? How is it that the living survivors in Romero's film have become less sympathetic to us than the zombies?

Romero has claimed that each of the *Dead* films was made in response to the social conditions of its time (Romero 2008), and this fact may help in making sense of the overall shift in sympathy that we see over the course of the cycle. The first film, *Night of the Living Dead*, was released in 1968, and it may be that the passive zombies in this film were intended to be evocative of what Romero considered the most pressing, current cultural danger: passive acceptance of US government overseas policies in Vietnam. When *Dawn of the Dead* was made in 1979, the war was over and the passivity of the zombies came to symbolise the mindless consumerism of that era. In this film the passive zombies appear robbed of much of their menacing power; perhaps because consumer culture is a problem somewhat more comical, and less urgently alarming, than is war. In *Day of the Dead*, which was released in 1985 while Ronald Reagan was president (a politician whose cold-war rhetoric was notoriously bellicose), unrestrained and aggressive military characters appear as the most prominent threat. In 2005 when George W. Bush was president, *Land of the Dead* was released, featuring an oppressive class of rich and privileged exploiters, thus evoking a common criticism of social inequality during that era. The zombies in this film appear as the heroic underdogs, representing a full inversion of our sympathies when compared to *Night of the Living Dead*. In *Diary of the Dead*, also made during the Bush era, the most threatening characters are, once again, actively aggressive military men and racist rednecks. In *Survival of the Dead*, released the year that Barack Obama was elected president (2009), it is the active, internal feuding of island dwellers that appears as the major threat, mirroring the ceaseless and vain squabbles between various factions in the US government that dominated headlines at that time. It is in this last film that the most memorable and entrancing figure turns out to be a zombie on horseback, suggesting that rescue from our situation, if it does come, will appear in the form of passive detachment rather than out of active and angry aggression.

Thus, as social conditions in the US have changed since the 1960s, Romero's zombies can be interpreted as symbols representing what he considers to be a shift in the roles appropriately played by activity and passivity in our culture. Initially, when passive acceptance of government policies threatened to keep the US embroiled in a futile and wasteful overseas war, passive zombies represented the dangerous threat of submission to authority. In this period, the zombies appear as an unsympathetic menace and danger. However, as social conditions have changed, and as there has been increasing public awareness and criticism of the actively aggressive economic and political policies of elite classes, Romero's sympathies appear also to change, and he increasingly depicts the passivity of the zombies with sympathy. In passive disengagement, perhaps he sees an alternative to our continued entanglement in a system demanding active allegiance in order to perpetuate the cruel oppression of those who are vulnerable and weak. The active exercise of human power becomes the more looming threat, and so, by comparison, the unreceptive passivity of the zombies becomes the more attractive alternative. Maybe it is better just to withdraw than to participate on the side of evil.

Whatever the political and cultural motivations underlying the shift in

Romero's sympathies, there is, nonetheless, a more fundamental, philosophical message inscribed in the *Dead* narrative. In a world where meaning and purpose are not found ready-made, the forces of activity and passivity gain value only in relation to the goals that we choose to pursue. Romero seems to suggest that activity is not a self-evident virtue. It only becomes virtuous if put into service of projects that lessen, rather than multiply, the amount of cruelty and torment that exists in the world. For this reason, in the end, an actively cruel human is less decent than a passively aloof zombie.

CONCLUSION

George Romero's cycle of *Dead* films dramatises the process by which passive nihilism eventually triumphs over active nihilism. The initial zombie invasion forces human survivors to face a topsy-turvy world in which the dead walk and pursue the living. The zombies, as lifeless creatures passively led by instinct, represent the forces of passive nihilism, while humans, in their attempt to fight, survive and explain this phenomenon, represent the forces of active nihilism.

Humans have different responses when confronted with the 'abyss', and the battle between active and passive nihilism is played out in the interactions of the main characters in these films. There is a progressive strengthening of the female, and a weakening of the male, characters throughout the series. In *Night of the Living Dead*, the weakest character is a woman and the strongest is a man. In *Dawn of the Dead* there is a development of the female lead from weakness to strength, while in *Day of the Dead* the strongest character is a woman and the weakest is a man. In the remaining films – *Land of the Dead*, *Diary of the Dead* and *Survival of the Dead* – men and women are treated as equally active and strong, though the women become sexualised in ways not present in the first three films.

Initially, it seems as if human activity is a real virtue, to be preferred over the passive onslaught of the living dead. However, as the series moves forward, a shift occurs in Romero's perspective. We find that the depictions of surviving humans as active and aggressive start to take on a more and more distasteful character and instead, the passive, shambling zombies become more and more sympathetic. This development in Romero's film-making suggests that in a world of nihilism, being active is not enough to salvage humanity. While the empowerment of women and minorities in general is a laudable aspiration, it is no less important that humans learn to be active in a way that makes the world a less awful place, rather than a more hellish one. If we are incapable of that, Romero seems to teach, maybe we are better off as zombies who, rather than exhibiting active cruelty, are simply passive 'nuisances'.

George Romero's *Dead* films are a warning against cruelty. When traditional ways of living and thinking are undermined or called into question by anomalous circumstances, people often respond either by ignoring the new developments and withdrawing passively from reality, or by actively trying to force the world into the mould of their own ready-made ideals. Romero's films try to persuade us that an active engagement with the world is admirable, even in the face of hopeless circumstances, so long as we avoid reintroducing needless cruelty into our world. If there is a choice between the production of pointless brutality and doing nothing at all, perhaps it is the latter choice that is preferable.

In the confrontation with nihilism, then, the victory of passive nihilism may not be the worst evil that can be imagined.

CHAPTER 5

The Lure of the Mob: Cinematic Depictions of Skinhead Authenticity

Figure 5.1 Derek Vineyard (Edward Norton) and his skinhead gang in *American History X* (1998).

INTRODUCTION

Skinheads are generally viewed, in contemporary Western culture, as symbols of violence, white racism and bigotry. In fact, the term 'skinhead' is taken by most academics and mainstream media consumers virtually to be synonymous with the term 'Nazi', and it has become almost automatic to associate images of young, white males sporting shaven heads with viciousness and racial intolerance. The media commonly utilise and exploit this iconic image in everything from television programmes and commercials to magazine ads and movies, reinforcing and strengthening its evocative power. The skinhead has thus become one of our culture's most recognisable images of contemporary malevolence.

A number of popular motion pictures, however, have expressed a remarkable ambivalence toward skinheads, depicting them in a sometimes very sophisticated and sympathetic light. In films such as *Romper Stomper*, *American History X* and *The Believer*, the skinhead is portrayed as a misguided, though passionate and rather intelligent, rebel; a sort of tragic, alienated and wounded character who is in search of, yet constantly failing to find, a place in the world. Because of these qualities, at the same time that we are encouraged to detest the way of life of the skinheads in these films, we are also encouraged to view them, and their struggles, with a sort of guarded sympathy and compassion.

The skinhead subculture has evolved over time, and though there is a great deal of diversity among the beliefs, practices and lifestyles of real-life skinheads, one characteristic that remains a stable feature of this subculture is its preoccupation with the ideal of 'authenticity'. The skinhead's concern with 'being authentic' helps to account for the sympathetic depiction granted to the neo-Nazi characters in such fictional films as *Romper Stomper*, *American History X* and *The Believer*.[1]

THE SKINHEAD SUBCULTURE

There is a large gap between the reality of skinhead culture and its depiction in much of the media and the academic literature. George Marshall, a Scottish skinhead and the author of two books on skinhead fashion and culture, writes:

> The media and its cohorts take great delight in focusing on the sensational aspects of the cult and by doing so present a totally false and distorted impression of skinheads . . . not all skinheads are the racists the media makes them out to be, and . . . not all skinheads are even remotely interested in being used as political footballs. Of course, there are skins who are racist, but they too are totally misrepresented in the media to the point where buzz words like 'Nazi' have lost any true meaning. (Marshall: 2003)

If we consider the history of the skinhead movement as a whole, it becomes very clear that the terms 'skinhead' and 'Nazi' are not interchangeable. The influence of racist, right-wing politics on skinheads dates back only to the revival of the style during the mid-1970s when in Britain the National Front and the British Movement actively began recruiting among skinheads, who then existed on the fringes of the new punk-rock music scene. Previous to this time, in the 1960s, skinheads were associated with the British mod youth subculture, and whatever racism they exhibited was neither systematic nor political in nature. Originally labelled 'hard mods', (Cohen 1980: 187, Hebdige 1981: 55, Knight 1982: 10, Wood 2006: 130) the first youths sporting skinhead style began to emerge around 1964. These 'hard mods' took to cutting their hair short and wearing heavy boots in order better to take part in street fights with the rockers, a rival youth subculture. The hard mod style solidified into the skinhead style, and eventually the subcultures split. Soon, as Marshall writes, the skinhead culture crescendoed in 1969 (Marshall 1994: 5).

With the skinhead revival of the mid-1970s, there appears to have developed a further schism between the old-style or 'traditional' sorts of skinheads and new-style, punk-rock influenced skinheads. The traditional skins tended to view the new-style skins as sloppy, overly political and not truly committed to the traditional skinhead culture, style and 'way of life'. What occurred between them is the same sort of conflict that commonly occurs between successive generations. As the older generation seeks to sustain and conserve the old ways, the new generation lashes out and seeks to overturn the conventions of the past. As a result, a great deal of animosity, rivalry and outright violence may develop, and that is what appears to have occurred between these two generations of British youth.

When the style was exported to America and other parts of the world, this schism between the old and the new was also exported. In America, right-wing political organisations, as they had in Britain, began to recruit members from among the new-style skinheads, and in reaction to a growing tide of racial attacks and violence, many non-racist skinheads banded together in order to fight against what they saw as a threat to skinhead culture and the skinhead image. In New York City during the 1980s, an organisation of anti-racist skinheads calling themselves SHARP (Skinheads Against Racial Prejudice) was formed with the intent of doing battle with gangs of Nazi skins and running them out of town. The SHARP movement had a degree of success and spread throughout the world, but ironically it also appears to have been viewed with some animosity by many other traditionally oriented skinheads who came to see it as just another diversion from skinhead style, culture and cohesiveness (Marshall 1994, 148–51, Cortez 2005–9).

Despite the regional successes of non-racist skinheads in actual turf wars, when it comes to the war for the attention of the mainstream media, it is Nazi skinheads who have won the fight. Today when the term 'skinhead' is used, the immediate association in the public mind is with Nazism and racism. However, there are skinheads that are right wing and those that are left wing in their political orientations, those that are white, black, Asian, Hispanic and Native American in ethnic backgrounds, and those that are straight and those that are gay in their sexual orientations. So, if not just Nazis, then precisely what are skinheads?

First of all, 'skinhead' refers to a type of fashion that has certain consistent and identifiable characteristics. Most obvious among these is length of hair. Skinheads either shave their heads or crop their hair very short. This hairstyle, it is often suggested, was originally adopted, in part, as a form of rebellion against the youth culture of the hippies, who went to the opposite extreme of growing their hair very long as a symbol of peace, love and naturalness. Among skinheads, length of hair also has a symbolic meaning. It speaks to the skinhead's advocacy of hardness and the desire for control and discipline as opposed to the hippy's 'let it be' attitude toward life (Knight 1982: 10–13, 38–9).

Skinhead style is also characterised by the wearing of 'boots and braces'. The most popular brand of boot is the Dr Marten, though there is no single type of shoe or boot that all skinheads wear all of the time. Normally, the trousers that skinheads wear are either turned up at the cuff or tailored to be short enough to expose and accentuate the boot. Next to the length of hair, it is perhaps the boots that are the most striking and eye-catching characteristic of skinhead style. Often they are highly polished and secured with laces of various colours that may or may not communicate some detail of the particular skinhead's belief system (Marshall 1994: 170–1; Cortez 2005–9, Cogan 2008: 301). The spaghetti-strap braces worn by skinheads often hang from their waists and dangle around their legs, apparently serving as ornamentation and as a symbol of the individual's attunement to skinhead fashion (Marshall 1994: 167–8).

Aside from the length of hair and the wearing of boots and braces, there is a wide spectrum of clothing that skinheads wear. Both Marshall and Knight devote whole chapters of their books to the varied and changing details of skinhead fashion (Marshall 1994: 167–74, Knight 1982: 36–47), and it appears that within the skinhead subculture itself, confusion and misunderstanding sometimes arise concerning style. For instance, Marshall reprints a cartoon that depicts two skinheads, neither of whom recognises the other. One thinks the other is a mod; one thinks the other is a punk. This particular type of skinhead fashion confusion is also the subject of the song 'The Ballad of Jimmy and Johnny' by the punk-rock group Rancid; and it reflects the fact that generally speaking, the mode of dress favoured by the traditional skinheads, taking their stylistic cues from the 1960s, is more focused on particular brands of clothing and the neatness with which they are worn than is that of the new style of skinhead, who is more influenced by the anarchic vogue of 1970s and 1980s punk rock.

While no single fashion element is either necessary or sufficient for identifying a skinhead as a skinhead, the style of dress that tends to be preferred on the whole is 'smart, clean and tough' (Knight 1982:10). It projects an attitude of rebellion, self-empowerment and self-discipline. The skinhead style is simple and almost militaristic in its appearance, reflecting readiness for action and an aspiration toward order, control and toughness in the face of chaos, disorder and anarchy. There is, it appears, a very particular attitude that underlies, and is expressed through, the adoption of this style.

'Most skinheads see themselves as straightforward blokes and birds, more honest than the soul boys, more working class than the punks and posers, rougher and tougher than the mods . . . Skinhead tastes are right "down to earth"', writes Dick Hebdige (Knight 1982: 28). Hebdige uses the term 'authentic' in order to characterise the skinhead attitude. In an ethnographic study of online skinhead chat rooms, Alex Campbell also identifies authenticity as an important element of skinhead identity (Campbell 2006). Scrutinising what it means to be 'authentic' helps to provide insight into the attraction of the skinhead style as well as helping to explain the frequently sympathetic depiction of Nazi skinheads in a variety of contemporary motion pictures.

THE CINEMATIC DEPICTION OF SKINHEAD AUTHENTICITY

The philosopher Martin Heidegger has explored the concept of authenticity with more profundity and nuance than most modern authors. According to Heidegger, authenticity is a distinctively human state of being in which we strive to understand, come to terms with and accept who we are, where we have come from, and take responsibility for what it is that we are going to be. Humans, Heidegger tells us, are not mere things or objects pushed this way and that by the forces of nature. Rather, humans differ from other, non-conscious objects insofar as they always are capable of mentally projecting into the future and of imagining new goals and objectives that they may then freely choose to pursue. It is this openness to possibility that lies at the essence of human existence and that distinguishes us from non-human objects. Humans are 'thrown' into the world as pure possibility (Heidegger 1996: 39–42). Though we have no choice concerning how, when or where we have been 'thrown' into this world, according to Heidegger, authentic human beings seek to cultivate an awareness of the fact that we always have a choice concerning what we do once we are here.

To be authentic, then, encompasses more than simply recognising and affirming one's origins. It also encompasses an affirmation of one's responsibility to incorporate those origins into a larger project of self-expression and self-discovery. Since human beings are not already summed up and defined by their past, the task of becoming authentic is an ongoing project. So long as we live, we must make the sorts of choices that pave the way for our own future. While those choices are affected by our past experiences, they are not wholly determined by them. Choice occurs in the present, not the past, and it is at the juncture of the past with the present that the course of our future is decided. Thus the human being always exists on the boundary at which the present pushes into the future, and then becomes the past. For this reason, Heidegger tells us that humans are not 'things' or objects but rather events or processes that unfold and develop up until the point of death. It is at the point of death that all freely made choices cease to be possible and humans, consequently, cease to be humans. Once dead, a human is transformed into a corpse and so becomes an object like all of the other non-human objects in the world, subject to the determining forces of nature. The awareness of impending death, furthermore, is important for the development of authenticity since it drives home the point that we will not 'be here' forever, and thus it encourages us to take our choices, while we are alive, seriously.

All human beings must struggle with the themes of authenticity in their own way, and the skinhead style and 'way of life' is just one of them. In the films *Romper Stomper*, *American History X* and *The Believer* this struggle is illustrated in an especially dramatic form. There is a common structure to all three of these films. In each, an especially intelligent and sensitive member of a Nazi skinhead gang becomes disillusioned with the inauthenticity of the other members. This disillusionment leads the main character down a difficult path of self-reflection, conflict and negotiation with others. Ultimately, each film culminates tragically, and the main character either dies or must confront the destructive consequences of his past actions and way of life. As with all genuine tragedies, however, there is something redemptive in the suffering of the main character who, in heroic fashion, resolutely faces and freely brings to a conclusion the series of events set into motion by his own earlier choices in life.

ROMPER STOMPER

Made in Australia in 1992, the film *Romper Stomper* stirred up controversy upon its release precisely because audiences were unsure about the nature of the director's sympathies. Anti-fascist organisations protested and picketed the showing of the film, ironically enough assaulting skinheads who were seen leaving the cinemas where it was being screened. On the other hand, many skinheads spoke out about how the film presented an inaccurate picture of their culture, and reportedly the director himself was assaulted by Australian skins unhappy with how they had been depicted. All of this controversy is a reflection of the fact that *Romper Stomper* avoids the delivery of any clear-cut, black-and-white moral message about its subject matter. Rather, the film attempts to wrestle with, and give voice to, some uncomfortable issues concerning how a group of underprivileged outcasts struggle with nihilism, alienation and authenticity.

The theme of alienation predominates throughout this film. At the very start of the movie a group of Nazi skinheads assault a group of Asian immigrants. The leader of the skinhead gang, Hando (Russell Crowe), tells one of the Asian youths 'This is my country. I don't want you here.' So it is that the scene is set for a conflict between the new immigrants and the native skinheads. Yet, as the film progresses, it becomes apparent that it is the immigrants who are better integrated into the mainstream of Australian culture than are the skinheads. The Asian characters own businesses and have families, contributing to the economic and social well-being of Australia. The skinheads, on the other hand, live in an abandoned warehouse, have no jobs or families, and make no contributions to mainstream society whatsoever. At one point in the film Hando criticises a member of his own gang for making the decision to join the army. 'At least I get a paycheck and I can keep the haircut', the skinhead responds. But Hando is cynical even about this, expressing distaste for the government and how it sends the poor off to die for the interests of politicians and the rich.

The idea expressed here is telling. According to Heidegger, the most powerful worldly force that encourages inauthenticity in human beings is the 'They', or society. It is unavoidable that we must become entangled in society to some degree, Heidegger tells us, because we are, before anything else, thrown into the world with others, and this is a launching pad for how we become who we choose to be. However, there is a common tendency for people to overemphasise the effects of society on the individual and to lose themselves in the They, becoming instruments of the group rather than agents of self-discovery. When humans 'fall prey' to society in this manner, they no longer view the tasks and assignments of social living as tools by which the individual may create and ennoble him or herself. Rather, social duties become final ends to which the individual becomes subservient. The individual then becomes a cog, a piece of the machine that must perform its proper social function in order to allow everything else to move along smoothly. When this happens, human beings become things, and therefore also become inauthentic. As Heidegger writes, when this occurs the human being 'stands in subservience to the others. It itself is not; the others have taken its being away from it' (Heidegger 1996: 118). Because of this, authentic human beings must constantly be on guard against the potentially distracting influences of the group. Yet at the same time, it is this very same group out of which humans emerged, and without the group they would not be who they have become. To completely pull away from the group would also entail a lapse into inauthenticity, since to do so would be a denial of the origins and conditions that have contributed to who we are. This is the delicate balancing act that Heidegger claims all authentic human beings must execute. On the one hand, we must recognise the social conditions out of which we have arisen, paying tribute to those circumstances that allowed us to be who we have chosen to become. On the other hand, we must resist being drawn into thinking that those same circumstances have inevitably determined who we are and what sorts of decisions we have made over the course of our development.

In *Romper Stomper*, Hando's participation in the gang is a defensive tactic against the corrupting forces of Australian society. Everything outside of the gang is viewed by him as a threatening 'They', and in *Romper Stomper* the most visible form of the They are the new Asian immigrants who originate from outside of the country and who aspire toward integration into Australian society. However, there is also a less visible They whose presence permeates this film. This They has no particular face but is a conglomeration of people originating from an economically privileged position and who have aspirations toward political, social and economic power over others. Though the skinheads might be able to get into gang fights with the more visible form of the They, the other form is impossible to pinpoint and rout. It is a looming and yet vague threat that we know, even at the beginning of the film, the skinheads will be unsuccessful in fending off.

Hando and his gang soon come to realise that their world is coming apart at the seams. First, their favourite hangout is bought by the family of the very immigrants they assaulted earlier in the film. Then, Hando's gang is physically overwhelmed by those same immigrants and run out of their squat. With nowhere else to live, the skinheads take over another warehouse by intimidating its occupants and kicking them out. It is during this portion of the film that the inner dynamics of the skinhead gang as a dysfunctional surrogate family are developed. Hando's epileptic girlfriend, Gabe (Jacqueline McKenzie), takes on the role of a mother, Hando takes on the role of a father, and Davey (Daniel Pollock) plays the role of an adolescent son who re-enacts an Oedipal drama when he falls in love with Gabe and rebels against Hando.

After being humiliated by Hando, Gabe leaves the gang. Davey, who has fallen in love with Gabe, also leaves, making his first attempt to break his association with Hando. Gabe, without Davey's knowledge, goes to the police and informs them of the skinheads' location; soon the entire gang is dismantled, with the members either being killed or put in jail. Only Hando escapes, and he hunts down both Gabe and Davey convincing them to commit a robbery, steal a car and to go on the run from the law. Yet again, both Gabe and Davey lose themselves by becoming entangled in a web of complications woven by Hando. However, Davey is gaining further insight into his own motivations for living his life, and we can see that his misgivings about Hando are finally percolating to the surface. It is at this point in the film that the character of Davey emerges as the film's key figure who, in his struggle for independence, will be compelled to resist and break free of

Hando's corrupting and oppressive dominance, ultimately achieving a sort of tragic authenticity.

At the film's end, Davey kills Hando, eliminating the last obstacle that stands in the way of his own independence. Yet in this action, Davey also eliminates the last person that offered him protection from the mainstream world. Now he is on his own and must confront the consequences of his past actions. At the finale of *Romper Stomper*, it is suggested that these consequences are the very ones that were feared by the skinheads all along. As Hando lies dying on an Australian beach, and as Davey and Gabe embrace one another nearby, a large group of Asian tourists pile out of a bus and, lining the cliffs overlooking the beach, snap photographs of the skinheads below. Thus it is demonstrated that the world of the skinhead is an anachronism. It is a world that no longer is a viable form of life, and the crimes that were committed in its name were simply vain gestures of defiance against the unstoppable forces of a changing society.

Despite the futility of the skinheads' struggles, we are left feeling that Davey, at least, has done what he must do. He was a product of the culture of his gang, he absorbed and accepted its ideals, and he finally acted on those ideals. When Davey eliminates Hando, he is freely choosing to carry out the logic of his gang. This logic is premised on the assumption that outsiders are a threat and must be resisted. In killing Hando, Davey brings to completion a drama that could not logically have ended in any other fashion. The gang had to self-destruct due to its fierce antipathy toward outsiders. Ultimately, every individual human being is outside of, and alien to, every other individual human being, and so, by the gang's own logic, only one human being could be left standing.

Davey experiences an epiphany of authenticity at the closing of the film. As is often the case with authentic revelations, Davey's experience is not a pleasant or a happy one. It is, however, redemptive insofar as it provides a platform for his future development. Davey, by bringing to completion the drama of his skinhead life, may now move on to explore the substance of his own uniquely human life. His life with the gang has contributed to who he has become, as is all too painfully obvious at the end of the film, but it has not necessarily closed the book on who he will be in the future.

AMERICAN HISTORY X

The theme of redemptive suffering is repeated in the struggles of the main character from *American History X*, the most commercially successful, but nonetheless controversial, of the skinhead films. Staring Edward Norton as Derek Vineyard, a Nazi skinhead living in Los Angeles, *American History X* draws on the dramatic imagery of skinhead culture in order to illustrate the difficult complications that result when one individual awakens to the fact that his freely chosen group affiliations have produced unanticipated and irreversibly destructive results for himself and those around him. A young man who has experienced a traumatic alienation from mainstream culture, Derek's skinhead affiliation is portrayed as an attempt to recapture a lost sense of belonging and at-homeness within a gang. Like Davey in *Romper Stomper*, Derek finds, however, that there are some very costly dues to be paid for his gang membership, and eventually it becomes clear to him that these costs outweigh the benefits of being a skinhead.

Unlike the characters in *Romper Stomper*, Derek is depicted as someone who initially has a legitimate and exploitable foothold in the mainstream world. He is part of a family that he cares about, and is a talented student with a potentially bright academic future. The story of his skinhead affiliation begins when his father, a firefighter, is randomly shot and killed while battling a blaze in a black neighbourhood. After his father's murder, Derek comes to blame non-whites not just for the death of his dad but for all of America's problems. This makes him sympathetic to the Nazi message of Cameron (Stacy Keach), a white supremacist organiser who sees strong leadership potential in Derek. Derek thus becomes the leader of the local skinheads, inciting his gang to terrorise and assault non-white members of his neighbourhood in hope of running them out of town.

Alienated from the mainstream, Derek finds comradeship and purpose with his gang of skinhead friends. It is in the gang that Derek feels potent and once again in control of his destiny. He reappropriates his world, taking charge of circumstances and bending them to suit his purposes. One key scene in *American History X* illustrates this new attitude by means of a basketball game between Derek's skinhead gang and a gang of black neighbourhood residents. Derek confronts the black players and makes a bargain with them: they will play a game of basketball and whoever loses will leave the court, conceding it as the rightful territory of the winning team. The challenge is accepted, and after a very close battle, the skinheads win, sending the black players away, defeated.

The contest on the basketball court is a pivotal scene in *American History X*, for it is here that the confidence of the skinheads becomes solidified and the resentment of the black gang members is further provoked. Both groups, ironically, see themselves as outsiders to mainstream culture. They come from the same working-class background, go to the same schools and struggle with the same sorts of economic challenges. Yet instead of feeling united in their social status, they instead feel at odds with one another, in competition for turf, prestige and power in the neighbourhood. Each sees the other group as a menacing They. The skinheads, in fact, feel as though they have become even more marginalised than blacks, since it seems to them that the government and all of liberal society has thrown its support behind blacks and withdrawn its support from working-class whites. Thus, association in the skinhead gang serves to set its members against the forces of both mainstream culture and the threatening, non-white forces within the working class itself. On the basketball court, the skinheads win their first tangible victory over the most visible threat from within their own class, and in so doing they become emboldened and infused with confidence that perhaps their struggle for white, working-class supremacy might be successful after all.

In retaliation for their defeat at basketball, members of the black gang attempt to steal Derek's truck late one evening. Alerted by his brother, Danny (Edward Furlong), that there are three black men with guns outside their house, Derek loads his own gun and confronts the intruders, shooting one dead, wounding the other and sending the getaway driver fleeing. In a rage, Derek drags the wounded gang member to the sidewalk and, forcing his open mouth onto the edge of the curb, stomps him to death. Derek thus kills the leader of the gang that he confronted on the basketball court, asserting final dominance within his own working-class kingdom. During this whole episode, Derek rants on and on about the sanctity of his home and about the fact that his truck was given to him by his dad, reinforcing the fact that what is at stake here is more than mere physical survival. This is a battle for territory, honour and status within the neighbourhood. Derek has proved that he is the top dog, capable of defending everything his father has left to him and his family. And yet, even as this drama plays out and Derek struts his tattooed, muscular frame through the street, smiling and smirking at his younger brother, the police arrive and arrest him, proving that there is an authority that outranks the leadership of the local gangs. Having defeated the street-level threat arising from within his own neighbourhood, now Derek is overwhelmed by the force of a more all-encompassing and powerful threat from outside his neighbourhood. The power of the state will now intervene in his life, depriving him of his freedom and imprisoning him for murder.

In a 1998 Washington Post review of *American History X*, Stephen Hunter claims that this last scene, in which Derek stomps a rival gang member to death, is an example of how the film glorifies the racism and violence of American skinheads. He claims that the powerful image of a half-naked Derek, tattooed with Nazi symbols and filmed in black and white, serves to imbue the main character with an aura of heroism, promoting a romanticised vision that may be attractive to some audiences. This, Hunter claims, is enough to condemn the film as a morally degenerate, 'taboo breaking' exercise. While it is undeniable that there is an air of romanticism about Derek in this and other scenes, what Hunter's criticism overlooks is that this is precisely one of the truths that *American History X* eloquently gives voice to. Thousands of youths are attracted to the skinhead image because it does give them a feeling of power. What this film does so successfully is to give the viewing audience a sense of why this subculture, terrible as it is in some ways, is also attractive in many other ways. As Dick Hebdige has pointed out, all subcultures are symbolic attempts by youths to 'recognize and rise above a subordinate position which was never of their choosing' (Hebdige 1981:139). It is the assertion of power and the refusal to remain subordinate that makes the skinhead image attractive, yet it is this same aspect that also makes it dangerous and potentially destructive. Derek is a character that illustrates both the seductive and the terrifying potency of the skinhead subculture. In it is embedded the potential for authentic self-empowerment as well as self-destruction

Derek's entanglements with the skinheads and the police cannot be undone. Even after he convinces his brother to sever ties with the gang, both Danny and Derek will forever bear the marks of their past affiliations. In one especially moving scene, this fact is illustrated when Derek, standing naked in front of a bathroom mirror, inspects the large swastika tattoo on his chest. He raises his hand to cover the symbol, imagining what it would be like no longer to have this image as a permanent part of his body. But when he lowers his hand, the tattoo is, of course, still there. Even if it was removed through surgery, or obscured with further cover-up ink, the memories, the resentments and the experiences that motivated him to get the tattoo in the first place would still remain in his mind. The tattoo is a bold and honest testament to what he once believed in and killed for. It is a symbol that brings to mind all of the pain, as well as the pride, that was involved in Derek's advance toward self-understanding. Though it might be comforting to remove or obscure it, such an action would also be a gesture of inauthenticity insofar as it would be an attempt to deny the past events, both good and bad, that contributed to who he eventually came to be. Likewise, when both Derek and Danny do decide to grow out their hair and change their style of dress, these measures prove only to be superficial actions that really change nothing that has already been set in motion. After leaving the skinhead gang, Danny is gunned down at school by the little brother of the black man that Derek stomped to death. At the end of the film, Derek cries and cradles his own dead little brother in his arms. Neither of them are skinheads anymore, yet they are still, like the rest of us, responsible to account for their past actions.

THE BELIEVER

The Believer is not only the most controversial of the skinhead films, it is also the most intellectually challenging and profound. Whereas the main protagonists in *Romper Stomper* and *American History X* sometimes come across as a bit too transparent and stereotypical, the main character in *The Believer* is always psychologically fascinating. While he is not someone that the audience ever comes to like, he is an individual that most fully exhibits the tragic conflict involved in the struggle for authenticity. As we watch this film, we feel an uneasy sense of admiration for the main character's fanatical dedication to the cause of philosophical purity, yet we also develop a sense of dread concerning where this dedication will lead him. At its conclusion, *The Believer* offers no simple resolution to the issues that it raises, and in fact its main message seems to be an especially nihilistic one. The world, and our life in it, is filled with irresolvable incongruities. We are thrown into circumstances not of our own choosing for no good reason, and when we die there is no final judgment about the type of life we have led. The best that we can do while alive is to be true to our personal ideals, defying human convention and rebelling against the absurdity of our existence.

The premise of this film is a strange one. Danny Balint (Ryan Gosling) is a Jewish Nazi Skinhead. This apparent contradiction in Danny's life is the basis for all of the conflict, struggle and eventual tragedy that characterises his story. Danny was brought up and educated in the traditional Jewish fashion. His schooling included detailed reading and interpretation of the Torah, and ironically it seems that his drift toward Nazism was encouraged by his understanding of this holy text. In it Danny found evidence of a God that was supremely powerful, 'a bully', as he tells his horrified teacher. This bully puts humans, like Abraham, through the most awful and horrifying ordeals simply because he can. 'I am everything and you are nothing!' is God's message as Danny sees it, and it is this message that Danny internalises and comes to embrace as his own ideal. Whereas his teachers and peers attempt to cover over and downplay the harshness of their faith by offering apologetic arguments and justifications for God's actions, Danny refuses to sugar-coat anything. If God made humans in his own image, then perhaps humans should be just as uncompromising, dogmatic and brutal as God himself. Danny's life thereafter becomes a fanatical battle against everything that he sees as fake and inauthentic both within and outside of the Jewish faith.

It is almost natural, given his antipathy toward mainstream interpretations of Judaism, that Danny should be drawn toward a movement that generally is seen as Judaism's polar opposite: Nazism. In the symbols and rhetoric of the Nazis, Danny finds an image and a vocabulary that helps him brashly to articulate everything that he has learned to hate about the traditional culture of his own Jewish heritage. He thinks Jews are sneaky, sexually depraved and money grubbing. They gain power over others by manipulating things from behind the scenes, yet they deny their own role in this manipulation. Instead, they play the part of the victim, pretending to be weak and put upon by the rest of the world. This mock weakness is a disguise that allows the Jews to become complacent and smug, blaming everyone but themselves for the hardships that they encounter in life. Danny finds this element of Jewish culture to be especially detestable, a fact that is illustrated again and again throughout the movie but perhaps most dramatically in the opening scene where he attacks a young Jewish student that he has encountered on the subway. When he sees this young man on the train, Danny goes out of his way to intimidate and harass him, trying to provoke some sort of a righteous response. Instead, the student slinks away and tries to escape from his aggressor. Danny follows him out onto the street where he knocks the boy's books from his arms; then after handing them back, Danny strikes the student, knocking him to the ground. He becomes more and more enraged as his victim becomes more and more passive. 'Hit me! Please hit me!' Danny yells at the cowering youth, but there is no response. It is this sort of passivity that makes Danny the most angry. A Jew should fight back. He is one of the chosen people, he has God on his side, and yet this student who should know all of this fails to act on his knowledge.

Something similar, however, is true of the gang of Nazi skinheads to which Danny attaches himself. While he seems to respect and admire their willingness to act out violently, he realises that their devotion to Nazism is just a shallow excuse for antisocial behaviour. The members of his gang claim to hate Jews, yet they don't even understand the philosophical basis of the religion. They have not read the Torah, as Danny has, they have not studied Jewish history and they have no understanding of Jewish customs and rituals. In fact, his fellow gang members at times become suspicious of Danny because of his well-developed knowledge of Judaism, a fact that Danny himself throws back in their faces. 'How can you claim to hate the Jews when you don't know anything about them?' he asks, pointing out that Nazi heroes such as Eichmann were deeply concerned with the study of Jewish religion and philosophy. The Nazis, it seems, are no better than the Jews. They are both, by and large, inauthentic.

Yet Danny is both a Jew and a Nazi. His Jewishness is something that he never chose, but it is a fact that he was born into. It is part of his cultural and spiritual heritage. His Nazism, on the other hand, is a freely chosen response to his Jewish heritage, and in some ways it is not such a strange reaction. An important aspect of the Jewish faith is the willingness to enter into an ongoing dialogue with, and criticism of, God and his design. The Jewish philosopher Martin Buber calls this affiliation between man and God an 'I and Thou' relationship. The Jew is supposed to engage in a conversation with God as one engages in dialogue with another human being. This involves the readiness actively to pursue an open, thoughtful and committed relationship with the Lord, and as Buber writes, 'Relation is reciprocity. My You acts on me as I act on it' (Buber 1999: 67). Thus, true Judaism is not a matter simply of blind faith but of an ongoing struggle with one's faith and a willingness to engage in the questioning, interpretation and the criticism of God's plan as expressed through Jewish holy texts, conventions and practices. Ideally, Jewish students are encouraged to argue with their rabbis, participating in a dialectical exchange through which a deeper and deeper understanding of God is developed. This process has no end but proceeds in Socratic fashion forever. The ultimate purpose is not to pronounce final answers but to gain a more textured and profound understanding of the subtleties of what it means to be Jewish. In these ways, Danny's Nazism is not at all incompatible with his commitment to Jewish theology. He takes up the banner of Nazism in order to express his discontent with certain aspects of Jewish faith and tradition, yet he still retains a distinctively Jewish commitment to understanding and doing justice to the profundity of the Judaic philosophy itself. In his Nazism, Danny thus becomes more of an authentic Jew than any of his Jewish peers who passively accept the way of life, the pronouncements and the dogmas of the mainstream tradition. 'Only Jews talk about the Jews as much as you do', says his girlfriend, Carla (Summer Phoenix). 'No', Danny responds, 'the Nazis talked about the Jews all the time.'

By associating with his gang, Danny has the opportunity to think about being a Jew without any interruption. He plots bombings, assassinations of Jewish businessmen and takes part in the desecration of a synagogue. It is during this last episode that Danny, unexpectedly, experiences a spiritual epiphany. After breaking into the synagogue, the skinheads begin to spray paint swastikas on the walls and to vandalise the building. Danny himself intends to plant a bomb in the pulpit at the front of the building. None of this is upsetting to Danny until one of the gang members discovers the scroll on which the Torah itself is rolled. It is only Danny who recognises this holy text for what it is, and he becomes agitated when his fellow skinheads begin to treat it with disrespect. He tries to explain to them that they must leave it alone, but the power of the Torah is lost on them. Danny, on the other hand, is instantly and profoundly affected by its presence. This is the text that he spent his school years reading, analysing, criticising and interpreting. It, more than any other influence, contributed to making him who and what he is. His fellow gang members, not knowing he is Jewish, have no idea how deeply important the Torah is to Danny, but when the gang finally leaves the synagogue, Danny takes the scroll with him. Once he is back at his apartment, alone with the Torah, he painstakingly repairs and cleans it, lingering over it and contemplating its meaning for him.

Danny is a Jew, and his encounter with the Torah proves to him how deeply this fact is inscribed in his soul. The Torah paints a picture of the Jews as God's chosen people, the people that He led out of slavery in Egypt and into the promised land. Their history is a story of homelessness, dispersion, conflict and harsh punishment for failing to keep their promises to God. God both loves and hates his people at various times, slaughtering them by the

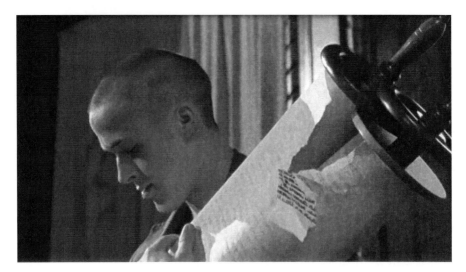

Figure 5.2 Danny Balint (Ryan Gosling) embraces the Torah in *The Believer* (2001).

thousands and then, conversely, rewarding them with fruitfulness. To be a Jew is to commit one's allegiance to such a God and never to rest in the desire to try and understand His expectations and plans. This is all done without the promise of a heavenly afterlife or even of happiness here on this earth. It is done only because of a blood-pact made by Abraham thousands of years ago. This blood-pact created an obligation that is now part of the essence of what it means to be a Jew. Its fulfilment does not entail contentment, riches or power. All it promises is that those who seriously devote themselves to the ceaseless task of trying to understand God will come closer to being what they were always meant to be: authentic Jews. Danny realises this, and like Jacob, the character in Genesis who 'wrestled with God' and was thus renamed Israel, Danny fights with his Lord right up until the end. At the conclusion of the film, Danny detonates a bomb as he reads from the Torah in the temple. After he is destroyed by the explosion, he finds himself running up an endless flight of stairs, and at each of the landings his Rabbi from childhood waits, telling him that he wants to discuss the Torah further. Danny continues running farther and farther upwards, and finally his Rabbi yells, 'Where are you going? There's nothing up there!'

CONCLUSION: THE FACT IN FICTION

The films *Romper Stomper*, *American History X* and *The Believer* are all controversial and thought-provoking motion pictures. While none of these films offers a literally accurate, documentary account of the skinhead subculture, each one uses the imagery of skinheads as a way to explore an issue of concern to real-life skinheads and mainstream audiences alike: the quest for authenticity. Each film utilises the iconic image of the skinhead as a focus, illustrating the sort of friction that ensues when an individual, immersed in a group movement, finds it necessary to break free of that movement for the sake of self-discovery and self-understanding. As this is a circumstance that all of us find ourselves in at one point or another, these films invite us to bridge the gap between our own way of life and that of a generally maligned and misunderstood subculture. The violence and wickedness of Nazi skin-heads is thus depicted as something that is not wholly incomprehensible, but that is rather an expression of a common impulse. This helps to explain why it is that, though the protagonists in these skinhead films are Nazis, they are all, nonetheless, received by mainstream audiences in a sympathetic manner.

In reality, the skinhead style transcends any particular set of sociopolitical beliefs or doctrines and is more properly seen as an expression of some very general, and not uniquely skinhead, ideals, feelings and values. Perhaps most important among these is the aspiration toward personal power and autonomy in a world that is seen as hostile to individual self-determination. As Heidegger has suggested, one of the most pressing concerns in human life involves the drive to become self-aware and to accept our essence as fully responsible agents. We can all too easily forget that authentic self-understanding and fulfilment are ultimately more important than money, prestige, power or even happiness, and in this forgetting we may lose ourselves and fall away from what we really are supposed to be. To avoid this trap often requires aggressive self-assertion, and at times it may even require that we affiliate ourselves with subcultures and movements that help us to consolidate our self-confidence and rebel against the mainstream. This is one of the grand ironies of the quest for authenticity. We are forged in a social context even as we seek to break free from its bonds. Paying tribute to the social circumstances that shape us, but refusing to allow those circumstances to define us, is one of the most impor-tant, and the most difficult, requirements of authentic self-realisation. It is a predicament that all human beings face.

NOTE

1. Almost without fail, the film productions exploring skinheads and their way of life have focused on Nazi skinheads and their gangs. The 2006 film *This is England* breaks this mould, focusing primarily on a gang of non-racist skinheads in 1983. Nonetheless, the gang is torn apart when it must deal with the return from prison of a racist member. *No Skin Off*

My Ass (1991) focuses on a gay skinhead. Other fictional films dealing with the skinhead subculture include: *Made in Britain* (1982); *Meantime* (1984); *Skinheads: The Second Coming of Hate* (1989); *Pariah* (1998); *16 Years of Alcohol* (2003); *The Green Room* (2015); *Imperium* (2016).

CHAPTER 6

Cultural Change and Nihilism in the *Rollerball* Films

Figure 6.1 Jonathan E. (James Caan), the nihilist superman in *Rollerball* (1975).

INTRODUCTION

In 2002, a remake of the 1975 film *Rollerball* was released in cinemas. It flopped at the box office, disappearing quickly from movie screens and reappearing shortly thereafter on home video. While aesthetically horrendous, the remake of *Rollerball* is instructive, as it provides a point of contrast to the original film, highlighting a change in our culture's mode of engagement with the problem of nihilism. Both films share a roughly similar plot, yet in the differing manners that they explore and develop that plot, we can glimpse two separate ways in which nihilism may be encountered, confronted and dealt with. The differences are quite striking.

In the original 1975 film, nihilistic melancholy is depicted as a situation stemming from individual strength and the aspiration toward excellence. The forces of culture, and of nature itself, are portrayed as conspiring against any individual who strives for absolute spiritual fulfilment, with the ultimate message that personal honour, nobility and success can be had only at the cost of forsaking public adoration and the economic rewards offered by corporate culture. In the 2002 remake, on the other hand, the encounter with nihilism is depicted as a result of personal inadequacy and individual weakness. This version portrays the entanglements of mass culture more sympathetically, in the sense that they offer the failing individual a way out of personal hopelessness. Whereas the original 1975 film ends with the main protagonist resolutely and fatalistically braving his destiny alone, the 2002 remake ends with the main character taking part in a mass movement against the powers that be.

The different sensibilities of these two films are best summed up in this last contrast, which also points to a characteristic difference between the ways that modern and postmodern cultures tend to view the issue of nihilism. Whereas modernists view nihilism as arising out of the individual's confrontation with a world naturally hostile to the innate strivings of authentic and self-reflective human beings, the postmodernist perspective sees nihilism as merely a transitional stage in the evolution of mass culture; one that might be overcome with the abandonment of older, more individualistic ways of thinking. Thus, in the relatively brief interval between the releases of the two versions of *Rollerball*, we can detect a shift from a modernist to a postmodernist rendering of the predicament of nihilism.

THE EXISTENTIAL AND ONTOLOGICAL AXES OF NIHILISM

Nihilism describes a distinctively human state of separation from the highest objects of aspiration. As human beings, we have the capacity to formulate notions of absolute Being, Truth, Justice and Goodness, yet so long as we live we must constantly fall short in our pursuit of these perfections. According to the nihilist, human finitude necessarily separates us from the full realisation of any form of absolute perfection, and so we must forever remain frustrated in our attempts to achieve those goals that are the most important to us. Human life, as Albert Camus puts it in *The Myth of Sisyphus*, is 'absurd', being characterised by an ongoing battle between the individual, human demand for meaning and fulfilment, and the resistance of the world around us to deliver on that demand:

The world itself, whose single meaning I do not understand, is a vast irrational. If one could only say just once: 'This is clear,' all would be saved. But these men vie with one another in proclaiming that nothing is clear, all is chaos, that all man has is his lucidity and his definite knowledge of the walls surrounding him. (Camus 1955: 20–1)

Though nihilists claim that all humans are necessarily alienated from the absolute, most of us are not fully aware of, or even interested in, this predicament. Humans commonly ignore their nihilistic separation from Being, Truth, Justice and Goodness, focusing their attention on more humble, and more attainable, worldly goals. While the pursuit of these sorts of modest objectives may produce feelings of potency and happiness in the short run, such pursuits also have the effect of distracting us from our actual state of alienation from the ultimate. This underlying alienation, claims the nihilist, can never fully be covered over. Though it may become obscured in the course of pursuing our everyday activities, it nevertheless reasserts itself and makes itself known in a number of different ways.

An existential feeling of alienation frequently offers us our first access to the phenomenon of nihilism. For an individual whose fundamental aspiration is for the absolute, the modest, attainable goals ordinarily pursued in the course of living life must at some point lose their sustaining power. It is then that life, as commonly lived, becomes shallow, flat and unsatisfying. Lived existence becomes 'a desert-like emptiness, a malaise, an illness of the spirit and the stomach' (Novak 1970: 11). These feelings of distress may provoke individuals to embark on an inquiry into the causes of life's deficiencies, and in the course of such an inquiry, they may be forced to recognise the pervasive scope of the phenomenon of nihilism.

From an existential encounter with personal meaninglessness, the nihilist discovers that all is not right with the world. As Camus asserts, 'We must despair of ever reconstructing the familiar, calm surface which would give us peace of heart' (Camus 1955: 14). The source of this existential discontent is the perception of an incongruity between the aspiration toward infinite perfection, on the one hand, and the finitude of human being, on the other. This incongruity is, in its very essence, irresolvable. Humans are finite, and so their very being is at odds with the state of being that they wish to achieve. The existential struggle with this state of affairs opens the way for an encounter with ontological nihilism. Ontologically we have 'fallen away' from Being. We are separated from the absolute and there is no hope of ever mending this rift. Our relationship to reality is naturally defective, and like puzzle pieces that fit nowhere, we are doomed to remain out of place and estranged from Being itself.

Ontological alienation and the existential sense of anxiety that accompanies it have often been pointed to as self-evidently negative aspects of nihilism. In modernist accounts of nihilism, these negative aspects are often viewed as grounds for a kind of despair that can only be faced with heroic or superhuman resolve. We find elements of such accounts in the writings of both Nietzsche and Camus. For Nietzsche, because humans are fated to struggle against the chaos of reality, and in the process eternally to suffer, they should develop the psychological capacity to endure this struggle and suffering, and even to take pleasure in it. Thus we find Nietzsche advocating the goal of the 'Superman'. The Superman understands 'every kind of "imperfection" and the suffering to which it gives rise [as] part of the highest desirability' (Nietzsche 1968a: §1004). Such an individual can endure recurrent feelings of alienation and despondency, utilising those feelings as a motivation actively and creatively to affirm life. For Nietzsche, while ontological nihilism is a reality, once faced this may serve the positive end of overcoming existential despair through the cultivation of individual strength and nobility of character. Likewise, Camus suggests that while the recurrent struggles and sufferings of life never end, a heroic and strong individual can resolve to rebel against the ontological injustice of the world and, like Sisyphus, take pride and joy in affirming that 'the struggle itself toward the heights is enough to fill a man's heart' (Camus 1955: 91).

The postmodern approach to both existential and ontological nihilism sees them as something to be left behind as quickly as possible, like bad dreams are forgotten upon waking from an unsettled sleep. Jean-Francois Lyotard provides perhaps the clearest and most straightforward articulation of this viewpoint when he characterises postmodernism as a 'war on totality' (Lyotard 1997: 82). Being, Truth, Justice and Goodness are viewed by Lyotard as outdated ideals and totalising 'metanarratives' that vainly attempt to sum up the absolute. In focusing our attention on these ideas and aspiring toward them, humans doom themselves to despondency and despair in pursuit of the unattainable. It would be better, then, to turn our backs on these traditional values and immerse ourselves in creative and ongoing play aimed at no final, totalising goal. According to the postmodernist, existential and ontological nihilism are both conditions of modernism that may be overcome and left behind if we can just give up on our antiquated aspirations. Nihilistic thinking is a sort of nostalgic longing for a bygone era, according to this point of view, and it is about time that we move on into the future. Once we abandon the desire for the absolute, we can get on with life, untroubled by the worries that accompany nihilistic alienation. The freedom to pursue diverse ways of thinking about the world will then be more frequently exercised, and we will no longer be concerned with dogmatic assertions concerning the 'reality', 'truth', 'justice' or 'goodness' of human creations. All of these creations will be understood as equally legitimate and not in the least bit substandard, since we will no longer judge them according to totalising and absolute ideals.

Whereas the modernist is an idealist, the postmodernist is a pragmatist. This, in a nutshell, defines their difference. The modernist is constantly struggling to attain the unattainable; the postmodernist finds satisfaction in what is attainable. While the modernist aspires to the ideal, and thus remains unsatisfied with the real, the postmodernist considers what has been made real, in all of its diverse forms, as good enough. There is, then, an inherent conflict between modernist and postmodernist approaches to the phenomenon of nihilism. According to modernists, nihilism (at least in its ontological guise) cannot truly be overcome, but must merely be endured and resisted. In this view, existential nihilism results from the awareness of an ontological reality that can never authentically be denied. For postmodernists, however, nihilism is simply a way of thinking, not a final description of reality, and so it may be overcome if we can become adept at creating new ways of thinking that are not reliant on absolutes. For modernists, it takes strength to endure the ontological truth of nihilism. For postmodernists, languishing in nihilism is a sign of weakness, as it indicates one's inability to break free from a nostalgic longing for the past. While both consider the struggle against existential nihilism to be a potential source of vital activity, they disagree on its ontological origins, and as a result, modern and postmodern perspectives tend to characterise the struggle with nihilism differently. From the modernist perspective, nihilistic struggle has a hint of fatalism and tragedy to it as the nihilistic superhero vainly battles reality alone and isolated from those who have chosen to ignore the Truth. From the postmodern perspective, on the other hand, the confrontation with nihilism is seen as a transitionary stage after which an individual might successfully break free from the outdated mode of thinking that had previously constrained his or her manner of being. In this liberating struggle, the postmodern nihilist tends to develop sympathy for the viewpoints and aspirations of others, accepting that there are many different and divergent ways of conceptualising the 'truth'.

In the old and new versions of *Rollerball*, we see these differences illustrated and played out to their logical conclusions. The 1975 version represents the modernist perspective, portraying the main protagonist, Jonathan E. (James Caan), as a professionally successful, yet tragic, individual who has no choice but to engage in a vain battle against the world around him. The 2002 remake, on the other hand, takes up a postmodernist perspective, depicting its hero, Jonathan Cross (Chris Klein), as a professionally unsuccessful, but opportunistic revolutionary who ultimately leads an insurrection against his oppressors. Contrasting and comparing these films produces several concrete illustrations of the internal vicissitudes of nihilism that are not only philosophically instructive, but which also offer insights into the shifting landscape of American culture.

ROLLERBALL 1975: A MODERN NIHILIST SUPERMAN

The original version of *Rollerball*, starring James Caan as the hero Jonathan E., begins and ends ominously with Bach's *Toccata and Fugue in D Minor* playing on the soundtrack. This is a significant detail that sets a tone quite different from that of the 2002 remake. *Toccata and Fugue in D Minor* is popularly associated with tales of terror, and so the feeling produced in the audience is one of foreboding and danger. At the very start of the film, as track lights and instrumentation are tested, as the audience for the game streams in, and as the corporate executives take their places, deeply menacing organ music dominates the soundtrack and creates a mood that will remain a major undercurrent throughout the course of the movie. We are not encouraged to feel excitement or enthusiasm by this mood-setting music, but rather anxiety about some sort of looming threat. Furthermore, the danger that represents the threat we are encouraged to be anxious about is not easily identifiable. It could be the violence of the game to come, it could be the crowd of spectators, or it could be the corporate executives dressed in suits and ties who seem somehow in control of all that is going on. In fact, it will turn out that the danger faced by the film's hero is composed of all these things. The very being of Jonathan E's life-world is made up of the culture that surrounds the ultra-violent sport of rollerball, and as the plot develops, we watch him become increasingly alienated from this world. His fall occurs not as the result of his choices, but rather is due to forces beyond Jonathan E's control and understanding. Ultimately there is nothing that he can do to change his fate, and though he is the captain of a championship sports team, he will end up alone as he rebels against his world and the forces that control it.

This opening scene of the 1975 version economically and artfully blends together many of the major elements that will be important to the rest of film. From the outset we know all is not well, and we quickly suspect that Jonathan E. is a sort of tragic hero on a collision course with destiny. According to Nietzsche, the tragic hero is a figure who 'prepares himself by means of his destruction, not by means of his triumphs', and as we watch him we, the members of the audience, experience 'an assured premonition of a highest pleasure attained through destruction and negation' (Nietzsche 1968d: §21). Jonathan E. embodies the tragic reality that there is always, even for the most successful individuals, an abyss that separates humans from Being itself. The longing for heavenly tranquility is doomed to failure, and even champions like Jonathan E. are destined to fall, no matter how heroically they assert their individual strength. We sense this as the first players assemble in formation on the rollerball track at the start of the film. As our hero stands with his team and impatiently endures the playing of the 'corporate anthem' (his impatience illustrated by the fact that he nervously beats his fist against his leg for the duration of the anthem), we get a feeling for what he is up against and how hopeless his struggles will be. Corporations rule the world now, and the game of rollerball is a rationalised, formalised and highly controlled substitute for the old-fashioned forms of warfare engaged in when political states dominated the earth. The corporate anthem is an organ piece, heard by the characters within the film, that reminds us, the audience, of the foreboding organ music we heard during the opening sequence. The multinational corporations, like God or Big Brother, are everywhere and control everything. Each time that the corporate anthem is played, we are reminded of the ever-present threat that Jonathan E's world poses to him. His destruction seems certain, yet we anticipate that he will exhibit the sort of personal authenticity and strength of character that we expect from a tragic hero.

The first rollerball game between Madrid and Houston (Jonathan's team) introduces us to the action, violence and frenzy that are integral facets of this sport. While the game is certainly vicious, it has strict rules of conduct that must be observed. Penalties are called for illegal moves and time limits for play are set. Players who violate the rules are pulled from the game, and in particular we see Jonathan's friend, Moonpie (John Beck), penalised for unnecessary roughness. The choreography of the players' moves, the colour of the costumes and the design of the rollerball rink (which is actually the Olympic bicycle stadium in Munich, Germany) all contribute to a sense of realism and energy that helps us to understand why Jonathan is led to exclaim toward the end of the match, 'I love this game!' It is in the midst of the action and the excitement of play that Jonathan feels most at home. He feels as one with this world that has predictable rules, a predictable duration, and clear-cut goals. Uniforms differentiate those who are with him from those against him, and he feels comfortable counting on the people around him to carry out their duties. Yet, as he leaves the arena, surrounded by chanting crowds of fans, the organ theme from the opening sequence booms out again. The camera pans upward and zooms in to reveal the looming presence of the office building of the Energy Corporation, the company that owns Jonathan's rollerball team. We are thus reminded that, despite his victory in the roller rink, all is not well. Though Jonathan may be a great team captain, his world is far more compli-cated than he can understand, and it is about to fall apart.

We soon see how uncomfortable and out of place Jonathan feels when taken out of the rollerball arena. A meeting with Mr Bartholomew (John Houseman), the head of the Energy Corporation, reveals that the game is only part of a much larger reality, and that this larger reality has 'rhythms' and 'rules' that override those within the world of rollerball itself. While Jonathan may be the consummate athlete, he is completely out of his element when it comes to understanding this world beyond his sport. As a symbol of this awkwardness, in the corporate office he stumbles, cuts his finger on a decoration, and generally feels ill at ease as Bartholomew proclaims rollerball to be a 'stupid game' from which Jonathan should be happy to retire. When Jonathan expresses his surprise at being asked to retire, Mr Bartholomew explains that the game was never supposed to be a tool for individual glory, but rather was designed by the corporations in order to demonstrate to the masses that team effort is what makes for greatness. Though not made explicit during this conversation, it later becomes clear that Jonathan has undermined this purpose by rising to superstar status. He has become too much of an individual figure, a sort of Superman in the sport. For this reason he must leave the game and eventually fade from the public consciousness. Jonathan is merely an instrument used by the corporations, and since he has ceased to serve his assigned purpose, the corporations want him out. It is interesting that even Bartholomew admits he alone is not fully in control of this decision concerning Jonathan's fate. Rather, there are a variety of corporate forces pressuring Jonathan to accept a generous retirement package that will include a television programme celebrating his life and career. What is important is not *why* Jonathan must retire, but *that* he must retire, for whatever reason.

After this first meeting with Bartholomew, an abyss opens up in Jonathan's world and he begins to fall away from all that previously brought him comfort and security. His entire identity and sense of self-worth stems from his rollerball-playing skill, and now all of that is going to be taken away. As it turns out, Jonathan had a sense that something was wrong long before this crisis. His wife, Ella (Maud Adams), was taken from him because a corporate executive desired her for his own. Presumably, Jonathan didn't make a big deal over this at the time, since the corporations were otherwise being so generous to him. But now that he is threatened with retirement, Jonathan starts to re-examine his feelings and he realises that these two episodes in his life – the loss of his wife and now of his career – result from some common cause. He repeatedly expresses a sense of bewilderment over just what this cause is, claiming that he doesn't understand why things seem to be falling apart in his life. He tells his friend Moonpie that 'someone is pushing' him and that 'something is going on' but that he doesn't know what it is. A sense of existential anxiety and emotional discomfort attune Jonathan to the fact that he is not in control of his own world, that something is out of joint, and that his spiritual health is deteriorating as a result. Jonathan's growing uneasiness, and his consequent reflection and meditation on his situation, are encouraged by the fact that now, like never before, the smooth functioning of his life's routines has been interrupted. These routines, in a Heideggerian sense, have now become 'unhandy', and so, like a carpenter clutching a broken hammer, Jonathan must stop and thoughtfully consider what to do next.

Moonpie laughs all of this off. Unlike Jonathan, Moonpie has no concerns other than the acquisition of more wealth and luxury. He tells Jonathan,

'We're living good! You know we are!', yet Jonathan is too far along the path of nihilism to take Moonpie's comments seriously. Moonpie is so distracted by all of the luxuries that his career brings him that he doesn't even care to question why he is of value to the corporation and the crowds that adore his team. Jonathan *does* wonder about this very issue, if only because now his personal strength and charisma have become more of a threat than an asset to the powers that be. As his relationships with those around him disintegrate, Jonathan is led to the realisation that although he is physically surrounded by people, he is also spiritually alone. His fans still adore him and cheer his victories, and his friends still profess their loyalty to him, but Jonathan nevertheless develops a progressively contemptuous attitude toward them and their placid manner of existence. He views them as participating in a way of life that makes them into tools of the system rather than fully developed and autonomous agents. While people like Moonpie cannot even conceive of leaving such a world behind, Jonathan is in the process of becoming ever more alienated from it. The further that this alienation progresses, the more isolated Jonathan becomes and the more suspicious and hostile he is toward the crowd and its complicity with corporate culture.

In the world that Jonathan and Moonpie inhabit, the masses and the corporations are mutually dependent on one another. The corporations require a large consumer base, which the masses provide, and the masses require easy access to goods and services, which the corporations supply. So long as products and luxuries are readily available, the crowd will continue enthusiastically to support corporate control and domination, regardless of how much freedom must be surrendered by particular individuals. In the event that someone did come forth to threaten the authority of the corporations, and consequently to endanger the economic comfort of the people, the 'herd' would instinctively defend the status quo, siding with their corporate benefactors in order to resist and subdue any threat to predictability and tranquility. Jonathan foresees this, realising that he will continue to be adored by the masses only so long as he submits to his role as an instrument of the corporation. At one point in the film we even overhear debauched partygoers at an Energy Corporation gathering who speculate that rollerball players are simply robots programmed for the purpose of playing the game. If Jonathan's rebelliousness were to result in any sort of decline in the efficiency with which the necessities and luxuries of life were delivered to these people, they would be certain to do away with him the way that they would do away with a malfunctioning machine. He himself would have become 'unhandy' to those around him. As Nietzsche repeatedly observed, the herd's love of the Superman is never unconditional. When working toward purposes and goals that promote their group interests, the herd loves the Superman. However, since his strength cannot invariably be controlled, the herd also fears the possibility that the Superman may go his own way, becoming an impediment, rather than an asset, to the group's way of life. Under such circumstances, the masses would turn against such an individual in an effort to protect their familiar and comfortable routines. Jonathan has now reached the point at which he is being forced to make a choice between retirement to the junk heap or resistance against the corporate machine. Furthermore, since the purposes of the corporate machine have the unwavering support of the herd, Jonathan, if he chooses resistance, is taking on the entire world, and this is a battle that he is bound, tragically, to lose.

The characters of Jonathan and Moonpie represent two aspects of the human attitude toward nihilism. In Moonpie, we see a character that doesn't care to reflect on the value or worth of his life. Since, unlike Jonathan, he has never been put in a position where he has to worry about his place in the world, he has never had the motivation to question the meaning of life. He remains content and happy with the things that he has earned and that have been granted to him by the corporation. Moonpie is mystified as to why Jonathan would even be curious about the behind-the-scenes workings of corporate culture, since he himself has never experienced discomfort or anxiety as a result of the outcomes of these workings. He represents that aspect of the human personality that doesn't want to make waves, but would rather take what the world has to offer without question. Moonpie desires stasis, predictability and the absence of anxiety, and he rejects anything that threatens to destabilise this contented state of being. Yet his state is one of ignorance and, in the terminology of Heidegger, it consequently 'covers over' the true nature of Being itself. In his contentedness, Moonpie refuses to raise the question of Being in the first place, and by refusing to raise such a question, he remains alienated from Being, and thus in a state of unreflective, though non-anxious, ontological nihilism. Thus, Moonpie exhibits the characteristics of an 'inauthentic' individual, or one who has become 'tranquilised' by the distractions of his world. As Heidegger writes, 'The supposition . . . that one is leading a full and genuine "life" brings a tranquilization to Da-sein, for which everything is in "the best order" and for whom all doors are open . . . This *tranquilization* is inauthentic being . . .' (Heidegger 1996: 166).

Jonathan, on the other hand, experiences a chronic state of anxiety throughout the film. At one point he too was like Moonpie, but now a sense of existential nihilism has become overwhelming for him. Though he may wish that he could turn back and become more tranquil like his friend, Jonathan is unable to do so. His existential angst has opened the doors of reality to him, revealing that there is more to life than just his own comfort. To remain passive and content is no longer an option now that he has caught a glimpse of the world beyond his rollerball career. What would he do once he retired? Certainly he would have luxuries, women and money. But Jonathan has come to realise that these sorts of things are not ends in themselves. For him, material goods are worthwhile only as measures of his individual struggles. As he says to his ex-wife at one point in the film, 'It's like people had a choice a long time ago between all them nice things or freedom. Of course they chose comfort.' For Jonathan, happiness and material goods are not equivalent. For him, happiness is to be found in struggle, contest and the freedom to push himself to new heights.

Despite their opposing reactions to the threat of nihilism, Jonathan nevertheless cares for his teammate. We see this when, in a game against Tokyo, Moonpie is injured and falls into a persistent vegetative state. Since Moonpie apparently has no other family to see to his affairs, it is up to Jonathan to sign the papers that would authorise ending life support for his friend. Jonathan refuses to do so. Earlier, Moonpie had tried to convince Jonathan that his life was perfect, and now Jonathan sees in Moonpie's brain-dead state the sort of stasis, predictability and lack of anxiety that Moonpie sought all along. There are beautiful nurses to take care of him, fresh flowers to add colour to his quiet room, nutrition provided intravenously, and perhaps even dreams to keep him entertained. When Jonathan tells the doctor to 'Just leave him as he is', he is, in fact, recognising that Moonpie's life is not substantially different *now* from how it *always* was. The corporation always did (and now always will) supply him with the comforts of life. Now, at least, he doesn't have to play rollerball to get them.

When Moonpie's doctor tells Jonathan that there are hospital rules that must be followed, Jonathan angrily responds 'No there aren't! There are no rules!' It is in this statement that Jonathan finally articulates an important insight that he has been grasping at throughout the course of the film. As he has fallen further and further away from his old, comfortable and predictable way of life, he has come to see that, as Nietzsche warned, 'the total character of the world is in all eternity chaos' (Nietzsche 1974: §109). Rules are human-created illusions useful only for fending off the chaos of reality. Though we often fool ourselves, taking comfort in the thought that there are objective guidelines and standards existing 'out there' in the world around us, the truth is that we, as individuals, are ultimately responsible for making our own way and carving our own path through life. There are no rules, no universal values, and no absolutely certain set of 'facts' about reality that can serve as the cornerstones of an authentic life. Instead, human beings are radically alienated from the totality of Being, and in our vain struggles to understand Being itself, the human mind always falls short of its goal. Anytime that we try to bring an end to our struggle with reality by claiming that one set of rules or facts is indisputable, we lapse into laziness, inauthenticity and self-deceit.

This point is driven home to Jonathan when he seeks out information about corporate decision-making and corporate history. Since all of the world's books have been summarised and digitised as computer files, he must travel to the world's storehouse of information: a supercomputer named Zero. Upon arrival, Jonathan is informed by the head computer scientist (Ralph Richardson) that Zero has misplaced the entire thirteenth century. 'Not much in the thirteenth century', he is told. 'Just Dante and a few corrupt popes.' The sheer volume of facts that Zero has been entrusted with is overwhelming, even for a machine. There are just too many details about the world to store or to recall, and Jonathan is told that Zero is continually confused as a result. Not even a supercomputer can recollect everything that has ever happened, and if there is no brain big enough to recall the truths of history, what good are those 'truths'? Jonathan is told, in fact, that it is as if Zero 'knows nothing at all'. When Jonathan asks Zero about corporate decision-making, the computer answers in a series of tautologies: 'Corporate decisions are made by corporate executives. Corporate executives make corporate decisions.' All of the bits of information, all of the 'facts' that Zero has stored, amount to nothing in the final evaluation. Absolute certainties are, when it comes right down to it, useless tautologies. As the Scottish philosopher David Hume observed, propositions that offer us certainty tell us nothing new or useful about the world, and those statements that *do* tell us something new or useful are always uncertain. But whereas Hume recommended a form of 'mitigated skepticism' in response to this state of affairs, suggesting that we go along with convention rather than struggling against it, Jonathan follows another path. He concludes that no authority, no so-called expert can tell you what is real. In the end, it is up to you as an individual to aspire to your own vision of the Truth, to struggle toward it and to ignore the distractions that always threaten to pull you away from it. It is up to each individual human mind to impart meaning, coherence and significance to the information that it collects. When our hero turns to Zero for an answer to his nagging questions about life, he is rewarded with nothing; zero. Here lies Jonathan's most profound lesson: no one, not even those who are the smartest, strongest and most erudite, are in touch with absolute Truth or Being.

At the end of the film, Jonathan will play one last game of rollerball, during which all rules have been suspended. This final match is intended as a fight to the death, and the corporation heads anticipate that Jonathan will be killed during its course; thus reducing *him* to zero. Jonathan, however, has learned his lessons very well, and as his awareness of ontological nihilism grows, so too does his resolve to fight even harder against it. In the final scene of the film, the ominous sounds of *Toccata and Fugue in D Minor* once again resonate. As the crowd of spectators chants his name, and the corporate executives angrily look on, Jonathan E. remains the last man standing in the rollerball arena. Alone, he skates around the track until the movie ends in freeze-frame, and we, the audience, are once again, as at the beginning of the film, left with the feeling that no good will come of this. Though Jonathan may have triumphed in the roller rink, he is still a stranger to the vast, hostile world 'out there'. When he steps off of the track, the qualities that allowed him to excel as a sports star – individualism, nonconformity, iconoclasm and a thirst for victory — will be the very qualities that are sure to bring him, yet again, into conflict with the herd and corporate culture. Nothing has been resolved at the end of the film, in other words, and our suspicion is that as one man against the entire world, Jonathan E. is certainly fated for eventual destruction. His struggles have led nowhere and accomplished nothing, and yet we are left with a feeling of admiration for Jonathan's integrity and strength of character. Herein lies his nature as a tragic hero.

ROLLERBALL 2002: A POSTMODERN NIHILIST OPPORTUNIST

The tone set at the beginning of the 2002 remake of *Rollerball* is more frenetic, more action-packed, and ultimately, far more superficial than that of the original. We are introduced to the main character, Jonathan Cross, as he rockets down the winding streets of San Francisco. Now transformed into a twenty-something airhead, in this opening scene Jonathan skillfully avoids collision with cars and eludes the police while taking part in an illegal streetluge contest. His competitor ends up losing control, smashing through a shop window while Jonathan is rescued from arrest by his friend Marcus Ridley (LL Cool J), who pulls him off of his street-luge board and into a speeding car. Instead of the ominous and unsettling tone of Bach's *Toccata and Fugue in D Minor*, all of this is played out against a rock-and-roll soundtrack that reinforces a feeling of speed, action and excitement.

It is in Ridley's car that we learn Jonathan is a failed hockey star. He has been unable to make it into the major leagues, and instead has had to pursue his quest for fame in the world of illegal extreme sports. Unlike his precursor in the original film, Jonathan Cross is introduced to us as an outsider who lacks the talent required to excel in his first choice of career. His friend suggests that he abandon hockey and instead sign up to play on a rollerball team. In this film it turns out that rollerball is no longer a product of corporate powers that rule the world, but is, rather, a moneymaking spectacle created by Eastern European gangsters who are riding the wave of chaos that resulted after the breakup of the Soviet Union. This is quite an interesting reversal. Recall that in the original film, rollerball was a means of social control, utilised by ruling corporate entities to demonstrate the futility of individual effort. It was depicted as a product of the artificial, yet strict order that corporate forces had imposed upon the world. In the 2002 version of the film, on the other hand, rollerball is a sport arising out of chaos and the breakdown of order.

The climate of corporate control has been replaced by the climate of anarchy. Whereas Jonathan E. struggled against a powerful, unified and omnipresent corporate threat, Jonathan Cross struggles against the threats of fragmentation and lawlessness.

Jonathan Cross, like his precursor Jonathan E., is caught in the grip of existential nihilism. However, the root cause of his malaise, and thus his response to it, is quite different from Jonathan E's. For Cross, his feeling of existential alienation derives not from being torn away from success, but from personal failure in his professional career. Cross, unlike E., never was a success. His desire to become a rollerball player is a second choice, pursued only after he fails at everything else that he really wanted to do. When he departs for Zhambal, Kazakhstan and joins the 'Horsemen', Jonathan discovers a sense of at-homeness that is new to him. He is transformed from an outsider and a criminal into an integral part of a bigger sports machine. Here we get to see a different, postmodern perspective on the problem of existential nihilism. The problem, it seems, is not that Jonathan has fallen away from his world, but rather that he never was part of any particular world in the first place. His feelings of unease might, hence, be alleviated by pursuing, and integrating himself into, *any* environment whatsoever. The particular sport, the particular set of rules or ideals don't really matter on this view. All that is important is to become a success, and in this remake, success is defined by all of the trappings that Jonathan E. rejected in the first film: money, possessions, sexy women and screaming fans. So it is that we see Jonathan Cross racing around in expensive sports cars, going to trendy nightclubs, sleeping with models, and so forth. He is happy here, and for a while, at least, his sense of existential angst dissipates.

As has already been noted, one of the characteristics of the postmodern response to nihilism is to reject old ideals and goals that, from the postmodernist's viewpoint, appear simply to be pipe dreams, incapable of fulfilment. Why torture yourself by working toward objectives that will never be reached? Why continue struggling to hit a target that is infinitely far away? As Lyotard observes, such a life can only end in despair, and the experience of nihilism results from the failure to realise this fact. Instead, Lyotard advises that we wage 'war on totality'. The postmodern hero, in this regard, is one who recognises the absurdity of struggling toward absolute ideals, and who rejects despair and frustration by lowering the bar, so to speak, setting new, attainable goals in place of the old, unattainable ones. Like Jonathan Cross, the postmodernist is a sort of opportunist and a pragmatist who is not committed to any particular vision of perfection, but is willing to bend in order to fit whatever world will accept him or her into its domain. Prewritten 'metanarratives' are to be rejected and instead we are encouraged to make up the rules as we go along. Success and happiness may be discovered in compromise, accommodation and flexibility rather than in single-minded commitment and determination.

Thus, for Jonathan Cross, hockey is no more desirable than rollerball. What matters is to find a niche, a home and a place to fit in. This is the only escape from existential nihilism according to the postmodernist. Because nihilistic feelings derive from a silly attachment to outdated ideals and old-fashioned goals, all that is needed in order to overcome these feelings is to reject the traditional pursuits that have led to frustration, and so Jonathan Cross leaves the US and finds his contentment in the chaos and anarchy of Eastern Europe. Though in his home country he is an outsider and a criminal, in another, more unstable culture, he can be a hero and a role model.

However, as he quickly distinguishes himself overseas as the star of the Horsemen, Jonathan begins to sense that his triumph is had at the expense of other people. The irony of Jonathan's newfound success is that the very conditions that allow him to prosper are also the conditions that are repressing those around him. His teammates are treated as expendable parts by the team's owner. Not only are their player numbers tattooed on their faces, marking them as property, but when the viewing audience enjoys seeing players killed in action, the owner organises the deaths of various members of the team. Furthermore, it turns out that the main audience for rollerball is composed of economically disadvantaged mine workers who toil like slaves for the very individual who owns Jonathan's team. It is here that we get a faint echo of one of the themes that was first sounded in the original film. There is some sort of nefarious force that is orchestrating rollerball in order to keep the proletarian masses placid and content. The difference in the remake, however, is that the force behind rollerball is a greedy individual who is out to exploit the current social disorder. In the original film, on the other hand, the force behind rollerball, though represented by Mr Bartholomew, is more shadowy and corporate. It was not out of greed that the corporations created the game, but out of a desire to maintain comfort, safety and security for the entire world. In the original film, the enemies are a corporate suit, a culture of conformity and a world in which the individual is subsumed by the masses. In the remake, the enemies are the leather-clad, unshaven Eastern European gangster Alexi Petrovich (Jean Reno), a culture of disorder, and a world in which the masses are exploited by greedy individuals.

Though the new version of *Rollerball* was obviously intended as an action-packed adventure film, the action sequences are so ill-conceived and executed that they are ridiculous rather than exciting. The rollerball matches take place on a roller rink that is tiny and too filled with gadgets and contraptions to give us a clear view of the contest as it takes place. Because there is no let up in the violence even outside the roller rink, the games do not shock us or even hold our attention for very long. Instead of the sombre and foreboding organ music of the corporate anthem, the matches are accompanied by rock bands playing on the sidelines. Instead of Bach, it is *Pink*, *Slipknot* and *Rob Zombie* that provide the soundtrack for the film. The mood that is thus conjured up is not contemplative, but frenzied and distracted. We are not encouraged to care about the feelings of the main character but to anticipate his next violent and audacious manoeuvre. Action instead of reflection is the keynote here. Whereas in the original version the three pivotal game sequences were masterfully executed, providing important anchor points around which the rest of the story unfolded, in the new version the game sequences seem almost incidental to everything else that is occurring in the movie. During the rollerball matches, the actors are filmed in close-up, so the audience misses out on the overall scope and sweep of the games. Each character is given an outrageous name, costume and personality, transforming them into cartoon characters that resemble contemporary professional wrestlers. There are even sequences during which trading cards of each of the players are superimposed over (and thus allowed to obscure) the rollerball action scenes. All of this contributes to a very particular vision of individuality that distinguishes the message of this remake from that of the original.

In the postmodern world, individuality is expressed through superficial diversity. To be a postmodern individual is to be unique in appearance, thought and orientation, though at the same time to be tolerant of the differences that others exhibit. As Richard Rorty puts it, the aim is to pursue 'an expanding repertoire of alternative descriptions rather than The One Right Description' (Rorty 1989: 39–40). For the postmodernist, one's individuality derives from the willingness to take action and resolutely construct a unique vision of reality. Such visions have no grounding in absolute Truth, but are simply interesting expressions of particular perspectives and viewpoints. The personal narrative, rather than the overarching metanarrative, is the model. The only real 'sin' for the postmodernist is to impose one's personal narrative too vigorously on others. Toleration, liberality and openness to the 'other' are defining characteristics of postmodern ethics, and in the new version of *Rollerball* we see an expression of this view. While Jonathan Cross searches for his place in the world, he is depicted as someone who is not content to occupy that place to the detriment of others. Though intent on fulfilling his individual desires, he does so with the presupposition that everyone else is free to do so as well. When he discovers that there is a domineering force behind the game of rollerball that is keeping others from their own desires, he revolts and vows to lead the oppressed in a war against this force. Thus Jonathan becomes a revolutionary leader precisely because he desires to be an individual among other individuals. The players and spectators that he rallies are of all different colours, nationalities, appearances, sexes and dispositions. This sort of diversity is good in itself, according to the postmodernist hero. On the other hand, the sort of individualism that the team owner embodies is of a different kind. It is the individuality of the tyrant, and this is a type of individual that the postmodernist detests. Such an individual disregards the diverse views of others, believing that his or her view is the 'One Right Description' of reality. But this is intolerable for the postmodern hero for whom there is no one right description, no overarching Truth concerning the nature of reality. The freedom to pursue diverse forms of happiness is what is important, and anything that gets in the way of this, including artificial standards of Truth, is rejected as oppressive.

The 2002 version of *Rollerball* ends, unlike the 1975 version, on an optimistic, and distinctively non-tragic, note. During the climax of the film, Petrovich trades Jonathan's teammate and love interest, Aurora (Rebecca Romijn-Stamos), to a rival rollerball team. As the final game commences, both teams turn their violence not against each other, but rather toward the owners and organisers of the match, leading the audience in a mass rebellion against the corrupt gangsters who have exploited them. Whereas the original version ends with Jonathan E. alone and in freeze-frame as that ominous organ music plays, this film ends with Jonathan Cross and Aurora in the midst of a mob of rioting mine workers. Aurora says to Jonathan (as they make their way through the crowd and into the back of a truck), 'You have started yourself a revolution.' She then tells him that she wants to take him home 'to her bed', kissing him as a rock song by *Rob Zombie* fills the soundtrack. The revolution is thus ushered in, not as a frightening and ominous prospect, but as a sexy, exciting and hopeful adventure.

THE ETHICAL, POLITICAL AND CULTURAL IMPLICATIONS OF NIHILISM IN THE *ROLLERBALL* FILMS

Traditionally, nihilism has been viewed as an unequivocally negative and life-denying phenomenon that should be avoided, left behind or overcome at all costs. Philosophers tend to emphasise the anguish, despair and torment associated with nihilistic struggle, suggesting that the experience of nihilism has nothing at all positive about it. If our examination of the old and new versions of *Rollerball* has taught us anything, however, it has taught us that this traditional viewpoint is simplistic. In truth, '[t]he essence of nihilism contains nothing negative' (Heidegger 1991: 221). While the separation of human beings from their highest objects of aspiration certainly is a situation that promotes frustration, torment and anxiety, at the same time it creates the potential for activity, struggle and the progressive pursuit of greater and greater levels of achievement. As finite creatures, absolute perfection always remains beyond our grasp, and yet the unending aspiration toward perfection may be the very thing that bestows dignity and worth upon us as human beings. Though this aspiration may often be accompanied by feelings of negativity, it would be a mistake, for that reason, to blind ourselves to the potentially positive power of nihilistic struggle. Both Jonathan E. and Jonathan Cross are examples of characters that use their experience of nihilism, not as an excuse to give up on life, but as a motivation for continued aspiration and activity. While the particular targets they pursue may differ, neither character simply gives up and rolls over in order passively to accept the injustices of the world. Rather, these characters remain alive, vigorous and vital in the face of a hostile environment.

While it is clear that both versions of *Rollerball* confront the threat of nihilism, neither film advocates the variety of nihilism that Nietzsche has labelled 'passive nihilism'. Passive nihilism is a symptom of 'decline and recession of the power of the spirit' (Nietzsche 1968a: §22). It occurs at the point when the individual is no longer motivated to pursue humanly created goals. Because all worthwhile goals seem out of reach to the passive nihilist, this individual comes to think that all actions in the world are inconsequential and therefore meaningless. For this reason, the passive nihilist withdraws, submissively giving in and renouncing any concern or care for the struggles of life, or for Being itself. This is, of course, quite unlike the attitude of either Jonathan E. or Jonathan Cross. Both of these characters are supremely active in their nihilism, finding in it an opportunity for the expression of strength, energy and concern for the world.

However, the mere expression of 'will to power' is not an unequivocally commendable thing, and so active nihilism is not, in and of itself, necessarily to be lauded. One of the dangers faced by the active nihilist is that this individual can all too easily fall into a distracted state of busyness, squandering his or her energies on pursuits and goals that lead further and further away from, rather than closer to, an attuned awareness of Being itself. This, I think, is the main distinction to be made between the activities of Jonathan E. and Jonathan Cross. Whereas Jonathan E. embodies the active nihilism of a modern Superman who retains an authentic, individual attunement to Being itself, Jonathan Cross embodies the active nihilism of a postmodern pragmatist who has become distracted by the world of the crowd. In his eagerness to overcome nihilism, the character of Jonathan Cross, ironically, becomes ever more entangled in it by losing himself and wilfully becoming an instrument for social revolution. As Heidegger writes, 'The will to overcome nihilism mistakes itself because it bars itself from the revelation of the essence of nihilism as the history of the default of Being, bars itself without being able to recognize its own deed' (Heidegger 1991: 240). Like Jonathan Cross, those who are too concerned with overcoming nihilism tend to forget that nihilism is itself an aspect of Being. As such, nihilism is not something to be avoided, or left behind as quickly as possible. Rather, it is a phenomenon that should be lingered over and taken as an opportunity to develop a greater, more authentic, understanding of ourselves, our world and the relationships that hold between the two.

By scrutinising the plots of both versions of *Rollerball*, we have revealed a number of common issues that are explored in these two films. In both movies we are introduced to a character caught in the grip of existential anxiety. This anxiety in both cases derives from the main character's inability to harmonise with the world around him, and this disharmony, in each case, provokes a search for solutions. In both films, furthermore, the main characters undergo a sort of philosophical transformation in the course of their search. By actively choosing to reflect on the underlying ontological circumstances that have contributed to their anxiety, these characters confront the issue of nihilism. But this is where similarities end, for the original version of *Rollerball* depicts the confrontation with nihilism from a modernist perspective, while the remake depicts it from a postmodernist perspective. In the former case, Jonathan E. is compelled by his conscience tragically to face his destiny alone, rejecting all of the social distractions that threaten to pull him away from the one thing that remains valuable to him: an authentic and conscious awareness of himself and his relationship to Being. Conversely, in the latter case, Jonathan Cross optimistically embraces the 'crowd', discovering an escape from the anxiety of nihilism through his entanglement with others in their common rebellion against tyranny and domination. Who he *is* is nothing more than who he *appears to be* to those around him. Whereas Jonathan E. attempts to reconnect with his own Being in the course of a struggle against the herd, Jonathan Cross attempts to find a place and function within the herd. In these differing approaches to the problem of nihilism, we see the initial development of a couple of themes that never gain full voice in the text of the films, but which deserve more extensive articulation nonetheless. One concerns the ethical implications of nihilism, and the other concerns nihilism's political ramifications. Before closing, I would like briefly to discuss these issues and to suggest that what we find here casts an interesting light on contemporary attitudes concerning Goodness, Justice and the meaning of life itself.

Implicit in the plot of the original version of *Rollerball* is an ethical message. That message states that the best way to live one's life is not in the pursuit of pleasure, prestige and fortune, but rather in the pursuit of personal authenticity. Jonathan E. is a tortured and profoundly unhappy man, an individual who, as his friend Moonpie tells him, 'has it all!', yet who finds no comfort in this fact. There is more to life than shallow pleasures, Jonathan seems to think, and insofar as we, the audience, are led to sympathise with this character, we agree with him. What makes him so sympathetic to us is his desire to understand himself and his purpose in life, even if this leads to professional and personal ruin. Public adoration, money and prestige are, for Jonathan E., all distractions that have pulled him away from an awareness of his authentic self. The powers of the corporation have transformed Jonathan into a 'thing', a marketable product, a veritable instrument that, in the end, has outlived its usefulness. It is only when discarded and cast aside by the Energy Corporation that Jonathan rediscovers his true life's ambition. It never was his purpose to acquire goods, fame and wealth. Rather, all along these were only ways to understand his place in, and his connection with, the world around him. By becoming too focused on things at the expense of an awareness of himself, Jonathan became distracted and forgot what is really important in life. His message to us, the audience, is that the best life is one in which the individual refuses to forget that the adoration of the crowd is incidental, and even detrimental, to understanding who you are. In the short story that inspired the film, Jonathan E. ineloquently sums up these feelings in a conversation with Mr Bartholomew:

> [Bartholomew] 'You don't want out of the game?' he asks wryly.
> [Jonathan] 'No, not at all. It's just that I want – god, Mr. Bartholomew, I don't know how to say it: I want *more*.'
> He offers a blank look.
> [Jonathan] 'But not things in the world', I add. 'More for *me*.' (Harrison 1975: 81–2)

This point is lost, and an entirely different ethical message is conveyed, in the remake of the film twenty-seven years later. Instead of pulling away from particular 'things in the world', Jonathan Cross actively pursues those things, finding happiness and purpose in his worldly entanglements. The crowd becomes a means of escape from his personal dissatisfaction. In solidarity with the group, Jonathan finds himself not only loved, but endowed with a purpose and meaning to his life. Whereas the open-endedness of the original film (and short story) suggests that the threat of nihilism has not been, and never will be, overcome, in the new version Jonathan's transformation into a revolutionary leader suggests that he has not only found his place, but that he will, in fact, change the world and make it a better place for everyone. Though the audience may find it hard to sympathise with this poorly drawn character, the message that he delivers is clear: we should not withdraw into ourselves and reclusively contemplate who we are. In fact, we are nothing until we *make* ourselves into something, and we make ourselves into something by *doing* things, making connections with others and bending the world to suit our will. The best way to live life, in sum, is to find a place in 'the crowd' and to make a contribution. In this we get the hint of a political message.

The original version of *Rollerball* takes place after the 'Corporate Wars', which presumably were times of chaos and disorder. After these wars, the world has become safe, comfortable and predictable. The inner, existential crisis that Jonathan E. faces is largely a reaction against the life of comfort and conformity that he otherwise enjoys. Jonathan E., in rejecting his success as a part of the 'establishment', is the type of individualistic rebel who wants nothing to do with corporate culture. We get the sense that he, like Socrates and Plato before him, holds a very dim view of the masses and their group choices. Most people would 'choose things over freedom', as Jonathan tells Ella, and so most people are not equipped to know what a good life really consists of. In this we sense a sort of anti-democratic sentiment. The masses are stupid followers. They chant slogans taught to them by those who give them what they want, and to put political power in their hands would be to produce a world where, instead of Justice, things, goods and consumer products are the targets of collective decision-making.

On the other hand, the remake of *Rollerball* takes place in the midst of political and social disorder. Jonathan Cross initially finds his place in this milieu, but he soon reacts against it, the way that Jonathan E. reacts against the stability of corporate culture, forming alliances with others in order to pursue effective revolutionary activity. Furthermore, it is with the working classes, the 'people', that Jonathan finds his allegiance, not with the exploitative gang bosses. The political message delivered here seems to be that it is only because of oppression that the people appear to be stupid followers. If given the opportunity, the means and the proper leadership, the masses will pursue the best course of action. This will draw them into a public realm where they will be less concerned with selfish desires, and more concerned with collective justice. Collective justice, furthermore, is understood as the freedom of each individual to be happy, and so, in the final analysis, political activity must be focused on the utilitarian ideal that the best government is one that brings the largest number of people the most amount of happiness.

One suspects that Jonathan E. and Jonathan Cross would not like one another very much. The change in how this main character has been depicted is quite interesting, not only from the perspective of a film critic, but also from the perspective of an American citizen. While it is difficult to fault the democratic sentiments of the remake, it is also hard to sympathise with the shallowness of its characters and the disregard that they seem to have for personal authenticity. American culture changed between the times that these two films were made, and not necessarily for the better. While Americans may be increasingly confident about group causes, and more aggressive about asserting their collective will, they have also become less philosophical and, perhaps, more concerned with 'things' and with manipulating the details of the world more than ever before. The two versions of *Rollerball* are not just movies. They are, in fact, symptoms of the way that Americans think about themselves and their relationship to Being itself. Made shortly after America's defeat in the Vietnam War, the original film was the expression of a people seeking a deep, personal and reflective understanding of who they are as individuals separate from the crowd. The remake, on the other hand, was made during a period of time when America was gearing up to fight terrorism and foreign enemies. In it we find the expression of a people more concerned with directing their attention outwards, away from the self, and with banding together in order to alter reality in accordance with collective desires. Whereas the original film is structured around settings of meditative quiet and reflection that are punctuated by action and violence, the remake consists of an uninterrupted barrage of violence, rock music and unreflective action.

Things certainly have changed quite a bit, and, it is worth repeating, not necessarily for the better.

PART III

Overcomings

Introduction: Overcomings

What would it mean to overcome nihilism?

Usually, this question is answered in an optimistic way, with the suggestion that in overcoming nihilism, we would accomplish something ultimately positive, productive and beneficial. If nihilism consists in the alienation of human existence from Truth and Being, then in its overcoming, we would find ourselves finally reconciled with that which is of the highest value and meaning. Human life would reach its supreme goal, our purpose for being here would become clear, and our place in the universe would no longer be a mystery. For these sorts of reasons, it has been taken as self-evident by many that overcoming nihilism is one of the greatest goods toward which humankind should work. If we could mend the rift between our real, finite existence and our highest aspirations once and for all, then we would truly be happy and fulfilled.

Indeed, throughout history this has been the aim pursued by those who have endeavoured to construct religious and scientific systems with which we might come to know the Truth. In religion, we find techniques and systems of worship that are intended to yoke followers together with the Holy, allowing them to experience the at-one-ment that comes from uniting with that which is ultimately True, valuable and meaningful. In science, likewise, we find techniques and systems of investigation focused on formulating testable hypotheses that might then guide us closer and closer to an understanding of True reality, thus releasing us from falsehood and superstition. In both of these traditions, different as they might otherwise be, the emphasis is on the endpoint. The goal pursued is final and objective certitude. To know the Truth is the highest good, and once this is grasped it is promised that we might rest content and glory in our success.

But is the attainment of our ultimate goals really an unequivocal good? On the face of it, this question might appear strange or even perverse. After all, isn't the motivation behind the pursuit of any goal the hope for its ultimate and successful attainment? The alternative would be failure, and failure strikes us as a self-evident evil. No one can be happy as a failure. Missing one's mark, failing to achieve one's goals (especially one's highest goals) seems a sure road to despair and despondency. And yet, in missing one's mark, if ambition still remains, the openness to potential endures. While in success we meet with finality, in failure possibility still remains. In success there is nothing more to pursue, and so we risk lapsing into smug passivity and tedious boredom. In failure, on the other hand, things remain uncompleted, and so we find ourselves with still more to be done. If we value the chase, the process, the pursuit, then perhaps there is something quite affirmative to be found in failure that cannot be found in success.

There is a further issue at stake. What if the value of our goals lies not in their consummation at all, but merely in their attractive power? Ever since Plato first established a philosophical direction for Western thinking, the assumption has been that the Truth is Beautiful and Good. These are the very characteristics that encourage and compel us to move closer and closer toward it; or so the Platonic argument assumes. But what if this assumption is wrong? Suppose that the Truth is neither beautiful nor good. Suppose that the apparent desirability of the Truth results precisely from the fact that we are so distant from it. Suppose that upon coming face to face with the Truth, we find ourselves in the presence of something so monstrous and horrendous that we couldn't bear it? Would it still be worth the breakthrough, or would we eagerly turn away so that we could once again distance ourselves from the hideous discovery and try to forget what we had seen?

Part III explores films in which nihilism is overcome, focusing on characters who successfully eliminate the gap between their ideals and aspirations only to discover themselves falling prey to abjection, fascism and death. In these chapters, we see that the drive to overcome nihilism does not necessarily culminate in positive outcomes. In fact, in their over-eagerness to repair the alienation, fragmentation and isolation of their worlds, the characters in these films demonstrate that overcoming nihilism can result in the obliteration of creative and positive potential.

In Chapter 7, 'The Abject Self: Apocalyptic Consequences of Self-Discovery in *Fight Club*', I consider the quest for self-discovery engaged in by the nameless narrator of *Fight Club* (1999). In his struggle for authenticity, this character uncovers dangerous and destructive drives within himself that, once unleashed, pursue an inexorable and destructive logic that is apocalyptic in scope. The chapter suggests that perhaps it may be better for humans to remain repressed and in the grips of nihilism rather than unleashing the primal drives of Eros and Thanatos; a liberation that could potentially result in the disintegration of civilisation.

Chapter 8 explores the fascistic themes in James Cameron's blockbuster film *Avatar* (2009), suggesting that in the utopian culture of the film's heroes, the Na'vi, Cameron has created a world in which the cultural overcoming of nihilism is made possible by a form of fascism in which individuals are subsumed to the collective. The pernicious thing about this is that the fascism in the film seems to have gone unnoticed by both the director and most audiences. By stripping fascism of its familiar face, Cameron has made this way of thinking appealing to a new generation of viewers seeking a way out of the nihilistic predicament of contemporary times.

In Chapter 9, 'Yukio Mishima and the Return to the Body', I explore the life, work and philosophy of the Japanese author Yukio Mishima. I argue that the most interesting and profound properties of Mishima's thought, his writings and of the films associated with his thought and writings, are those that leave us with a sense of the open-ended and ambiguous struggle involved in his efforts to define himself. The case of Mishima illustrates how in the overcoming of nihilism, spiritual peace and union with Being are prizes won at the cost of ongoing activity, struggle and creative aspiration. For Mishima, the defeat of nihilism literally entailed the commission of suicide, which he saw as the only way to bring his entire life project to a final close.

As a whole, the chapters in Part III consider the potentially deleterious consequences of the defeat of nihilism, offering a counterargument to the widespread contention that overcoming nihilism is an unequivocal good. It is here that we are forced to consider that the nihilistic problematic is far more complicated than commonly claimed. While psychological, political and existential integration may sound like noble and worthy goals, in their achievement we might run the risk of suffering something far worse than nihilism itself.

CHAPTER 7

The Abject Self: Apocalyptic Consequences of Self-discovery in *Fight Club*

Figure 7.1 The unnamed narrator (Edward Norton) and his alter ego, Tyler Durden (Brad Pitt) in *Fight Club* (1999).

INTRODUCTION

Is it possible that there might be some truths about ourselves best left undiscovered?

Thousands of years ago, the admonition to 'know thyself' was inscribed at Delphi, and it came to be regarded by philosophers as a guiding principle, promising to lead in the direction of authenticity and spiritual fulfilment. Beyond all else, so this ancient wisdom claims, it is the soul that is important, and to take care of the soul, one must reflect upon and interrogate one's self in order finally to uncover who one truly is. This was the message of Socrates, still considered by many to be the most fully perfected philosopher in the history of the West. According to Socrates, 'the unexamined life is not worth living', (Plato 1997a: 38a) and so he became dedicated to questioning himself and all of those around him in hope that by clearing away the accumulated pretences and falsehoods of popular belief, he would reveal something true and real about the human condition. So important was his quest for self-perfection that Socrates preferred death to silence when presented with this choice by his fellow citizens.

If we believe Plato, Socrates' most faithful student, what Socrates ultimately revealed was that the Truth is both beautiful and good. Human reality, when properly understood, is a reflection of an immutable, unchangeable and magnificent ideal that illuminates our inner, spiritual world, the way that the sun shines down on the outer, physical landscape of the earth. We lose sight of this ultimate Truth due to the distractions of our base appetites and emotions, but, the Platonic Socrates teaches, we might reconnect with this Truth – The Good – if we diligently engage in a systematic, dialectical investigation into the depths of our being. By degrees this Truth might be recovered, and when it is, we may potentially be transformed into something better and more pure. Philosophy, in this Socratic/Platonic sense, is the path toward spiritual perfection. This optimistic message has, to varying degrees, been the message of all philosophy ever since. Even when the truth articulated by some later philosophers – such as Schopenhauer and Nietzsche – appears to be painful and terrible, it is still cherished precisely because it is true, and in this there is presumed to be something both noble and virtuous.

But what if this is wrong? What if the Truth is neither beautiful nor good, but rather abject, horrifying, destructive and evil? Would it still be advisable to love such a Truth or would it rather be advisable to recoil from it, reject it and struggle to forget it? Supposing this Truth was a truth about the self? Would coming face to face with it spur one to renounce the inscription at Delphi, flee from self-realisation and instigate the desire to reassert some sort of comforting, soothing lie?

We no longer live in optimistic times, and so these sorts of questions are raised with increasing frequency. Our world seems permeated with a fear of the Truth and a suspicion that all is not well in the depths of existence. Consequently, our culture has produced an increasing number of popular parables warning us of the danger that threatens if we peek too persistently into the human soul. These parables suggest that what is potentially revealed by such scrutiny may be enough to destroy the philosophically curious individual while also potentially unleashing forces powerful enough to annihilate human civilisation itself. The lesson they teach is that perhaps it is best to keep the ugly Truth lying at the foundation of the human soul hidden, locked away and chained beneath consciousness.

Fight Club is one of these contemporary parables. Both the novel and the film have enjoyed tremendous popular success, becoming woven into the fabric of popular culture. It is clear that this story has struck a very deep and meaningful chord in audiences; not just among young men, but among males and females of all ages who resonate with this angry and ironic story of an unnamed narrator's struggle against the forces of civilisation and his absurd attempt to reclaim his authentic self. The story is both revolutionary and conservative at the same time. On the one hand, it appeals to the longing for individual liberation; the freeing of base and primal desires and the unfettered expression of libidinal urges. On the other hand, it also depicts the frightening consequences that follow from the emancipation of repressed human fury, and how once unleashed this fury propagates according to its own logic, threatening to dismantle civilisation itself. Personal authenticity, in the end, has fearsome consequences for collective living, and the question that *Fight Club* asks its audience to consider is this: Are you willing to give up the comforts and safety of civilisation in order to become individually free?

CIVILIZATION AND ITS DISCONTENTS

The question presented by *Fight Club* was also previously posed by Sigmund Freud in his book *Civilization and Its Discontents*, a work that could have served as a philosophical blueprint for *Fight Club*. According to Freud, civilisation is a development that keeps in check the natural, primal urge toward aggression that lies buried in every individual human consciousness. Civilisation helps to sublimate our most animalistic desires and inclinations, directing them toward useful and socially acceptable ends. It also produces in us a superego that triggers feelings of guilt when we feel inclined to transgress against the legal and moral rules that function to keep society running efficiently. All of this is certainly a benefit for collective living, but the psychological cost of this sublimation is a vague and chronic malaise that hangs over all societies; a discontent stemming from the repression we suffer in order to get along with one another. 'Civilized man has exchanged a portion of his possibilities of happiness for a portion of security', writes Freud (Freud 1961: 62). In this sense, he claims, we are neurotic creatures who have surrendered our own deepest desires in exchange for communal safety.

If our primal drive toward aggression was not so strong, the trade-off might be well worth the reward. However, Freud holds that the benefits of social living do not always pay back the costs of repression. While our safety gives us comfort and leisure, this situation also allows us the luxury to linger in reflection on the meaning of our lives, and as we do so, we inevitably ruminate on what it is that is missing, why we feel unfulfilled and why nothing that we do seems to satisfy our deepest longings. The reason, of course, is because the goals we pursue as civilised human beings always miss the mark. They are stand-ins and replacements for what it is that we, in the dark night of our unconscious minds, really want. And so long as we struggle and strive toward superficial substitutes for our true urges, we are doomed to neurosis and dissatisfaction; disorders that threaten the stability of the very civilisation that produced these ailments in the first place. It is because of this contradiction, internal to all civilisations, that 'civilized society is perpetually threatened with disintegration' (Freud 1961: 59). Since our most powerful wishes never gain direct expression, they inevitably become dammed up, over time building to dangerous proportions until the opportunity arises to grant them relief. And any excuse will do. With the slightest provocation, individuals will leap at the opportunity to tear one another apart in order to act out their aggressive desires and to kick down the walls of social order in search of liberation.

This is precisely the situation of the narrator (Edward Norton) in *Fight Club*. He is a 30-something white-collar professional, obsessed with the accoutrements of middle-class success. This nameless character is preoccupied with buying designer clothes, state-of-the-art appliances, gourmet condiments and decorating his condo with furniture purchased over the phone from IKEA. In an early scene from the film – contemptibly hilarious in its evocation of consumerist superficiality – the camera pans around his living space while the catalogue descriptions and prices of his domestic belongings appear superimposed over his collection of things. All the while he wonders, in voice-over, 'What kind of dining set defines me as a person?' Clearly he is living a lie, mistaking materialist consumption for 'knowing thyself'. His is a civilised man's version of a cave; both in the sense of his dwelling, but also in the sense that his lifestyle is a prison. His is a world of illusion, insulating him from true human needs. As in Plato's allegory, the main character in *Fight Club* is chained by his preoccupation with materialism, which distracts him from confronting the truth of who he really is.

While the work of ancient cave men was to hunt for and gather the necessities of life, facing physical danger and potential death as they dragged their hard-won earnings into their dwellings by their own physical efforts, the narrator of *Fight Club* buys his things with money earned at a job that deals wholly with abstraction. He is an actuary for a major car company, tasked with calculating the economic costs and benefits of either paying out claims or actually fixing defects in the vehicles that have led to deadly accidents. Life and death are nothing but numbers to him, and his livelihood is only possible in a world where humans are isolated from the primal realities of violence. His is an artificial world built out of intangible social and economic arrangements that enable him to buy superfluous goods, valuable not for survival or for their intrinsic worth, but for what they symbolise. He desires fashionable designer clothes, trendy furniture and sleek appliances because these are the sorts of things that show the world he is a social success. And yet, the more that he buys, and the closer he thinks he finally is to completing his wardrobe, or the decoration of his condo, the emptier he feels. None of these things – his clothes, his furniture, his condo – are really the point, since as Freud suggests, they are all stand-ins for something else that civilisation denies its members. His materialist entanglement is a distraction that keeps him from thinking too deeply about who he really is. As he himself states, 'Then you're trapped in your lovely nest, and the things you used to own, now they own you' (Palahniuk 1996: 34).

The narrator's malaise manifests in insomnia. Unable to sleep, the events in his world, ironically, start to blur together like a waking dream, and as Freud observed, it is in dreams that the mind's internal censor drops its guard, allowing our real obsessions and concerns to emerge from the unconscious. At the suggestion of his doctor, the main character starts attending various support groups for people with deadly illnesses in order to 'see what real suffering is'. Significantly, it is in a meeting for survivors of testicular cancer that he experiences his first real catharsis. Here he finds other men who have literally been castrated, just as he has symbolically been castrated by society. In particular, it is in the arms of Bob (Meatloaf), an ex-bodybuilder whose steroid use led to cancer, that the narrator is able to cry and lose all inhibitions, finally experiencing a release that allows him to express his deepest feelings and thus finally overcome his insomnia and sleep soundly once again.

Bob is a perfectly overdetermined dream symbol for the modern, civilised man. As a bodybuilder, he represents the sort of artificial masculine aesthetic that can only be developed in circumstances divorced from nature. The use of steroids, which helped him develop his artificial physique, calls to mind the sorts of poisonous and unnecessary extravagances modern humans are encouraged to consume in order to become more socially and professionally attractive and successful. These extravagances – like processed foods, liquor, tobacco and various chemical additives – while beneficial to the economic well-being of society as a whole, are nonetheless destructive to individual health. In the case of Bob, his quest for masculine perfection ironically leads to feminisation: he loses his testicles and grows breasts that are the result of his body's natural attempt to balance his hormone levels. This seems to be the reason why the narrator finds what he really needs in the arms of Bob. Bob is a concretisation of everything that modern civilisation has done to him. It has taken away his 'balls' and made him soft, woman-like. Indeed, throughout *Fight Club*, the theme of castration recurs often: in the testicular cancer support group, in a scene where a group of men attack the police chief, and toward the end of the story when the narrator himself is attacked by a group of his own followers. The theme of castration anxiety is clearly a preoccupation here, emphasising civilised man's fear of lost virility.

While Bob helps the narrator finally to confront and understand his social predicament, it is the figure of Tyler Durden (Brad Pitt) who offers a solution to this predicament. First breaking into the narrator's awareness in brief, dreamlike flashes that are at first almost imperceptible, Tyler Durden represents everything the narrator is not. Tyler owns nothing, he has no career, he is uninhibited, and he engages in acts of vandalism and mischief aimed against mainstream society. As it turns out, Tyler Durden really just is a manifestation of the narrator's own unconscious drives; a buried urge toward rebellion that he doesn't recognise as part of himself. Tyler represents the deep, primal and aggressive part of the narrator that has been repressed by civilisation, but which starts to break through as his mental defences become more and more worn down by insomnia and as he starts to understand the real conditions of his own oppression. It is through Tyler that the narrator tries to reclaim his masculinity. And yet, as Freud warns, the cost of this reclamation will imply the dismantling of civilisation's comfort and safety. The narrator will have to decide if this cost is worth the benefit.

In *Fight Club*, soap appears as the quintessential symbol of civilisation. As Tyler Durden explains to the narrator, soap was first discovered in ancient times when women, doing their washing in a river, found that clothes got cleaner at a particular spot downstream from where human sacrifices were performed. As it turns out, the fat from the sacrifices seeped though the ashes left over from the sacrificial fires, mixing with lye and creating a basic detergent. Civilised cleanliness, thus, has its roots in the rot and filth connected with death. But the modern process of making soap helps us to forget this, as the product itself bears so little resemblance to its source. Packaged in nice, neat little cakes, today's soap is associated with health, purity and hygiene rather than with death, decay and waste. Civilisation, like soap, has an ugly, unpleasant and hidden basis. Embracing this irony, Tyler manufactures expensive, artisanal soaps out of human fat that he steals from liposuction clinics. In stealing this waste, he literally harvests the excess fat made possible by civilised life and transforms it into a product craved by the very people who cast it off in the first place. 'It was beautiful. We were selling rich women their own fat asses back to them.' This is what civilisation is all about: forgetting the awful origins of our cultivated ways of life while unconsciously craving the reclamation of the very things that we have cast away.

Tyler and the narrator invent their own support group for men called 'Fight Club'. This is a sort of underground boxing club, meeting in parking lots and basements, where participants beat one another with their bare fists rather than crying and talking with one another. The idea is spawned by an intuitive realisation that the problem with civilisation lies in the repression of raw, primitive aggression. By getting to the source of the modern male's malaise, and by offering an outlet for bottled-up fury, the participants discover real release and comfort. This is not an activity that offers any mainstream benefits, however. In fact, it actually threatens the social and career standing of participants, leaving them with visible wounds, injuries and black eyes. Polite society would not approve, and so for this reason it is something that cannot be shared with more civilised neighbours, friends or families of the members. 'The first rule of Fight Club is that you don't talk about Fight Club. The second rule of Fight Club is, you don't talk about Fight Club!' This is something private and intimate that is only to be shared among the members. Just as it would be impolite to discuss one's sex life in public, so too is it taboo to discuss Fight Club. The release enjoyed in this activity is too primal and raw to be tolerated in good-mannered company.

The problem is that once unleashed, the aggressive drive pursues a logic of its own, unfolding in ways that become terrifying. Unbeknownst to the narrator's conscious mind, fight clubs begin springing up all over the country and a bigger agenda starts to take shape. 'Project Mayhem' is a terrorist organisation formed out of the various cells of Fight Club, first carrying out prankish acts of vandalism, but then escalating to carry out bombings of buildings that house centres of economic activity. The movement's plan is that once the banks and credit card companies are destroyed, civilisation will crumble and human beings will once again live in a state of nature. It is then that the aggressive urge will no longer be repressed, and a new age of individual freedom and fulfilment will be ushered into existence.

At this point the narrator realises Tyler Durden is not a separate person at all, but an aspect of his own personality spinning out of control. Now that it has been allowed expression, and the sensation of full, primal catharsis has been felt, this urge toward destruction proves impossible to stop. With the constraints of society falling away, no safety net remains and the narrator comes to understand the real implications of absolute individual freedom: 'the complete and right-away destruction of civilization' (Palahniuk 1996: 116). When the aggressive drive is unleashed and becomes its own end, rather than being harnessed for the accomplishment of other ends, there remains no welled-up energy that can be sublimated into art or literature, into industry or technology, governments or economies. All that remains is an honest but ferocious fury of violent activity seeking instant purgation. Anything lasting that threatens to dam up this passion will be swept away in a rising tide that only gains increasing momentum as it flows forward with greater and greater force. Personal liberation is thus accompanied by a sense of abject terror, and as the narrator is swept up by uncanny forces he can no longer control, he panics, longing to go back to his old, repressed identity. He wants to erase Tyler Durden from existence. But this, of course, entails killing a part of himself.

EROS AND THANATOS

In *Fight Club*, the narrator's aggression finds its final and most destructive manifestation in the activities of Project Mayhem. This revolutionary group emerges from his repressed desire to dismantle civilisation and thus to liberate humans from the chains of socialised oppression. Project Mayhem, however, undergoes an ironic evolution over the course of the story, beginning with the plan to liberate individuals, but then morphing into a sort of fascist-styled organisation in which members (including its creator) become cogs in the service of a new ideology. The followers don't even have names – except in death, when, having given up their own personal existence for the cause, they regain an identity as martyrs. As the narrator's aggressive drive becomes refined, turning away from sublimation and rushing toward an increasingly aggressive attack on mainstream social and institutional structures, a new sort of tyranny begins to emerge. This new tyranny, though directed toward the destruction of civilisation, is much like the old form, as it also harnesses individual fury, channelling it into a collective project. The success of Project Mayhem is, thus, also its failure, as it oppresses its membership in the name of absolute liberation. The utopia that the narrator and Tyler Durden long for, it seems, can never be accomplished so long as human beings feel the need to bond with one another and sacrifice their own personal gratification for collective ends.

The counterbalance to Project Mayhem's destructive plan is the narrator's relationship with Marla Singer (Helena Bonham Carter). When the narrator first meets Marla, he resents her. She frequents some of the same support groups that he also attends, but he knows she is a 'faker'. It is very obvious that, as a woman, she does not suffer from testicular cancer; or from brain parasites, or TB for that matter. It is the fact that she is so clearly faking these conditions that he feels exposed as a faker as well. In her gaze he sees himself reflected, and so he is unable to cry in her presence; his own self-consciousness intruding upon his ability to express deep feelings. And yet, despite his anger toward Marla, he is also attracted to her. The aspect of his personality that manifests as Tyler Durden actively pursues Marla, having sex with her and allowing her to stay at his house. In one sense, Marla offers a primal outlet for Tyler's aggressive sexual impulses. However, in another sense the narrator is repulsed by her because she is a moderating influence on his own behaviour, channelling his aggression into sexual activity and feelings of self-consciousness, thus threatening to domesticate him once again. The narrator complains at points in the story that he is part of a generation raised by women, and that this feminising influence is what has led to his alienation from his own aggressive masculinity. His malaise, as symbolised by Bob, has to do with castration anxiety, and Marla represents precisely this threatening force. For this reason, the narrator is jealous of Tyler's relationship with Marla; not because his conscious self is sexually attracted to Marla, but because his conscious self is attracted to Tyler, the conduit for his repressed aggression. Any relationship with Marla is a distraction from the purity of his own rage, and thus she threatens the goals of Project Mayhem as well as his search for authenticity. At the end of the book, it is Marla and members of the various support groups who appear to banish Tyler Durden. In the film, it is Marla alone who remains with the narrator. In both cases, it is the feminising influence of this woman that pulls the main character back from unbounded fury and violence. He escapes Tyler Durden by embracing Marla Singer.

Marla is the force of Eros, which is a drive toward civilisation and connection with others. Tyler Durden and Project Mayhem are the forces of Thanatos, which is a drive toward destruction and disintegration (Freud 1961: 69). While the narrator is caught between these forces, he is vital and alive. Eros holds him back from complete immersion in the abyss of violence, while Thanatos keeps him from utter capitulation to domesticity. Torn in a struggle between these forces he creates, he acts, and he engages in projects. From the perspective of either extreme, it might seem as if the narrator is acting as a double agent, but the cost of abandoning one or the other of these influences would be the collapse of creative vitality. Take away Eros and he is left with pure mayhem. Take away Thanatos and he is left with pure stasis. It is only by existing in-between these forces that something creative happens.

In the book, bombs planted by Project Mayhem fail to detonate, suggesting that the explosive aggression bottled up in the narrator's consciousness remains pent up and unexpressed at the conclusion of the narrative. Here the story ends in frustration, and thus the narrator's revolutionary anger, apparently, continues to lurk dangerously beneath the surface, waiting for the opportunity again to break free and tear down the barriers of oppression. This is why, in the book, he finally ends up in an insane asylum. By the story's conclusion he is not fit for life among others. He still imagines that his followers continue the fight, and that they look forward to getting him back. Nothing has really been resolved, nothing has changed; and while civilisation wins the first round and the narrator is locked away in an institution where he continues to suffer the loss of personal freedom, the potential for future revolt remains.

In the film, on the other hand, the bombs do detonate; to the tune of the *Pixies*' song 'Where is my mind?' The main character and Marla embrace against a backdrop of falling buildings, and the narrator's voice expresses a kind of hopefulness missing from the tone of the novel. In the conclusion to the film, the explosions are a cathartic release, purging the narrator's aggression and making him ready once again to become safely integrated into polite society. He has been made safe by the film's end, getting rid of his suppressed

Figure 7.2 The unnamed narrator (Edward Norton) and Marla Singer (Helena Bonham Carter) watch as buildings crumble in *Fight Club* (1999).

aggression. He now longs to flee back to a life of domestic comfort and civilised security.

SICK SOCIETIES

The book and film versions of *Fight Club* pursue contradictory solutions to the problem of repression. In the book, the revolutionary urge remains because society wins. In the movie, the revolutionary urge is dissipated because the individual has won. But could there be a third option between passively following the logic of unleashed aggression to its end, on the one hand, and the complete repression of primal human fury, on the other? Is there a middle ground between absolute capitulation and absolute revolt? Might it not be desirable to embrace the incongruity existing between our beastly and civilised selves while never fully giving in to either extreme? Taking this middle path might be viewed by purists as a kind of 'cop out', as a passive acceptance of nihilism, but it would have the advantage of catering to both sides of what seems like a real, ongoing contradiction involved in human life: the contradiction that Freud refers to as 'the struggle between Eros and Death, between the instinct of life and the instinct of destruction' (Freud 1961: 69). Perhaps it is best that neither instinct ever fully wins, but that human beings continue life in a self-alienated, neurotic but productive state of ongoing anxiety. Perhaps nihilism is our natural condition.

Freud concludes his book *Civilization and Its Discontents* by proclaiming that he will remain impartial as to the 'value of human civilization' (Freud 1961: 91). He does, however suggest that like individual human beings, cultures can become sick, and that it might be worthwhile, one day, for someone to construct a 'pathology of cultural communities' (Freud 1961: 91). This is a task that Freud must have been aware had already been undertaken by thinkers he himself admitted as influences, such as Plato. In Plato's *Republic*, the question of cultural imbalance is a central concern, but unlike Freud, he quite clearly offers his own evaluations concerning the healthiest and the most sickly ways that civilisations can be organised rather than simply remaining 'impartial'. It is interesting that in *Republic* we find diagnoses of sick civilisations that very much describe the dynamics depicted in *Fight Club*. We also find a plan that gestures toward the possible cure for these pathologies.

Plato diagnoses at least four sorts of sick civilisations. Drawing, as Freud does, upon an assumption that communities mirror the inner dynamics of the individuals that make up their populations, Plato is very critical of societies that are organised democratically. In this case, it is the lowliest appetites and desires that drive the community, creating a situation largely indiscernible from mob rule. Just as an undisciplined individual seeks immediate gratification, chasing pleasures indiscriminately with no regard for the greater Good, so too in a democracy we find policies, rules and institutions constructed on the basis of majority opinion. In the language of Freud, it is in this sort of community that the 'id' instincts run free, guided by the pleasure principle. Nothing is intrinsically valuable independent of the whims and desires of the crowd, and since the crowd, according to Plato, is largely uneducated and vicious, democracies also tend to value that which is superficial, fleeting and easy. This is one of the sickest forms of culture according to Plato, exhibiting the kind of collective foolishness that derives from a lack of discipline and wise leadership. If everyone is a leader, then no one is a leader and society becomes crippled, being pulled this way and that by base aggressions and emotions.

Plato's description of democracy casts it as among the worst, and sickest, forms of cultural community – very close to a bad kind of anarchy, or mob rule – precisely because it is driven by the worst, and sickest, individuals within society: those with unbalanced souls, those who are led by their appetites, those who are the most unrepressed; the 'drones' (Plato 1997b: 559c). While such individuals feel that they are free when they are doing what they really want, their freedom actually is a form of slavery. They are enslaved by their beastly natures, and so doomed to lives of unreflective servitude to desire. The problem with this is that while such servitude may bring a kind of vulgar happiness, it also undermines the potential for spiritual and creative growth. If one always acts on impulse, never deferring gratification, never repressing libidinal urges, then one never has the opportunity to develop the ability to experience and appreciate the sorts of 'higher' pleasures associated with self-discipline and philosophical contemplation. And this is what is truly 'sick' about a democratic society according to Plato. In its toleration of everyone's desires, it drags down the collective community, catering to the lowest common denominator. The world longed for by the narrator of *Fight Club* appears to be precisely this kind of world, and (at least in the film version) it is not until the consequences of this way of life become apparent to him that he recoils from it, the same way that Plato recoiled, fearing the destructive implications of appetite and aggression set free. While Plato was horrified to witness the appetites and passions of his fellow Athenians become unleashed to persecute and kill his own beloved teacher Socrates, in *Fight Club* the main character, likewise, becomes horrified by his own eagerness to be swept up by passions and feelings that threaten the destruction of civilisation itself.

Freud certainly was aware of Plato's diagnosis of the cultural sickness of democracy. And if he was, then he must have been aware that Plato also diagnosed another form of cultural pathology that he termed 'timocracy', or military rule. While not as dire, this form of collective sickness also results from an imbalance. Whereas in democracy it is the appetites that rule, in a timocracy it is the 'spirited' people who dominate. Emerging from the decay of the best form of government – the aristocracy – a timocracy develops when honour, rather than wisdom, becomes the governing ideal. In the soul, as in the community, when the spirit dominates over the appetites, discipline results. Soldiers, for instance, harness their spirited motivation to conquer fear and lack of comfort in service of ordered regimentation. While the appetites may rebel against the imposition of this kind of discipline, since it hinders their free expression and immediate gratification, the result for the individual – as well as the collective – is the emergence of long-lasting structure in opposition to fleeting impermanence. For these reasons, Plato believed that a timocracy, while still pathological, is not as corrupt as a democracy.

In *Fight Club*, the development of Project Mayhem offers a parallel to Plato's diagnosis of timocratic sickness. Project Mayhem emerges almost automatically out of the mob-like anarchy that precedes it, as if those experiencing the cathartic release gained through participation in Fight Club are instinctually drawn to the need for leadership and order once their appetites have been appeased. As in fascism, Project Mayhem develops around a charismatic leader who acts as the 'head' of the collective body of followers, offering guidance, direction and a channel for their combined aggression. There are rules and structure that delay the followers' gratification. They live in barracks. They have chores and duties. They must obey orders unquestioningly. In all of this they find a kind of happiness not discovered through simple, appetitive gratification. Plato, indeed, comments that those attracted to this form of life often come out of families in which mothers denigrate the manhood of fathers, thus influencing their sons to become obsessed with honour and victory (Plato 1997b: 549d–e). Like in *Fight Club*, sons raised under these circumstances fear their own feminisation. They harbour, in Freud's terminology, castration anxiety, and so compensate by seeking ways to demonstrate their toughness and manliness.

According to Plato, timocracy itself eventually deteriorates into oligarchy, where money rather than honour becomes the ruling principle. In *Fight Club*, this devolution describes the initial state of existence that the narrator finds himself living in at the start of the narrative; a state in which none of his real desires are adequately catered to because he is so focused on material wealth. This is, indeed, the state of being that precipitates his nihilistic discontent and resulting rebellion against the constraints of society. It might also be speculated that this is the state that he falls back into after the events depicted in the movie when the narrator and Marla presumably settle down into domestic bliss. By suggesting this at its conclusion, the film's message seems to be that the only other option to the complete liberation of desire (and its dangers) is to lapse back into domesticity and firm censorship of aggression in the individual. The only cure for unleashed aggression, the film seems to say, is to crush it and once again to endure the malaise of sublimated yearning.

According to Plato, the relationship between the various types of society exist on a continuum, with one emerging out of the other. An aristocracy, which he deems the best form of government, devolves into a timocracy, then into an oligarchy, a democracy, and finally into the worst form of social organisation: a tyranny. Tyranny is not really a legitimate form of government at all, according to Plato, but the utter collapse of legitimate government altogether, resulting in the enslavement of everyone, including the tyrant himself. 'A real tyrant is really a slave' (Plato 1997b: 579e). This is because in the tyrant, desire and passion are completely unchained from all social constraint, and in this 'the soul adopts madness as its body-guard and becomes frenzied' (Plato 1997b: 573b). In the concluding sections of the book *Fight Club*, as the narrator descends into utter insanity, we see a mirror of Plato's concern that the complete liberation of repressed desire results in individual 'madness' and the destruction of society. For Plato, without civilisation humankind is doomed to maladjustment.

But there is an important difference between Plato and Freud on the subject of humankind's relationship to civilisation. While Plato suggests that there is a healthy form of social organisation in aristocracy, Freud seems to suggest that *all* civilisations are, to one degree or another, 'sick'. The reason for this radically different position stems from a fundamental difference in their assumptions about human nature. According to Plato, the faculty of reason is the highest of human capacities, not tied to the body, and capable of being detached from the lower, passionate aspects of the soul. In the best form of government – the aristocracy – it is the dispassionate, fully rational 'philosopher kings' who lead, guided by the ideal of Justice, and seeing to it that society is organised in such a manner that all people occupy appropriate, useful and fulfilling roles. According to Freud, on the other hand, reason is something not detachable from the lower passions, but necessarily rooted in the irrational drives of Eros and Thanatos. There is no way, thus, fully to detach ourselves from the lower appetites, as all of us – even those who are the wisest – are rooted in the world by our bodies. If Plato is correct, then there is hope for us, and through philosophy we may overcome our beastly nature. However, if Freud is correct, then the internal struggles of the psyche ultimately have no solution. If an ongoing conflict between the incongruous forces of Eros and Thanatos is part of our basic psychological constitution, then it is a fundamental mistake to think that this state of being is something that can be dissolved, either individually – through absolute rebellion – or collectively – through absolute submission to civilisation.

CONCLUSION

Fight Club is more influenced by the Freudian description of human nature than it is by the Platonic one. This story assumes that humans are fundamentally beastly, and that if our authentic, primal nature is exposed, then a logic will be initiated that unleashes humanity's repressed libidinal energies, which in turn will threaten to topple polite society with all of its safety, comfort and contentment. On the other hand, as long as the buried core of our nature remains covered over, our lives will continue to be inauthentic and ignorant of the Truth.

It is interesting that the book and movie versions of *Fight Club* conclude with seemingly different answers to the question concerning which one of these options is more desirable. In the book, the narrator ends up in an insane asylum, musing about how he doesn't want to go back to the world he left behind. Imagining that Project Mayhem goes on without him, he seems certain that it will eventually succeed in its revolutionary goal to 'break up civilization so we can make something better out of the world' (Palahniuk 1996: 199). Here, Chuck Palahniuk's original anti-establishment sentiment dominates. In Jim Uhls's screenplay version, on the other hand, a more conservative note is sounded. While buildings are destroyed, and while the main character shoots himself in the mouth, he is, nonetheless, finally reunited with his girlfriend, Marla, whom he reassures everything will be OK. All talk of revolution and the destruction of civilisation comes to an end, and the narrator and his girlfriend, it seems, will reunite, somehow building a regular relationship together. 'You met me at a very strange time in my life', he tells Marla in the film's concluding scene, suggesting that things will now be different – more normal – for the two of them.

I think one of the dangers involved in characterising the conditions of human self-alienation and nihilistic separation as sicknesses or diseases is that such thinking naturally encourages us to demand a cure. As we see in *Fight*

Club, such 'cures' are potentially worse than the conditions they purport to correct. If the choice is between self-alienation, on the one hand, and either fascism or anarchic chaos, on the other, then perhaps we should choose self-alienation. Perhaps the utopian ideal of a perfect society, made up of individuals free from neurosis, conflict and self-alienation, is the real disease. Maybe a bit of expression tempered by a bit of repression is the best that we can hope for. Perhaps this intermediate state of hovering in the void between self-knowledge and self-deception is the one most appropriate to us.

Perhaps, in the end, it is best to avoid really 'knowing thyself'.

CHAPTER 8

Rooting for the Fascists in *Avatar*

Figure 8.1 Jake Sully (Sam Worthington) subdues a dragon and leads the Na'vi into war in *Avatar* (2009).

INTRODUCTION

James Cameron's *Avatar* depicts the invasion of a planet called Pandora by human forces in search of a rare mineral called 'unobtainium'. The native inhabitants of Pandora, the Na'vi, are part of a primal culture that has no modern technology, worships nature and lives in mystical interconnectedness with all other things on their planet. They initially are no match for the human invaders, who mobilise a powerful, modern, mechanised, paramilitary force, which is used to attack the Na'vi, destroy their home and uproot them from their territory. However, when one of the human characters named Jake Sully (Sam Worthington) becomes disillusioned with his mission, he joins the Na'vi and leads them in a successful war against the human invaders.

Conservative American critics have united in attacking James Cameron's blockbuster for its 'liberal' political message since *Avatar* clearly is intended as an allegory highly critical of imperialism, militarism, corporate greed, exploitation of the environment and capitalism (Khan 2010). The overall, manifest message of *Avatar* appears to be that primal, organic cultures, with their lack of technology and harmonious attitude toward nature, are morally praiseworthy while modern, mechanical cultures (like the US), with their aggressive technological development, dominating attitudes toward nature and capitalist motives, are fanatic and corrupt. It's no wonder that conservatives have become so upset with this movie.

But underneath all of the manifest liberalism of *Avatar* there is also a latent message, no doubt unintended by Cameron, and yet still lurking in the shadows nonetheless. In his valorisation of the organic, primal, interconnectedness of Na'vi culture and his denigration of the mechanical, modern, disconnectedness of human culture, Cameron comes very close to advocating a form of fascism.[1]

The term 'fascism' is normally used today as a derisive label; a way of discrediting governments, policies or personality types that are considered to be overly authoritarian and aggressive. In what follows, I will steer clear of this evaluative usage of the term and attempt simply to describe the philosophy of fascism in order to understand the world view that it promotes. Once I have described the overarching philosophical perspective of fascism, I then will draw on the work of Jay Y. Gonen, who, in his book *The Roots of Nazi Psychology*, has distilled Hitler's foundational ideological values to nine basic principles. As we scrutinise these principles of Nazism, we will begin to see how greatly they overlap with the ideals that Cameron attributes to the culture of the Na'vi. My intention here is not to discredit Cameron's ideas or to malign what is an outstanding piece of film-making, but rather to understand the implications of the world view presented in this motion picture and perhaps gain a better understanding of why fascist ideas remain appealing to many people today.

FASCISM

While there are many forms of fascism, some more threatening than others, they all share in common a monistic and totalitarian view of society. All fascist ideologies promote the view that the best form of social organisation is that in which people and their leaders are 'bound together' into a functional whole, the way that, in ancient Rome, the lictor's rods were bound together around an axe-head, forming the handle by which the blade could be wielded. The lictor was a bodyguard to the Roman magistrates, and his axe was called a 'fasces'. Hence, the term 'fascism' derives from the weapon carried to protect Roman judges. It is intended as a 'symbol of unity' according to Benito Mussolini, the man with whom the term 'fascism' originated (Mussolini 1932).

The unity of those in fascist societies is ensured by a hierarchy that is envisioned as the organic and natural outgrowth of the 'will' of the people. Although it is in many ways anti-democratic, fascism imagines that the people consent to the rule of a leader on the basis of their instinctual understanding of the rank order found in nature. Some people are naturally born to lead and some people are naturally born to be led. There is a place for everyone, and under fascism, all people gravitate toward their proper positions. The state is conceived as a living being in which the people are organs (Mussolini 1932). The leader is not better than those that follow. He is simply thought of as the 'brain' while others serve equally necessary functions. Some people are like the hands. Some people are like the eyes. Some people are like the heart. An organism needs all of these parts in order to function properly, and so too does the healthy nation. Those who do not serve a function in the state are likened to a disease or to a parasite (Hitler 1971: 225–83), and like a disease or a parasite, such individuals must be removed and neutralised in order to ensure the integrity of the national 'body'. In fascism, it is the collective welfare of the people that is most important, and anything that is thought to interfere with the well-being of the people is targeted as an enemy.

United behind a supreme leader, all members of the fascist state are as one. Hannah Arendt has claimed that the growth of fascism during the twentieth century developed as a reaction against existential feelings of 'isolation', 'fragmentation' and 'atomization' (Arendt 1976: 317). The loneliness of humans during this 'age of anxiety' created a circumstance of nihilism and meaninglessness. In response, fascism offered a solution by reinvigorating a lost sense of rootedness in nature by encouraging people to work in concert with others who share a common bond of blood, race or purpose. While the modern age of technological industrialism encouraged people to view themselves as autonomous individuals, separate from nature and in competition with one another for jobs, wealth and resources, fascism, on the other hand, is a counter-movement to this trend that encourages people to think of themselves as part of some greater whole in which they play an indispensible part. It is 'primal' in the sense that it harkens back to a time before modernity when all individuals existed as part of an organic, rather than mechanically organised, community.

Because the individual is so completely integrated into the life of the whole community, in fascism there is the sense that while each human being plays an important role in the health of the society, it is also the case that each individual should be prepared to sacrifice him or herself for the good of the collective. The individual is encouraged to identify with the welfare of the state rather than to think about self-interest, and so the instinctual readiness for action and the willingness to give one's life in service of the nation, state or race is held as among the highest virtues imaginable. Fascism, thus, 'glorifies surrender; it exalts mindlessness; it glamorizes death' (Sontag 1975). It encourages a non-rational, felt connection to the whole for which the individual is willing to fight and kill. Fascism is suspicious of intellectualism, which tends to encourage analysis and calculation. Instead, under fascism, feelings of primal unity are encouraged among the people so that the individual becomes absorbed into something greater than the isolated self (Hitler 1971: 457).

Mussolini writes, 'The Fascist conception of life is a religious one' (Mussolini 1932). But the concept of religion that fascism promotes is not belief in a God that stands outside of and separate from the universe, acting as the ultimate lawgiver. Fascism, as a totalitarian system, has no room for that sort of God. Rather, the religion of fascism is a kind of pantheism that finds the holy within the state and within nature. It is pagan and primal in character, viewing the Abrahamic religions as superstitious, other-worldly fantasies that cover over the only true reality: it is the struggle and sacrifice of human beings within the universe that determines the destiny of our world. The vicissitudes of 'will to power' replace the Ten Commandments as a guide to proper behaviour and the supreme leader becomes the mouthpiece of God.[2] This is a more thorough and consistent form of monism than that promoted by any other religion before or since. Because everything is one and interconnected, there is nothing that stands above and beyond the tug-of-war struggle of life in the here-and-now. Rewards and punishments are doled out in this life, not in heaven. The strong are good. The weak are evil. That is fascism's holy law.

Under the total control of fascism, all parts of society are unified and mobilised toward action. Fascist dictatorships exercise complete oversight in order to insure that not only the people, but all branches of government, all art, all business, all religion, all food production — everything — works in concert and coordination so that the state is able to act and move toward its goals efficiently and effectively. Control of all parts of society is total. In this way fascism does away with alienation, nihilism and fragmentation at the expense of individual autonomy. And yet, in the fascist way of thinking, the individual only becomes fully and authentically realised through the operations of the state. In the words of Mussolini:

Liberalism denied the State in the name of individual; Fascism reasserts the rights of the State as expressing the real essence of the individual. And if liberty is to be the attribute of living men and not abstract dummies invented by individualistic liberalism, then Fascism stands for liberty, and for the only liberty worth having, the liberty of the State and of the individual within the State. (Mussolini 1932)

Fascism is more than just an anti-liberal political philosophy, however. It also describes a way of thinking about reality that may, to greater or lesser degrees, be present in any person. I'd like to suggest that we imagine fascism on a continuum, and that we gauge differing levels of fascism in relation to what Jay Y. Gonen has identified as the nine 'basic ideological principles' that underlie fascist, and specifically Nazi, psychology (Gonen 2000: 167–73). The more of these principles that we find operational in a person, the more fascist we might say that person's way of thinking tends. This is useful not just so that we may identify tendencies toward fascist thinking in others, but also so that, as Wilhelm Reich suggests, we can see it, and come to terms with it, in ourselves (Reich 1946: xii).

In what follows, I will examine each of Gonen's nine principles and consider how they compare to the world view of the Na'vi culture from *Avatar*. What emerges is a great deal of similarity, and as Cameron, the writer and director of *Avatar*, seems to be suggesting that Na'vi culture is morally praiseworthy, it appears that his film tends toward the advocacy of something resembling fascism. The popularity of this film, furthermore, might thus be an indicator suggesting America's enthusiasm for, and susceptibility to, fascist ways of thought.

THE NINE PRINCIPLES OF NAZI PSYCHOLOGY

In his book *The Roots of Nazi Psychology*, Gonen argues that Hitler's success in German politics during the 1930s and 1940s was not simply the result of coercion and oppression, but was also due to his intuitive, psychological resonance with the German people. Hitler was a man of his culture who shared with other Germans a way of thinking and a set of values. Far from being an aberrant monster, Hitler was a leader who understood his people and helped them to act on a set of principles that they already believed to be true. There are nine of these principles, according to Gonen, and they lie at the foundation of fascist/Nazi forms of thinking. These principles are not unique to Germans of the 1930s and 1940s, but are held by many people across national borders and periods of time, either consciously or unconsciously. The principles are as follows:

> Principle #1: The world is permeated by an ill-understood mortal danger. At this eleventh hour, the historical clock for removing this danger is about to run out. (Gonen 2000: 169)

This principle was expressed in Nazi Germany as a fear and hatred of the Jews, Slavs, communists, capitalists and other perceived threats to the German 'race'. Hitler acted on this fear by targeting various groups, both internal and external, that were thought somehow to be dangerous to the health of the German national 'body'. In a more general, psychological sense, this principle is rooted in a feeling that there is a 'we', meaning those who are like 'us', who share our ways of life, beliefs, values, traditions and so forth, who are under attack by a 'them', meaning those who are different from 'us' and who do not share our way of life. This 'us' versus 'them' mode of thought paints the world as split between friends and enemies. It also characterises the enemies as waiting at the gates, ready to pounce and to dismantle 'our' way of life. 'Our' world is in crisis and it is 'our' way of life that is at stake. This feeling of emergency, of impending disaster, primes those who adhere to this principle for action and defence.

In our own time, we have seen the activation of this principle in the thinking of Americans and Westerners more generally speaking. Especially after the events of 9/11 and the worldwide financial collapse, Americans feel as if some 'ill-understood' force is planning our downfall. This threat originates not only from outside of our borders in the Middle East, Mexico and South America, but is also living among us in the form of illegal aliens, religious radicals, corrupt politicians and greedy business executives. We are in imminent danger, and if we do not take action to combat this force, 'our' way of life will come to an end. It is a matter of 'us' or 'them', and if we wish to continue enjoying the American way of life, we had better get busy, get tough and take defensive measures.

In the film *Avatar*, this mode of thought is embodied in the Na'vi, who quite literally find themselves under attack by the violent, greedy and technologically superior forces of the invading humans. The humans are viewed by the Na'vi as 'crazy', suggesting that they cannot be understood, that they are dangerously irrational and incapable of being reasoned with. The Na'vi, whose society is represented as seamlessly interconnected with nature, are soon to be uprooted and their organic relationship with the planet broken by the disease-like invasion of the human threat. This threat, furthermore, has a foothold within their society. The 'sky people' are humans, like Sully, Grace Augustine (Sigourney Weaver) and Norm Spellman (Joel David Moore) who have infiltrated the Na'vi by occupying avatars, which are clones of the Na'vi, in order to study, manipulate and if need be destroy their culture. Thus the threat, like that of the Jews in Nazi Germany or of today's terrorism, is both an inner and an outer one. And time is running out for the Na'vi; the humans are poised to strike and take what they want unless something is done quickly.

Principle #2: To cling to the magic substance of life is to cling to biomystical health. (Gonen 2000: 170)

Among the Nazis this principle applied to the preservation and propagation of Aryan 'blood'. Hitler and his officers conceived of Aryan blood as a magical substance that ran through the veins of the German people in greater or lesser concentrations. All great things originate from the preservation of the purity of this magical substance and all terrible things spring from its pollution. 'All the human culture, all the results of art, science and technology that we see before us today, are almost exclusively the creative product of the Aryan', Hitler writes (Hitler 1971: 290), and furthermore, 'Blood mixture and the resultant drop in the racial level is the sole cause of the dying out of cultures; for men do not perish as the result of lost wars, but by the loss of that force of resistance which is contained only in pure blood' (Hitler 1971: 296). Blood is a holy fluid that is the mystical and magical source of the German nation's power. If it is not kept pure, the power of the race will be lost. For this reason, it is absolutely imperative that the people resist the forces, referred to in principle #1, that wish to adulterate this precious substance.[3]

In the United States today there is a variation on this kind of thinking in the myth of the 'melting pot'. America is popularly thought of as a place where people of all races, beliefs and backgrounds may productively live together as one. The American 'spirit' has always been associated with individual opportunity, freedom and the energy to get things done regardless of social class or background. President Barack Obama thrilled listeners when he characterised himself as a 'mutt', by which he intended to point out that there is nothing more American than someone who draws strength from diversity and intermixture (CNN 2008). The strength of the nation is thought of as emanating from something less literal than blood, but no less mystical. The 'magical substance' of America is a mysterious infusion that has been distilled in the melting pot of our culture. Ironically, today there seems to be a widespread fear that this magical substance is somehow being adulterated by non-Western forces, like Islam, as well as by immigration from poor countries and other internal threats. Somehow, these new elements in the mix threaten to neutralise the magic that once served to energise the American nation.

In *Avatar*, the Na'vi are depicted as existing in perfect harmony with nature and possessing the ability to access the collective consciousness of their planet's history by means of a neural interface that grows out of their heads. Like a plug that enters a socket, each individual member of the race is endowed with the capacity to tap into the consciousness of nature. The force of this collective consciousness is represented in the film as a kind of glowing light that pulses through their world and that is centralised in a magical 'tree of souls'. This tree channels the power of 'Eywa', which is something like the God of the Na'vi. This concretisation of 'world spirit' in pulsing light parallels the Nazi's concretisation of the people's strength in blood. In both instances, this mystical, flowing force is the source of power, vitality and life. The humans in the movie threaten to destroy this well of magical potency, and toward the end of the film, the efforts of the natives are directed toward defence of the all-important tree of souls. As the reservoir of the people's spiritual life, it must be protected at all costs.

Principle #3: The omnipotent leader confers magic power. (Gonen 2000: 170)

The 'leadership principle' holds that hierarchies are natural, and that in human relations, society is best organised around the inborn capacities of its members. Some people are suited to be workers. Some people are suited to be leaders, but there is only one person suited to be the supreme leader. In this supreme leader all power culminates. If society is organised in this natural, hierarchical fashion, the 'magic substance' may flow efficiently and unimpeded and amazing things then become possible. In Nazi Germany and other fascist nations, the supreme ruler channels the will of the people and directs it toward domination of enemies and the pursuit of national glory. Anything is possible when the people are unified and when they put their unquestioning faith in their supreme leader. If it is otherwise, then confusion, inaction and defeat are the result.

Americans are in many ways suspicious of authority, and especially of supreme authority. The whole basis of democracy rests on the idea that no one person should be allowed to impose his or her will upon all people. Fascists, of course, do not conceive of the supreme leader as someone who *imposes* his will on others, but rather as someone who *channels* the collective will of the people into action. In fact, Mussolini writes that fascism is a kind of 'organized, centralized, authoritarian democracy' (Mussolini 1932: 7). American representative democracy is certainly hierarchical, with the people voting for representatives, senators and for a president who sits at the top of the national chain of command. The President, however, is not a supreme leader, as the other branches of government balance his or her power. Americans do, nonetheless, have an almost religious reverence for various kinds of leaders who exert their will and get things done, even if this means breaking the rules. Americans love mavericks and nonconformists who prove the opinions of naysayers and pessimists wrong. They love leaders who take chances by going against the trends of popular opinion, so long as the purposes they pursue are, ultimately, thought to be worthwhile. Americans love pragmatists who cobble together solutions to problems that others thought unsolvable. Such individuals seem to possess a special, almost magical power that draws from the vital mixture of the American spirit. But in the end, Americans generally tend, I think, to remain suspicious of anyone who holds *absolute* power. In America, it is always the people, and sometimes the mob, that has the last word.

In *Avatar*, the primal society of the Na'vi is naturally hierarchical. It is led by a king and his wife, who serve as the spiritual heads of the tribe. The members of the tribe, as in fascism, seem to have taken roles on the basis of their natural born capacities. At one point in the film, Neytiri (Zoë Saldana) enumerates to Sully all of the skills of the various female members of her tribe as a prelude to mating with him. She mentions that one person is the tribe's best singer. Another is the best hunter. Part of the primal appeal of the Na'vi is the fact that all of its members naturally fit into useful slots in their society. Everyone is valuable and serves a purpose. But the real message of the film emerges when the tribe places its faith in the power of Sully himself, who leads them in battle against the invading human enemies. In a plan to establish himself as the supreme leader, Sully, like a Germanic knight, dazzles the natives by subduing a fearsome dragon that is a symbol of tribal leadership. He then directly channels the mystical wisdom of the tree of souls in order to mobilise all of the planet's living creatures in total war against the invaders. Against all odds, Sully magically engineers the defeat of the enemy and as in all fascist societies his true glory is achieved in warfare, domination and the expulsion of a threat to the people's purity.

> Principle #4: The urge to merge is nature's way of making people feel both good and powerful. (Gonen 2000: 171)

This is, perhaps, one of the most important of all the fascist principles. It holds that by merging into one corporate body, individuals lose themselves in collective unity, which brings not only individual ecstasy but also collective power. The proper hierarchical ordering of society creates a circumstance in which the magical powers of blood may come to full expression through the body of the nation and this is accompanied by health, happiness and the expansion of power.

Just as Americans tend to be suspicious of supreme leaders, they have also traditionally been suspicious of the loss of self within the collective. Think of the chronic American fear of socialism or communism and you get a sense that Americans prefer to stand alone rather than being bound together with others. All governments to some extent or another must unite individual members into a group possessing a collective identity, but in America this seems rarely to last long. There have been, of course, points in the history of the country during which a group consciousness has emerged, for better or for worse, and America has acted as a single, unified organism. Usually these times occur, in accordance with principle #1, when there is a perceived threat, such as during a catastrophe, war or when responding to terrorism. However, these episodes wax and wane on an ongoing basis in the US. When Americans have the 'urge to merge', they tend to turn toward religion, to participate in sports or go to rock concerts. These outlets, in fact, may act to dissipate what might otherwise be transformed into fascist political tendencies.

James Cameron's depiction of the Na'vi, on the contrary, characterises them as a group whose members are naturally inclined to merge with one another and with their world as a whole. The very physical structures of these individuals are configured to allow them to fuse with other organisms and with their planet's magical essence. In doing so, these natives are able to share in the collective wisdom of their race, experiencing a mystical unity this is both pleasurable and from which they draw their power. The Na'vi are so identified with the overall cycles of nature that they do not even fear their own personal deaths. They accept death as a part of the rhythms of reality, conceiving of personal mortality as just a moment in a larger overall process. The life energy of Eywa is given and taken away. It is not the personal possession of any one person, but something that is borrowed for the span of time that one is alive. This understanding invigorates the Na'vi, and it is because they abide by it that they are ultimately able to repel the technologically advanced human invaders who have an analytic, disconnected and individualistic approach to reality. United as one people behind a powerful warrior-leader, the Na'vi are able to draw on the magic of nature to defeat their enemy.

> Principle #5: It is only just that no one should do it to us, but we should do it to them. (Gonen 2000: 171)

Gonen characterises this as the Nazi 'justice principle'. It depicts the world as a place in which any struggle for power is a zero-sum game. If one side wins some sort of benefit, then that means others must lose something. Since in fascist societies the people imagine themselves as magically special and meritorious, it follows that justice requires such people enforce their will and claim as many of the world's 'material and cultural assets' as possible for their own. Thus in Nazi Germany there was no question that the German Third Reich was entitled to the resources of its neighbours; especially if those neighbours were Slavs, Jews, communists or capitalists. Such 'decadent' peoples had no right to nature's resources or territory, and the only way that they had ever been successful in amassing these things was through trickery and fraud. After WWI, there was a widespread myth among the Germans that the only reason why they lost the war, and thus had burdensome conditions imposed upon them under the Treaty of Versailles, was because they had collectively been 'stabbed in the back' by traitors and sub-men both within and outside of Germany (Shirer 1960: 31). Justice therefore demanded that the Germans take back what was rightfully theirs all along. It was unjust for others to take from Germany, but because Germany is special, it may legitimately take whatever it wants.

The US also has at various times in its history been led by a similar 'justice principle'. Beginning in the 1840s, leaders promoted the idea of 'manifest destiny' as a justification for the westward expansion of US territory and the subjugation of Native American tribes. There was no way, it seems, that European immigrants could possibly live together and share resources with the natives, who, it was thought, were backward, living in a state of anarchy without the 'magical substance' embodied by democratic institutions of government. The displacement and murder of these people was, thus, justified. Later, during the Cold War with the Soviet Union, America once again experienced this sort of thinking. President Eisenhower, in a 1954 speech, articulated what became known as the 'Domino Theory'. It justified US involvement in the Vietnam War by claiming that if Vietnam were to fall to the communists, this would lead to the loss of all of Southeast Asia and of Japan. The world, in other words, cannot be shared with non-democratic nations. If the communists win, we lose. Additionally, we know that the only way the communists can win is through trickery, force and intimidation. Therefore, we ourselves must use these tactics in order to insure that our own much more meritorious way of life triumphs and prospers. It is against nature to stop the march of democracy, and so we should fight for it by any means necessary. Most recently this way of thinking seems to have emerged, and to have come under question, during the US wars in Iraq and Afghanistan.

In *Avatar*, Cameron executes a clever somersault of perspective in order to justify the totalitarian claim of the Na'vi to the planet Pandora. The humans are depicted as outside invaders who come to Pandora only because they have already destroyed their own environment on Earth. The element that they seek is called, appropriately, 'unobtanium'; a name that suggests these humans will never be satisfied in their exploitation of the universe. If they are granted anything, they will take everything. This is a zero-sum game, since the humans are corrupt, greedy, decadent and insatiable in their desires; all characteristics that the Nazis attributed to the Jews, Slavs, communists and capitalists. In this movie the humans, in fact, have been trying to negotiate with the Na'vi, who refuse to broker any deal with the outsiders because the entire planet and everything in it is sacred to them. They have a natural birthright to the resources of the planet, and it would be unjust to concede any territory or resources to the invaders. After all, even if the humans do *need* the resources, they still don't *deserve* them. Thus, the Na'vi come to feel that they themselves are entitled to everything and the humans are entitled to nothing. The Na'vi have a special connection to Pandora that cannot be shared with outsiders. Consequently, at the end of the film, the only outsiders who are allowed to stay on Pandora are those who have, through the magic of the tree of souls, been transformed into Na'vi. The Na'vi are special and thus have a unique claim to the 'material and cultural assets' that they command.

Principle #6: We can do it. (Gonen 2000: 172)

This is the principle that expresses a people's confidence in its own 'will to power', and it is a belief that contradicts what I have, in the Introduction to this collection, identified as a principle of nihilism. Whereas in nihilism there is a fatalistic conviction that nothing can be done to change the world for the better, in fascism there is an optimistic conviction that the world can be improved. The people, bound together and under the direction of their supreme leader, are in a position to channel their special powers for the enhancement of the community. Here we have an indication as to why fascism was such an attractive alternative to the alienated feelings of nihilism that Arendt describes in her monumental work *The Origins of Totalitarianism*. In the fascist way of thinking, anything is possible.

Americans share this 'can do' attitude with fascist societies. One of the iconic WWII images in American propaganda is the Rosie the Riveter poster, which proclaims, 'We can do it!' During war time such an attitude on the part of a nation is crucial, but the overall character of American culture has always tended toward the pragmatic, leading George Santayana to refer to Pragmatism as the only truly American philosophy. Only after the Vietnam War ended in failure did America experience a period of defeatism and lack of confidence in its capacities.

The Na'vi also exhibit confidence in their powers and a resolve to resist the forces that threaten them. They are never depicted as giving up or lapsing into fatalistic passivity. The closest that they come to despair is after their 'hometree' is destroyed by the human gunships. However, even then, they do not abandon hope. Instead they immediately retreat and regroup, eventually uniting behind Sully in order to fight back against what appears to us, the audience, to be impossible odds. There is never an indication, however, that it ever crosses any of the tribe members' minds that the struggle is lost. They always seem to retain the belief that 'we can do it'.

Principle #7: We shall gobble up! (Gonen 2000: 172)

One of the primary Nazi doctrines was the push for *Lebensraum*, or living space. The aggressive expansionism of the Nazis was motivated by the belief that the nation needed space, not only to accommodate more pure-blooded Aryans, but also in order to supply them with room for agriculture and with natural resources like oil. This seventh principle is an imperative that describes the German desire to incorporate more and more land into the empire. Ultimately, the Nazis envisioned their Reich dominating the entire world. 'Gobbling up' land, of course, raises the issue of what to do with the subhuman inhabitants of those lands, and the Nazi solution to this is now infamous. Those who are not pure of blood must be enslaved, expelled or exterminated.

Imperialistic 'gobbling up' of territory is not unique to Nazis, and the US has engaged in its own share of this sort of activity. Manifest Destiny has already been mentioned, but such behaviour, many people argue, continues today whenever the US attempts to expand its military sphere of influence overseas. In another sense, the economic nature of America is unstoppable in its capitalist drive to open up and exploit new markets for the consumption of American products and culture. Even when it is not literally gobbling up territory, then, the US is gobbling up new markets and opening them up to capitalist exploitation.

In *Avatar*, it is most obviously the humans who are intent on gobbling up the planet of Pandora in order to exploit its resources. The whole purpose of their mission is to mine unobtainium and bring it back to Earth as a solution to a global energy crisis. In this sense, it is the villains in the film who resemble the Nazis and their aggressive, militaristic desire to open up *Lebensraum*. However, the noble Na'vi are also quite insistent that the entire planet of Pandora is theirs, and it is precisely because they refuse to negotiate or to compromise with the humans that they come into inevitable territorial conflict with the invaders. From the perspective of the humans, this need not be a zero-sum game since all that they desire is the unobtainium. They neither need nor desire to occupy any territory. From the perspective of the Na'vi, however, this is a zero-sum game since to them the conflict is about living space and not about unobtainium at all. Once their dominion over the planet is threatened, they must gobble back up all of the things they have lost; like the Germans after WWI. This is why they are eager to fight, kill and, as will be observed in regard to the next principle, expel the outsiders.

> Principle #8: We shall spew out evil since the urge to purge is nature's way of healing. (Gonen 2000: 172)

The most horrendous atrocities in Nazi Germany occurred as a result of the government's concerted, organised and wilful attempt to 'spew out' those people who were identified as poisonous to the national blood. In nature, those organisms that are unfit to survive perish. Since the Nazis believed Jews, Slavs, homosexuals, the mentally retarded and the physically deformed to be unfit, they must, by the law of nature, be eliminated. Such subhumans were a threat to the purity of the Aryan race, and were thus thought to be evil. Only by purifying the species could the race heal and reclaim dominion over the world. This was nature's way.

Nazi doctrines about race were influenced both by mystics like Madame Blavatsky and by Charles Darwin's scientific theories of evolution (Shirer

1960). These influences, however, were not isolated to Germany. They had an impact worldwide. The US actually began instituting eugenics laws before Nazi Germany, and it was only in 1979 that all of these laws were repealed (Rogers 2009). The Nazis studied and emulated American policies concerning eugenics, racial segregation and the destruction of Native American tribes. In the US, until the repeal of Jim Crow laws in 1964, black Americans were considered inferior to white Americans, and thus needed to be kept separate so as to avoid contamination. The visual differences between the races were thought to be an indication of the fact that nature intended for blacks and whites to remain segregated. Any mixing of blood was thought to contaminate the white-skinned offspring, and thus the 'one drop rule' was followed. Anyone with even a trace of black ancestry was, and still is, considered to be 'black'. Though the US never went to the extremes of the Nazis to purge the 'evil' of those thought to be inferior to whites, it is clear that there was, and still is to some degree, a sense in which Americans think it natural for those who are different from the white majority to be isolated and separated so as to retain some strange sort of biological and cultural health. The 'urge to purge' remains.

In *Avatar*, this urge is clearly present in the Na'vi. At the end of the film, they quite literally expel the humans from Pandora, only allowing those who have magically taken on a Na'vi body to remain. The expulsion of the human invaders is depicted as the first step toward healing the planet, which has been violated and damaged by the outsiders. The natural environment of the planet, furthermore, makes it impossible for non-natives to survive and prosper on Pandora in the long run, and so the presence of outsiders is something that cannot naturally be sustained. Nature dictates that the physically fragile, and morally wicked, human race must leave. It must be 'spewed out' and purged so that the planet and its rightful inhabitants may regain dominion.

Principle #9: Sacrifice is the best investment. (Gonen 2000: 173)

Connected with all of the previous principles is the idea that the individual should be prepared and eager to sacrifice him or herself for the overall well-being of the nation. In Nazi Germany, such sacrifice was expected of both men and women. Men were required to contribute their skills to the Reich in industry, warfare, art and business. Ultimately, all men were expected to be willing to sacrifice their lives in the defence of Germany. Women were expected to contribute by bearing pure-blooded children, whether they were married or not. In the infamous *Lebensborn* program, women were even encouraged to mate with members of the SS in order to produce Aryan babies and then to hand them over to SS families once the children were born. Sacrifice was the name of the game for both men and women under the Nazis. As organs in the collective body, individuals contributed what they could so that the national organism would continue to function properly. The individual was merely part of a larger whole, and the more that individuals were willing to sacrifice for the benefit of the whole, the more secure their investment in the future became.

Americans admire sacrifice, but they do not expect it. Rather than the individual existing for the state, in the US, it is the state that is thought to exist for the benefit of citizens. Americans conceive of themselves as living in a melting pot rather than functioning as organs within a national body. Individuality is valued to the point that we sometimes even admire the most anti-government of types. Many American national heroes are rebels who have resisted going along with the collective in order to pursue their own personal interests. On the other hand, Americans also bestow a great deal of reverence upon those who willingly sacrifice their own well-being for what they see as a good cause. Just one example is Pat Tillman, who after 9/11 gave up a spot playing football in the NFL in order to join the army and fight in Afghanistan, where he was killed. Americans almost universally admire Tillman for his voluntary sacrifice; even those who otherwise did not support the war. Whereas the Nazis expected everyone to sacrifice themselves for the good of the nation, Americans admire those who voluntarily sacrifice themselves so that the rest of the population doesn't have to.

Like the Nazis, the Na'vi consider all members of their tribe to be integral parts of a larger organism. The individual is a functioning part of the tribe, and the tribe itself is a part of the planet. Each organism is instinctually inclined to sacrifice him or herself for the well-being of the whole. We see this dramatised during the war between the humans and the Na'vi when not only do the members of the various Na'vi tribes willingly sacrifice their lives as they fight against the invaders, but so do all of the animals on the planet. All persons and animals are depicted as sharing a mystical bond that leads them to feel one another's pain and to feel compelled to come to one another's aid when threatened. The sacrifice of each individual is an investment in the long-term health of Pandora.

Clearly, there is a profound resonance between each and every one of Gonen's nine principles of Nazi fascism and the world view of the Na'vi. In fascist cultures, the people unite behind a supreme leader who channels the magical energy of the collective will-to-power in order to fight internal and external enemies. These enemies are thought to be especially dangerous because they threaten the purity of the race or national character. Members of the community, thus, are moved to sacrifice themselves for the good of the collective, and in so doing they ensure the success of their people, securing living space and expelling or exterminating the evil, contaminating forces. This world view describes not only the perspective of Nazis and fascists in general; it is also an accurate summary of the situation facing the Na'vi as depicted, and valorised, by James Cameron in *Avatar*.

CONCLUSION

Does the similarity between the names of the heroic Na'vi tribe and the nefarious Nazi movement somehow reveal James Cameron's recognition of the robust overlap between the world views of these two cultures? It is no secret that fascism and Nazism still possess a strong psychological fascination, if not an outright attraction, for many people today. This allure extends beyond the realm of fringe political movements and racist subcultures into mainstream media and society. In her essay titled 'Fascinating Fascism', Susan Sontag suggests that this magnetism is the result of the fact that fascism is theatrical, dramatic and, above all, erotic (Sontag 1975: 13). In our examination of Gonen's nine principles, we have seen that the erotic allure of fascism is not necessarily related to any sort of overt sexuality, but rather to a widespread erotic desire on the part of people to bond with others in order to merge into a larger unity, and thus to overcome distressing feelings of alienation, fragmentation and nihilism. Freud described this psychological tendency as indicative of 'Eros' or the 'life instinct', and he distinguished it from 'Thanatos', or the death instinct (Freud 1990). It is ironic that this libidinal drive toward life would also ultimately culminate in the death of the self under fascism. But while fascists threaten the integrity and autonomy of the individual, they also offer a solution to loneliness and the despair of nihilism. For some people this may be a tempting trade-off.

Perhaps by depicting an idealised, alien fascist culture and stripping it of all negative historical baggage, Cameron has been successful in tapping a deep well of fascist sympathy in American culture. As we have seen, although American values diverge in some ways from those of fascist cultures, there are still many principles of fascism that resonate with the US population, and indeed with all people. Perhaps in the present historical period of change and uncertainty, as the phenomenon of nihilism makes one of its recurrent appearances on our cultural scene, Americans are especially susceptible to the lures of fascist thinking.

CNN reports that there have been over 1,000 posts on an *Avatar* fan site from people who describe falling into a state of depression and suicidal thinking after seeing *Avatar* (Piazza 2010). The reasons given for the onset of these dark thoughts have to do with a realisation that our real-life Earth in no way matches up to the beautiful cinematic images of Pandora. Interesting is the fact that these feelings of depression occur when viewers leave the cinema, not when they are actually viewing the movie. When viewing the movie, they report feeling happy. It seems that temporary immersion in the idyllic setting of Pandora, where all living creatures share a mystical interconnectedness, is the perfect antidote to our everyday world where people are disconnected, alienated and cut off from nature. Of course, this is what fascism was designed for. It binds people together into a unity so that no one is ever alone, everyone always has a purpose and people always know who the enemy is.

NOTES

1. Cameron is, obviously, not completely against technology. His movies are among the most technologically advanced films ever made. In an interview with David Chen, Cameron says, 'For me, technology in and of itself is not evil, but there is great potential for evil in the human misapplication of technology . . . I'm not trying to make people feel guilty. I just want them to internalize a sense of respect and sense of taking responsibility for the stewardship of the earth . . . and I think this film can do that by creating an emotional reaction' (Chen 2009).
2. This is given dramatic illustration by the proposed 'thirty point program for the National Reich Church' authored by Alfred Rosenberg under Adolf Hitler's Nazi government. Among the provisions were the following: '5. The National Church is determined to exterminate irrevocably . . . the strange and foreign Christian faiths imported into Germany in the ill-omened year 800. 13. The National Church demands immediate cessation of the publishing and dissemination of the Bible in Germany. 19. On the altars there must be nothing but *Mein Kampf* (to the German nation and therefore God the most sacred book) and to the left of the altar a sword. 30. On the day of its foundation, the Christian Cross must be removed from all churches, cathedrals and chapels . . . and it must be superseded by the only unconquerable symbol, the swastika' (Shirer 1960: 240).
3. Mussolini was less literal when it came to the idea of race. 'Race: it is a feeling and not a reality' (Mussolini 1932: n. 19).

CHAPTER 9

Yukio Mishima and the Return to the Body

Figure 9.1 Yukio Mishima (Ken Ogata) commits seppuku in *Mishima: A Life in Four Chapters* (1985).

INTRODUCTION

Yukio Mishima was a controversial Japanese author who, in 1970, disembowelled himself in an act of ritual seppuku. A self-avowed nihilist,
Mishima devoted his career to finding a cure for his own lifelong spiritual
alienation through an eccentric assortment of activities, including: writing,
bodybuilding, political action, and an antiquarian return to Emperor worship
and samurai ideals. Through the integration of art and life, he sought to transcend the decadence of his cultural inheritance, purifying and finally perfecting himself with a heroic death. In Mishima's life, work and death we find

dramatic examples of the creative potential, as well as the dangerous temptations, involved in the struggle to overcome nihilism.

Part of Mishima's wide, international appeal came from his eagerness to embrace popular culture – including film – as a vehicle for the propagation of his own ideas and personality. In addition to writing for the stage, TV and movies, Mishima acted in a handful of productions, and also acted, directed and produced the short film *Patriotism* (1966), which was adapted from one of his own short stories. In Japan, many of his works have been made into movies, and in 1976, his novel *The Sailor Who Fell From Grace With the Sea* was produced in the UK as a major motion picture starring Kris Kristofferson. In 1985, Paul Schrader directed *Mishima: A Life in Four Chapters*, in which portions of Mishima's fictional and non-fictional works were dramatised in order to tell the story of the author's life and extraordinary death.

The case of Yukio Mishima offers a unique opportunity to scrutinise the complicated operations of nihilism on at least three interrelated levels of analysis.

First of all, as he advocated and strove toward the unification of 'action and art' (Mishima 1982: 50), Mishima's involvement with literature, film, the stage and TV highlights and dramatises the obscure gap always lurking between representations and the reality they purport to depict. Mishima's art was never mere entertainment, but always evocative of the deeper existential struggles and issues with which he himself was engaged. This inevitably leads us to ask, 'How close do we get to the "real" Yukio Mishima through his works, including the films that his writings inspired?' We sense that there is an important relationship between the 'real' Mishima and the words on the page or the images on the screen, but we also feel that such representations inevitably fall short of depicting the full nature of this Truth. We feel that these artefacts must somehow represent Mishima and his ideas about the world, but just how well or how poorly do they do so? In the case of an artist like Mishima, this always remains a question, and as a result the ontological dimension of nihilism chronically and insistently intrudes upon our experience of the various works with which his name is associated.

Secondly, as Mishima was himself a nihilist, there is a further, ideological level to the literature and films with which he shares a connection. These works tell us something about how the man thought, reasoned and felt, and so the content (no less than the form) of these works encourages us to meditate on the actual, conceptual dynamics of nihilistic alienation and despair. In this, we are plunged into the philosophy of nihilism and the desire for its overcoming. As we follow along with its logic, we potentially come closer to a concrete understanding of how Mishima himself may have reasoned through the choices that ultimately led him to his unique end.

Third, and finally, in encouraging audiences to think through Mishima's step-by-step march toward perfected oblivion, his writings and the films with which he is associated offer cautionary examples of the potentially poisonous results that might occur as a consequence of being swept up in the enthusiasm to defeat nihilism. While Mishima's suicide can be seen as the culmination of his life project – the final step in his unification of 'action and art' – it is also the case that it was this very act that brought his creative life to a close forever. In eradicating the nihilistic gap between his real life and the ideal for which he longed, Mishima also decisively obliterated his future potential. If the truly interesting part of human existence rests not in the successful achievement of our final goals, but in the process of ongoing, creative struggle, then we might question Mishima's suicidal desire to overcome nihilism. Perhaps a life of unresolved contradictions, failed aspirations and ongoing struggle has its advantages over a life in which success is connected to finality and the closing off of possibility. Maybe, indeed, nihilism is something that we should not seek to overcome.

In what follows, I shall address these three interrelated themes as I explore the life, work and philosophy of Yukio Mishima. The thrust of my argument will be toward the conclusion that the most interesting and profound properties of Mishima's thought, his writings and of the films associated with his thought and writings, are those that leave us with a sense of the open-ended and ambiguous struggle involved in Mishima's efforts to define himself. It is this 'in-between' area of creativity that makes Mishima's nihilism interesting; not his premature and impatient desire to overcome his nihilistic despair. In this, I shall be critical of Mishima for too eagerly pursuing a resolution to the problem of nihilism and consequently of diminishing the profound depth that is potentially found in one's struggle with – rather than one's overcoming of – the void. The case of Mishima illustrates how in the overcoming of nihilism, spiritual peace and union with Being are prizes won at the cost of ongoing activity, struggle and creative aspiration. My contention is that these prizes are not necessarily worth the costs, since defeating nihilism entails the commission of either literal or metaphorical suicide.

BOUND TOWARD MISHIMA

Kimitake Hiraoka was born in 1925. He adopted the pen name Yukio Mishima at the age of sixteen when his story *The Forest in Full Bloom* appeared in the literary magazine *Bungei Bunka* (*Literary Culture*), a publication inspired by the right-wing nationalism of the Japanese Romantic School. The name Yukio Mishima was created by the editors of the magazine who regularly met at an inn near the town of Shuzenji. To get there from Tokyo, a transfer was required in the town of Mishima. The word 'yuki' means 'bound toward', and so Yukio Mishima literally means 'bound toward Mishima' (Inose 2012: 91). This turns out to be a fitting name for an author who would self-consciously spend his entire life working toward the formation of a unique identity for himself. In a way, he was 'bound toward Mishima' up until the moment he died on 25 November 1970.

While initially expressing confusion as to why his story was to be published under a pseudonym, Mishima was also apparently relieved, as his father was not at all supportive of his son's literary aspirations. The adoption of this pseudonym, then, offered one of the first screens, or masks, behind which he might hide. Already, at the age of sixteen, the young Mishima was becoming accustomed to splitting and segmenting his identity, alienating one part of himself – and of his life – from another.

Previous to the adoption of this pen name, Mishima had already experienced an unusual degree of alienation in his family life. As a sickly and frail young boy it was thought that he needed to be protected from physical hardship. Consequently, in a perverse attempt to shelter him from the dangers of the 'real' world, until the age of twelve Mishima was separated from his mother and father and lived instead with his grandmother, who demanded that her grandson refrain from physical exercise or sports, avoid contact with other children, and spend most of his time indoors attending to her needs. He lived in this unnatural manner, apart from his family and the world outside of his grandmother's supervision, for years until finally his grandmother became so incapacitated that Mishima's parents took their son back into their own home and care.

His return home to live with his family was marked, portentously, by the commencement of hostilities between Japan and its neighbours, ultimately leading to the country's involvement in World War II. Mishima attended school and continued writing throughout these war years, publishing his first book, a collection of stories, in 1944. His father, who remained hostile to his son's literary pursuits, told Mishima at the celebration dinner for the book's publication that he shouldn't get too excited about his accomplishment since, 'You'll soon be dead anyway' (Flanagan 2014: 72). The conviction at the time was that all young Japanese males would inevitably die either in battle or as a result of Allied bombing raids. Despite this expectation, Mishima survived the war. Ironically, his frail constitution seems to have saved his life. Because of his fragility and poor health, he was never inducted into the armed forces, and though he worked in the wartime factories, he escaped falling victim to the Allied bombardments.

The end of the war arrived for Mishima, when he was twenty years old, not as a relief, but as yet another challenging transition. He had become accustomed to living with the assumption that he was fated to die young, but with the war over, that assumption appeared to be faulty. Here, once again, it seems that Mishima experienced a jarring incongruity between his expectations and reality. On the one hand, his own consciousness had been formed and given shape against a backdrop of looming oblivion. On the other, he was now thrust into a world where that backdrop had been torn away. The world failed to deliver on what he had anticipated was his destiny, and now in the post-war world he was set free to pursue an unknown future in a defeated country that was becoming increasingly westernised.

Under the Allied conquest of Japan, the Emperor was forced to renounce his divinity, the Japanese military was dismantled, and traditional Japanese cultural institutions were subject to control, suppression and censorship. The nationalist literary movement of which Mishima had been a part predictably fell out of favour, and so his past writing efforts, the basis of his identity as Yukio Mishima, became anachronistic; part of a defeated and disgraced past. Thus, at twenty years old Mishima found himself yet again thrust into a hostile and unfamiliar world. Both his psychological and his literary personae were out of place in this post-war environment, and so if he was to survive as a writer he would have to enact yet another shift in self-conception.

CONFESSIONS OF A MASK

This shift came with the publication of his powerful and disturbing novel *Confessions of a Mask* in 1949. As Roy Starrs writes, 'In a single stroke, the wartime romantic had turned himself into a post-war realist' (Starrs 1994: 30). Considered to be the first (and some say the best) of Mishima's major works, *Confessions* has consistently been interpreted by critics as an essentially autobiographical account of Mishima's own struggles with his sexual identity beginning from birth and moving into young adulthood. It is often concluded on this basis that what we find in *Confessions* is as close as we ever come to encountering the genuine man, raw and honest in the revelation of his true inner desires, thoughts and feelings. Consequently, critics regularly rely on *Confessions* as if it gives us a clear window into Mishima's 'real' self. Henry Scott-Stokes 'relies heavily' on it as a 'single source' for the author's early life (Scott-Stokes 1974: 56). Marguerite Yourcenar likewise treats it as a reliable source for details about the 'traumatic episodes' in Mishima's childhood (Yourcenar 1987: 5). In the BBC documentary titled *The Strange Case of Yukio Mishima*, the narrator, John Hurt, reads passages from *Confessions* as if they are facts of Mishima's biography that are not taken from a novel.

This way of approaching *Confessions of a Mask* is dramatically illustrated by Paul Schrader's *Mishima: A Life in Four Chapters*. In this film, Mishima's childhood is visually depicted in black and white; a technique used throughout the rest of the movie to highlight episodes that are supposed to be biographical rather than fictional. In the film's first 'chapter', 'Beauty', we see the young Mishima with his grandmother; his first instance of masturbation while gazing at a portrait of St Sebastian pierced by arrows; and also his military physical examination. The words that act as narration in these scenes come from *Confessions*, and the use of black-and-white photography serves to compartmentalise and to set them apart from the scenes drawn from Mishima's other literary works, suggesting that what we are seeing here is different, and somehow more real than the novelistic fantasies constructed in books like *Temple of the Golden Pavilion*, *Kyoko's House*, or *Runaway Horses*. In these other 'chapters' of the film, the dramatised episodes are presented in colour and with staging that highlights their non-reality. Titles intrude at the beginning of each chapter to remind us of the particular book that acts as source material and its publication date. The scenes are enacted on literal stages. This is not so with the scenes featuring narration from *Confessions of a Mask*, however. The lack of titles or of artificial staging, along with the black-and-white photography, work together to produce a feeling of documentary verisimilitude that is absent from most of the other parts of the film (except for the framing scenes depicting Mishima's final day). Schrader's stylistic choices, thus, serve to mark the material from *Confessions* as different – indeed more biographically veridical – than the material drawn from Mishima's other novels.

Perhaps the recurrent inclination to read *Confessions of a Mask* as presenting a more 'real' Mishima than do his other works is a consequence of the unflattering subject matter that the book contains. There is nothing heroic in *Confessions*. Instead, the main character is presented as despairing, self-loathing and pitiable. The assumption that many readers, critics and interpreters may understandably form is that since the book is written in the first person, and since it reveals such a convincing and yet unflattering portrait of the inner thoughts of the main protagonist, what is revealed here must be true. After all, who would falsely 'confess' to having sado-masochistic, homosexual and cannibalistic desires? Couple this with the fact that in a later, more clearly autobiographical work like *Sun and Steel*, Mishima refers to some of the same facts about his childhood as appear in *Confessions*, and it may be tempting to draw the conclusion that this latter book really is a literal memoir of Mishima's life, rather than a work of fiction that merely takes *inspiration* from, and only dimly reflects, his childhood feelings and experiences.

But the conventional readings of *Confessions* underestimate how much of the book really is a self-conscious, yet incomplete, attempt by Mishima to refashion his literary persona in accordance with Japan's changing cultural zeitgeist. With increasing westernisation, popular tastes in Japan turned away from the old romanticism and moved toward the more modern form of psychological and existential soul-searching popular in post-war European literature. Mishima's book was clearly intended to fit in with this trend; a fact that he himself later comments on in *Sun and Steel*:

> The literary works written or put before the public around that time were dominated by night thoughts – though their night was far less aesthetic than mine. To be really respected at that time, moreover, one's darkness had to be rich and cloying, not thin. Even the rich honeyed night in which I myself wallowed in my boyhood seemed to them, apparently, very thin stuff indeed. (Mishima 1982: 21)

As confirmation that his book did, in fact, fit in with the spirit of the times, shortly after its publication, six of Japan's top writers and critics selected *Confessions of a Mask* as one of the year's top three novels (Inose 2012: 177).

While *Confessions of a Mask* does indeed take the form of a sort of Augustinian confession of 'sins', it also clearly (as the very title suggests) concerns the narrator's adoption of various concealing 'masks', none of which ever perfectly fit him comfortably or correctly. In this regard, Naoki Inose and Hiroaki Sato have suggested that the 'perversions' confessed in this story might perhaps themselves serve as masking cover for deeper, unstated and more painful issues in Mishima's real life; like his unrequited love for Mitani Kuniko (Inose 2012: 178–88). If this is the case, then surely it complicates the widespread penchant for reading the book as a literal documentary account of Mishima's own life. If in focusing on the narrator's sexual fetishism and sado-masochism Mishima is really engaging in a conscious act of distraction from his own preoccupations, then it may be a mistake to think that we come anywhere close to finding the 'real' Mishima in *Confessions*. Perhaps the most that we can determine is that the author is someone with something to hide; and that what he has to hide is, to him, far more psychologically threatening than sado-masochistic homosexuality.

Indeed, there is something tremendously frightening, yet unstated, at work in this novel. Behind the narrator's admissions to perverse feelings and thoughts, one finds consistent, terrifying inner confusion, self-deception and a general sense of meaninglessness:

> it was not my maturity but my sense of uneasiness, my uncertainty, that was forcing me to gain control over my consciousness. Because such consciousness was simply a stepping stone to aberration, and my present thinking was nothing but uncertain and haphazard guesswork. (Mishima 1958: 104)

Everything the narrator 'confesses' is, he tells us, merely a 'stepping stone', 'uncertain' and 'haphazard'. The voice in *Confessions*, it seems, is a voice of confusion. It is the voice of someone who does not really know who he is, but who feels pushed this way and that, haphazardly, by drives and forces beyond his own control. I don't believe that there is any comfortably clear or unambiguous diagnosis that we can reach either about the narrator or about Mishima's 'true' self from this book precisely because the story's protagonist has no 'true' self at all. And this seems to be the novel's unspeakable message: the self is an illusion. There is no such thing as the 'real' you.

The character in this book just is the series of 'masks' presented outwardly to the public. These masks find continuity with one another only because they are connected by an unfolding project 'bound toward' an uncertain fate, not by some underlying, pre-existent essence. This shadowy, amorphous and far-off destiny can only become solidified, taking on a finalised shape, with the narrator's own extinction when there is no longer any future potential to be realised. 'It was in death', he thus writes, 'that I had discovered my real "life's aim"' (Mishima 1958: 183). Death is his aim precisely because death signals the end of life, and it is only with the end of a life that the multitude of masks and identities accumulated over the course of one's existence can be totalled up once and for all. The construction of an identity is an ongoing process for which death supplies the conclusion. Therefore, so long as one lives there is no 'true' self that is set, stable and unchanging. At any point in time, a person's identity is merely another creative facade conjured through artistry with words, images and appearances. This is part of a line of reasoning that Mishima struggles to articulate in *Confessions;* a line of reasoning that becomes increasingly more lucid in his later works.

In *Confessions*, readers are introduced to the narrator's embryonic awareness that the ongoing development of his 'self' is characterised by a hopelessly strained relationship between the 'real' and the 'ideal'. Reminiscent of Plato's claim that the physical world is simultaneously a conduit as well as an impediment to the attainment of the highest ideals, the narrator of this story starts to understand that his existence as a body both allows him the opportunity to conceive of a perfected self while also holding back and frustrating his non-physical aspiration toward the absolute. This awareness becomes manifest through the narrator's self-loathing, which is prompted by the tension between his own sexual arousal by men's brutalised bodies and his non-sexual, platonic love for the pure spirit of Satoko, a woman. These incongruous inclinations cannot be reconciled with one another, and yet they are descriptive of how the character actually experiences life and comes to conceive of himself. As a maturing bodily organism caught in the grip of incongruous longings for sexual passion, on the one hand, and longings for purity and spiritual perfection, on the other, the narrator is a vessel of unease and distress. He needs the body in order to actually exist, and yet it is the body's finitude that separates him from infinite purity. The only resolution to this conflict would be, on the one hand, to abandon the aspiration toward the absolute, or, on the other, to destroy the finite body. Later, in writings like *The Temple of the Golden Pavilion*, *Runaway Horses*, as well as in both the short story and film *Patriotism*, it is the destruction of the body that accomplishes a final overcoming of this ontological incongruity. In Mishima's own life, it was his ritual seppuku that achieved the same goal. But in *Confessions*, there is no such resolution. In this work, the narrator's experience serves only to indicate the fundamental, problem of human existence: that the construction of the self is a process in which embodied minds struggle, strive and suffer toward the realisation of ultimately unrealisable ideals.

This is why *Confessions of a Mask* is merely a beginning rather than an end in itself. It marks Mishima's first clear statement of his personal nihilism, marking a step in the construction of a philosophy that will allow him to make sense of who he is by discovering what he is not. He is not any one of the time and space bound 'masks' that serve to sum up his identity to the outside world. Those are merely finite conduits for the expression of his creative energies, and thus each of them is, in the end, an imperfect expressive failure. Only the infinity of nothingness is perfect and absolute, summing up all contradictions. And while creativity thrives in the pursuit of this nothingness, it would also die if this nothingness were to be successfully achieved. Completed perfection implies the end of creative struggle, and thus realisation of a final and fixed identity would also be accompanied by the extinction of the generative, striving self.

THE TEMPLE OF THE GOLDEN PAVILION

This nihilistic theme becomes more clearly developed in the book that many critics consider Mishima's true masterpiece: *The Temple of the Golden Pavilion*. This story concerns a Japanese college student named Mizoguchi who serves as an acolyte at a Zen Buddhist temple in Kyoto during and shortly after World War II. Mizoguchi is a stutterer; a disability that – like the sado-masochistic homosexuality of the character in *Confessions* – is symbolic of his separation from the world around him. He is preoccupied with the incongruity that exists between his own inner, subjective experiences, and the world that exists beyond his subjectivity. He is alienated from everything and everyone outside of himself, feeling alone and misunderstood until he becomes friends with Kashiwagi, a club-footed student who attends the same college. Mizoguchi's friendship with Kashiwagi pushes Mizoguchi to confront his own alienation and finally to overcome it through an act of destruction: the torching of the Temple of the Golden Pavilion.

The Temple of the Golden Pavilion represents the impossibility of all abstract notions of idealised perfection. When Mizoguchi was a child, his father described the Golden Temple to him as the most beautiful thing on earth. This description, which resides only in the mind, set a criterion against which the actual, concrete temple was doomed to fall short once Mizoguchi was finally to see it in actuality:

> 'Well what do you think?' said Father. 'It's beautiful isn't it?' . . .
> I changed my angle of vision a few times and bent my head in various directions. But the temple aroused no emotions within me. It was merely a small, dark, old, three-storied building. The phoenix on top of the roof looked like a crow that had alighted there for a rest. Not only did the building not strike me as beautiful, but I even had a sense of disharmony and restlessness. Could beauty, I wondered, be as unbeautiful a thing as this? (Mishima 1959: 24–5)

His disappointment with the appearance of the actual temple provokes a desire to explore further, to look harder and to expend more effort in order to discover what he had missed. Mizoguchi is not satisfied with only the ideal of perfection; he wants to see that ideal reflected in the world of objective reality. His frustration with this quest comes to an end only when he discovers the logic of destruction and nothingness.

The beauty of the Golden Temple rests in its lifelessness. Living things, like humans, cannot truly be beautiful since they lack the quality of being eternal and 'rigid'. Beauty is infinite, and so nothing finite can be absolutely beautiful. The Temple, then, is only beautiful to the degree that it exemplifies a timeless ideal. Yet, the materials out of which the Temple was constructed are subject to decay. These physical materials – the timbers and the gold foil, the nails and the planks – provide a medium through which the eternal may speak, but they also hold back the infinite by binding it to something that is itself finite. This is the source of Mizoguchi's disappointment upon first seeing the Golden Temple, and he comes to realise that it is only through destruction of the physical manifestation of the Temple that its essence can be liberated and finally achieve immortality.

In *Sun and Steel*, Mishima explicitly applauds the kind of nihilism that Nietzsche called 'active nihilism', which strikes out at the void in order to create, destroy and act. The character Mizoguchi is an exemplar of just this sort of nihilistic impulse. Unlike the narrator in *Confessions*, who passively acquiesces to the fractured condition of reality, Mizoguchi strives to resolve the problem through action. Since the ideal of infinite Beauty trapped within the finitude of the Temple's actual structure contributes to an unacceptable 'uneasiness', it becomes clear to him that this offence against true Beauty can only be resolved by reducing the physical manifestation of the Temple to nothing. In the destruction of the physical Temple, he hopes to eradicate the real, concrete barrier that separates him from participation in the infinite. As Mizoguchi himself reasons, 'The beauty of the individual detail is always filled with uneasiness. It dreamed of perfection, but it knew no completion and was invariably lured to the next beauty, the unknown beauty . . . Nothingness was the very structure of this beauty' (Mishima 1959: 255).

The 'nothingness' that is the real structure of Beauty is the only principle capable of synthesising the 'struggles and the contradictions and the disharmonies' (Mishima 1959: 254) found in the actual, physical structure of the Temple, and so in burning down the Temple, its real form may be revealed. This form is the same structure, curiously, that Mizoguchi discovers trapped in a young woman's breast; a fleshy mound whose true beauty resides not in its outer appearance, but its inner darkness. As depicted in Schrader's film, *Mishima: A Life in Four Chapters*, when Mizoguchi first sees this woman's breast, it grows to immense proportions, filling his consciousness and becoming one with the Temple itself. The point here is not that the actual, physical breast or the actual physical Temple are beautiful, but that true Beauty is impossibly large and unitary. It only exists in the mind of the observer, and so is incapable of being corralled or contained by any finite vessel. It is, in other words, not a 'thing' at all, but 'no-thing'. Beauty and nothingness are the same.

It is this last point that seems to escape many of the critics who have addressed *The Temple of the Golden Pavilion*. The key to understanding the philosophical point that Mishima is driving at in this work is to recognise that it is not the actual, physical Temple itself that is beautiful, but the ideal that is made manifest through the physical Temple. It is a mistake to think that the main character destroys the Temple out of a 'hatred of beauty' (Yourcenar 1987: 34). It is quite the opposite. It is the character's love of real, infinite Beauty that leads to the destruction of the very thing that falsifies and holds that infinite Beauty in abeyance. Likewise, it is not, as is suggested in Schrader's film, that the 'Temple is *too* beautiful'. Again, it is quite the opposite. The Temple can never be beautiful enough to give perfect expression to real Beauty. The message here is nihilistic: nothing in the actual, physical world is Real, True or Beautiful. The only way to achieve these ideals is to destroy what is actual.

The Temple of the Golden Pavilion was inspired by real historical events, but critics have generally been more attuned to the gap that exists between this story and its historical inspiration than they have been to the gap that exists between the events in *Confessions* and Mishima's real life. Perhaps this is due to the cynical, unimaginative assumption that anyone who would really burn down a national treasure must have been motivated by insanity rather than philosophical purity. Of course, no one really knows what went on inside the mind of Hayashi Shōken, the monk who, in July 1950, actually did burn down the famous Temple of the Golden Pavilion in Kyoto. Nonetheless, it is obviously the case that Mishima's story does not map perfectly onto reality. It is not a mirror of actual events, but a novelistic interpretation intended as a vehicle toward the further explication of his own developing nihilistic philosophy. Damian Flanagan is, in this regard, quite correct when he observes that the book is less about the monk who burned down the Temple than it is about Mishima himself (Flanagan 2014: 138). I would, however, go even further to emphasise that the story is not even really about 'Mishima'. Like *Confessions*, it is a stepping stone, a feeler that is reaching out and attempting to find its way toward an articulation of a philosophy that, while emanating from the author, is still distinct and independent of him. What we find in this book is no more the 'real' Mishima than it is the 'real' Hayashi. It is simply one more step in the direction of a consciously articulated and developed philosophy of nihilism, which, though emanating from the thought processes of a particular flesh-and-blood human being, nevertheless is on the path toward its own growing and independent existence.

In *Sun and Steel* Mishima writes that from the outset he was concerned in his 'literary life with methods for concealing rather than revealing' himself (Mishima 1982: 71). *The Temple of the Golden Pavilion* is one more step in this direction, building upon the nihilistic revelations of *Confessions of a Mask*. The 'true' Mishima is not to be found in either of these stories, expect by way of an uncomfortable void that refuses to be filled by the characters, acts of violence and suffering depicted within their pages. When these stories are translated into images and viewed on the movie screen, as we see in Schrader's *Mishima*, we are pulled even further from the source, and so become ever more removed from the underlying nothingness that grounds and sustains the creative power behind Mishima's life project of identity construction.

THE SAILOR WHO FELL FROM GRACE WITH THE SEA

While Schrader's *Mishima: A Life in Four Chapters* gives cinematic voice to fragments from a variety of Mishima's literary works – including *Confessions of a Mask* and *The Temple of the Golden Pavilion* – interpreting them as keys to understanding the 'real' author, the film adaptation of *The Sailor Who Fell From Grace With the Sea* is a story told independent of the author's life. In this story, nonetheless, we find a further step in the development of Mishima's logic of nihilism, which extends and intensifies the shift toward destructive activity articulated in *The Temple of the Golden Pavilion*.

Mishima's novel, *The Sailor Who Fell From Grace With the Sea*, and its filmic interpretation, are in their details very different from one another, and yet in the general thrust of their narratives, they explore similar territory. The theme that permeates both the novel and the film involves the tragic pursuit of perfection. This, as has already been noted, is the same theme first sketched out in an uncertain and halting fashion in *Confessions*, and then which was more fully developed in *The Temple of the Golden Pavilion*. In *The Sailor Who Fell From Grace With the Sea*, this theme is very explicit, and as in *Temple*, the story articulates an actively nihilistic stance toward the alienated and broken nature of reality. In this tale, it is a group of young, idealistic boys who take violent action in order to repair what they conceive of as the betrayal by a sailor of his own heroic identity. In order to 'rescue' him from this betrayal, the gang of youngsters decide that his body must be destroyed so that his spirit may remain pure. Like Mitsoguchi, they represent the actively violent forces of nihilism that strike out at the concrete world, which always inhibits and holds back the expression of infinity. But unlike in *Temple*, here the violence is directed toward a human body rather than toward an inanimate building. This is an important, but also a dangerous, advance in Mishima's logic. In his quest to think through and solve the problem of nihilism, Mishima moves from lashing out at the non-living world and now begins to consider the implications of lashing out at human beings. After moving from mere confusion to vandalism, his mind now turns to murder as a solution to nihilism.

The infinite is symbolised in this story by the sea. In the novel, the setting is a Japanese seaside town, while in the film the action takes place in a small English fishing village. In both cases, it is the vast, dangerous, dark and looming presence of the ocean that acts as a backdrop; both geographically and conceptually. The physical presence of the ocean waves lends a sense of foreboding while also reminding us of the past history of the main protagonists: a mother and her son who live together in a house overlooking the waters. The man of the house, the owner of an upmarket import business, is now absent, having died young. His absence evokes the aura of death that hangs over the story. Everything that happens seems compromised by a tenuous sense of impermanence and impending ruin, and it is the dark waters of the crashing ocean that keep this thought in the forefront of our minds. The movie itself begins with an extended montage of dark, crashing waves peaking and breaking on the shoreline, thundering with loud and sublime grandeur. These waves rise up out of the abyss, formless and fluid, powerfully overwhelming anything that challenges their might. Like infinite Being itself, which both sustains and destroys the finite objects in our world, the ocean is a vast concretisation of nothingness whose boundaries cannot be contained by the physical bodies of the earth.

In the novel, the central protagonist is a young Japanese boy named Noburo, while in the film the same character is a young English boy named Jonathan (Jonathan Kahn). Early in the story, this young boy discovers a peephole in his bedroom wall that allows him to spy upon his mother in her bedroom. Mishima's book emphasises that Noburo only watches his mother through the peephole on those nights when she has been mean to him, but never after she has been kind. This suggests that there is an aggressive motive behind his voyeurism. He is making his mother into an object; something to be held at a distance and scrutinised dispassionately as if she were a mere thing. Nonetheless, as he watches her masturbating in front of her mirror one night, he senses (as is articulated in the film) something sad in her movements. The sadness here is connected to the absence of her husband. With his death she has become separated from the one she loved, and now her longing is turned in upon itself, bringing, however, no sense of catharsis or satisfaction, but instead a sorrow that Noburo associates with 'emptiness' and 'ugliness'. It is then that he concludes, 'A man isn't tiny or giant enough to defeat anything' (Mishima 1965: 9). Noburo, here, reiterates the sentiments of the narrator in *Confessions*. Humans, he thinks, are powerless to repair the world's damaged nature.

Bodies, both human and non-human, are evocative of the ocean's topography in *The Sailor Who Fell From Grace With the Sea*, and since the ocean is itself a symbol of infinity in this story, it becomes apparent that bodies evoke an awareness of infinity at the same time that they hold the infinite at bay (so to speak), containing it and giving it a concrete form. Thus, his mother's shoulders remind Noburo of the shoreline (Mishima 1965: 7), while the 'zone of black' between her legs makes him think of 'a pitiful vacant little house', and he wonders 'if it has anything to do with the emptiness of his own world' (Mishima 1965: 8). His mother's body is like the ocean: the life it contains exists in a state of tension stretched between form and formlessness. The curve of a shoulder sweeps downward only to disappear into the void of nothingness that describes her reproductive organs. This is like the waves, which peak before melting back into the dark depths out of which all life first emerged. It is as if Noburo somehow understands that he himself was born from that 'zone of black' that is contained within his mother's body, which in turn recalls the sea itself. In this way, we come to entertain thoughts of how in one sense, all bodies are separated from one another while, in another sense, they also are all united insofar as they share a common origin in infinite nothingness.

Both the book and the film focus a great deal of attention on the first act of violence perpetrated by Noburo and his gang of friends against a cat. In this scene, it is the cat's body that acts as a conduit for the infinity symbolised by the ocean. In the book, Noburo smashes the cat against a log, feeling a sense of power in taking the animal's life. 'I killed it all by myself . . . I can do anything, no matter how awful', he thinks (Mishima 1965: 61). This is the first inclination he has of the transformative power of destruction. Instead of feeling impotent and sadly removed from the world, Noburo now feels as if there is some hope for him. He is empowered, and now gripped by a dangerous optimism that he can change the world. Unlike the scene in which he passively observes his mother, separated by the hole in a wall, here he experiences a sense of exhilaration and a confidence that he can immerse himself within the flow of reality to experience a connection with Being itself. This is indicated when the cat, now dead, is dissected by the boys, and within its entrails they find the infinity of the sea:

> The liver, limp beside the corpse, became a soft peninsula, the squashed heart a little sun, the reeled-out bowels a while atoll, and the blood in the belly the tepid waters of a tropical sea. Death had transfigured the kitten into a perfect, autonomous world. (Mishima 1965: 61)

The cat's body is like a microcosm of the universe, reflecting in its details a miniature world filled by the waters of Being. In revealing these details, the gang of children proves that they are capable of potency and action. By violently seizing reality, they force it to open up and reveal its infinite secrets. But this is merely a prelude to bigger things. After having tested themselves on the dissection of an animal, the boys now turn their attention to a human being: a sailor – named Ryuji in the book; Jim (Kris Kristofferson) in the film – who has betrayed the Truth of the sea for a conventional and safe life on land.

Noburo's mother, falls in love with the sailor when his ship docks for repairs in the small village in which they live. When he sets sail, Noburo is gripped by a sense of romantic mystery, imagining this sailor to be a heroic superman who has passed through their lives only to disappear into infinity once again, like some sort of magical and faultless vision. However, when the sailor returns, expressing his desire to marry Noburo's mother and give up his life on the sea, Noburo is devastated. This heroic superman is just a man after all, merely like all other conventional fathers. In this, Noburo and his friends believe that the sailor has not only disappointed them, but that he has betrayed himself and so must be saved from his own decision. Noboru's friend, the Chief, asks him, 'would you like to make the sailor a hero again?' (Mishima 1965: 135). With this, the young group sets out to do with the sailor what they have already done with the cat. They will drug the sailor and then dissect his body, revealing and releasing the infinite ocean that hides trapped inside of his physical shell.

In both the book and the film, the dissection of the sailor is merely hinted at, but Mishima apparently did originally intend to include a description of this violence in the book. His friend, Domoto Masaki, recalls the content of the omitted section:

> The description of the cruel dissection was full of metaphors of glittering oceans and exotic foreign sights, as intoxicating as the stories of Arabian Nights. The pubic hair is seaweed that enwraps a pearl shell, the manroot and glans turn into the minaret and roof of an Islamic mosque and are torn and peeled even as they glitter blindingly in a golden sunset. A perfection by a solemn collapse. (Inose 2012: 502)

And so, within the sailor's body the boys find and reveal the mysteries of the sea and all of the exotic truths that it touches. They have performed their duty, reasserting order in a universe that threatens chaos and nothingness by rescuing the sailor from his impending fall from grace. In this they carry out the only thing that is important in an otherwise empty world: 'to try to maintain order in that emptiness' (Mishima 1965: 162–3). In the film, there is no real intimation of the sailor's last thoughts, but in the book Mishima makes a point of letting readers know that the sailor understands 'the immensity of what he had abandoned', and that he understands how 'Noburo imagined him' (Mishima 1965: 179). As he sits on a hilltop with the young boys who have poisoned him, he slips slowly into dark nothingness, watching his ship sail off into the sea without him. He dies, engulfed in a dream of storms, sharks, the sea and death. We are left with a sense that the sailor may actually appreciate what is happening to him.

What *The Sailor Who Fell From Grace With the Sea* does is to advance Mishima's logic of nihilism in the direction of murder. What started as a confused and despairing sense of alienated separation from the highest ideals becomes transformed here into a course of optimistic action. The message that Mishima has now articulated is that the world can be repaired by violence. But unlike in *The Temple of the Golden Pavilion*, the sort of violence that is really effectual is violence against the only beings who truly can be held responsible for betraying their ideals: human beings. The building in *Temple* was a misguided target it now seems since, not being capable of formulating ambitions of its own, it was never really capable of falling short of its aims. This sort of failure can only happen to beings that long for the concrete manifestation of pure perfection itself. Since it is only humans who are capable of both formulating ideals and recognising their failed realisation of those ideals, they are the ones against whom action is appropriately taken if nihilism is to be overcome. Either their ideals of infinity or their finite existences must be obliterated to alleviate the problem at the core of nihilism.

But there is one last step in this logic, taken when Mishima recognises that it is not other people who are responsible for the production of nihilistic incongruity, but in fact it is he himself who has generated the problem. If this is the case, then the solution to nihilism comes not from wielding violence against others, but in turning it against one's self. This is a step in thinking that Mishima executes both in his literary writings and, ultimately, in the act that brought about the end of his own life.

PATRIOTISM

The story *Patriotism* is inspired by a real-life event from Japanese history. In 1936, factions within the Japanese military came into dispute over strategy and planning. One of these factions – the Kodo-ha – sought to have their rivals – the Tosei-ha – deployed to Manchuria in order to reduce their numbers, and thus their influence, at home. Seeing through the plot, the Tosei-ha assassinated three government officials and occupied Tokyo, declaring their actions in the name of the Emperor. The uprising was, however, condemned by the Emperor and quickly defeated. This became known as the Ni Ni Roku Incident.

Mishima's short story focuses on an army officer, Lieutenant Takeyama, ordered to attack the Tosei-ha rebels, but who, because he sympathises with their aims, instead makes the decision to commit seppuku along with his wife, Reiko. The story deals only with the officer's disembowelment and its preparations, leaving the historical backdrop as a schematic pretence for Mishima to describe the minute and grisly details involved in the lieutenant's suicide. This was, in Mishima's own words, 'the only work which, from start to finish, was born of my own brain and which realized its world through words' (Inose 2012: 371). While the story's setting retains a superficial connection to actual events, the content of what occurs in the pages is more closely related to the author's own obsessions than it is to the historical incidents only dimly lingering in the background. In an interview for a magazine in 1966, Mishima explained that the Ni Ni Roku Incident was 'a big spiritual influence', and that 'My hero worship and feeling of collapse, which I experience now, are both derived from that incident' (Scott-Stokes 1974: 237). The events of his childhood, it appears, lingered with him as he wrote *Patriotism*, and while childhood memories and impressions have a formative power that sets us on a path toward who we become, they also rarely (if ever) accurately reflect the real, objective nature of historical fact. As in *Confessions of a Mask* and *The Temple of the Golden Pavilion*, the historical setting for *Patriotism* thus serves mainly as a pretence to orient Mishima's own thinking in space and time, thus permitting him to operate in a literary world imperfectly reflecting two simultaneous realities: the outer, objective world that shaped the author's psychology and the inner, subjective world of his own ideas. In any event, it is Mishima's own thought process, rather than objective history, that is the real focus of this story. And this thought process is forward-, rather than backward-, looking, advancing the logic of Mishima's solution to nihilism toward its final conclusion.

The historical realities reflected in *Patriotism* are so dim as to be almost imperceptible. The main significance of this simple tale is to offer Mishima an opportunity to work out the logic of suicide and to imagine, in clinical detail, how his own seppuku might be carried out. The officer in the story, in this regard, appears to serve as a stand-in for Mishima's idealised self, and by projecting himself into this role, he begins to rehearse his own heroic demise. After the confused nihilism of *Confessions of a Mask*, and failed attempts to overcome nihilism – through vandalism in *The Temple of the Golden Pavilion*, and through murder in *The Sailor Who Fell From Grace With the Sea* – in *Patriotism* the author seeks to articulate his own vision of a completed, finalised and dignified solution. In an imperfect world, Mishima reasons, the only way to avoid compromising, and thus betraying, one's ideals is to destroy one's own body, the vessel that ties the perfection of conceptual ideals to the finitude of an impermanent, physical world. In working through this process of thought, the author takes a fateful step in the direction of solidifying who he is to become and how he is to be remembered. He moves further down the road toward becoming who we now think of when we hear the name 'Yukio Mishima'.

Patriotism reads like the author's not so tender fantasy, and indeed, in 1966, when Mishima produced and directed a short film version of this story, he cast himself in the role of the lieutenant, taking yet another step toward personally acting out his dream. Both the short story and film are structured around five sections, and although the content of the chapters in the story and film do not have an exact correspondence, their overall trajectories, as well as many of their details, reflect one another very closely. The tale begins with a prologue enumerating the events to come, indicating that Mishima does not intend this narrative to contain any surprises. It will simply be the story of a couple who together commit heroic suicide so beautiful 'as to make the gods themselves weep' (Mishima 1966: 93). We are told of the purity of their love, the beauty of their bodies and their passionate physical attraction to one another. The perfection of their relationship, along with their utter happiness, is repeatedly emphasised by Mishima, altogether setting a tone that, far from realistic, gives the story a fairytale-like sense of make-believe.

When they learn of the Ni Ni Roku uprising and its defeat, Reiko sees in her husband's face a 'determination to die' (Mishima 1966: 96), and she immediately understands that she must also die. The fascinating thing about both the short story and the film is that there is no psychological complexity or conflict in the thoughts of Reiko or the lieutenant. Their decisions to commit joint suicide are not depicted as involving any sort of inner struggle, but rather as the necessary consequences of the situation in which they find themselves. Everything is dutiful ritual, from the drinking of sake, to bathing, to the final act of lovemaking. All of these acts are performed as if in obedience to a rule of nature that cannot be questioned, begrudged or regretted. In describing their submissive obedience to these rituals, the narrative offers a matter-of-fact description of each minute detail in the procedure leading up to the bloody conclusion. Everything appears to unfold according to an inner logic that the two protagonists both clearly understand and are compelled to see through. We, as readers and audience members, also understand the direction this must all go, as in the prologue to both the story and the film the entire narrative has already been summarised. This foreknowledge gives the tale a sense of inevitability, and if there was any exercise of what appeared to be 'free choice' on the parts of the characters, it would no doubt feel to us as if an absurdity had been committed; as if the chain of logical necessity had been violated.

Both Keiko and Lt Takeyama experience the rebellion and its denunciation by the Emperor as the trigger propelling them toward suicide. But while there is a sense of betrayal on their part, this feeling is not the focus of the story. The incident itself is treated as part of the world's facticity; something that has occurred but that cannot be changed. All that the couple can do is to carry out their own obligations, which first consist of lingering gratefully on thoughts of Beauty, Love, Happiness and Fidelity. In this regard, Keiko sorts through a collection of china animal figurines, recalling a time when she 'genuinely loved these things . . . Now she merely loved the memory of having once loved them' (Mishima 1966: 97). When the lieutenant arrives home, he is mesmerised by Kieko's loyalty, as well as her physical beauty, rejoicing that he will never see her 'crumble in death' (Mishima 1966: 105). This is because Keiko, in the one departure from ritual, will die only after watching her husband disembowel himself. The lieutenant scrutinises Kieko's 'face minutely, with the eyes of a traveler bidding farewell to splendid vistas which he will never revisit' (Mishima 1966: 103). Husband and wife make love, staring adoringly at the details of each others' bodies and then they write their last words. All of this is carried out in the presence of a banner hanging on the wall of their apartment bearing the Chinese characters for 'sincerity' or 'fidelity', highlighting the ideal at the centre of this story. There is no irony, no cynicism, no anger here. These characters are driven by an earnest commitment to an ideal that their world will not allow to exist.

And so they kill themselves. While the film version of the story goes quite far in depicting the consequences of disembowelment by showing the lieutenant's intestines spilling out of his belly, it in no way matches the ghastliness of Mishima's original description:

By the time the lieutenant had at last drawn the sword across to the right side of his stomach, the blade was already cutting shallow and had revealed its naked tip, slippery with blood and grease. But suddenly stricken by a fit of vomiting, the lieutenant cried out hoarsely. The vomiting made the fierce pain fiercer still, and the stomach, which had thus far remained firm and compact, now abruptly heaved, opening wide its wound, and the entrails burst through, as if the wound too were vomiting. Seemingly ignorant of their master's suffering, the entrails gave an impression of robust health and almost disagreeable vitality as they slipped smoothly out and spilled over into the crotch. (Mishima 1966: 115)

'Was this seppuku?' (Mishima 1966: 113), the lieutenant thinks as he draws the sword across his belly. The question is really Mishima's, who in his detailed description is clearly fascinated by the simple mechanics of the act. Indeed, in writing this story and then playing the lieutenant's part on film, Mishima performs a dress rehearsal for his own real, final performance. Having failed to die in World War II, and having failed in changing the world around him, through words, into one of perfected Beauty, Mishima now imagines that in seppuku, he has discovered 'a death of no less degree and quality than death on the front line' (Mishima 1966: 111). His search for the absolute comes to its conclusion when he discovers that all of his highest ideals were hopelessly unattainable precisely because of the finite constraints of the body. In returning to the body, and then destroying it, Mishima releases the infinite within. This brings his nihilistic logic to its completion.

Keiko follows her husband in death, stabbing herself in the neck and falling, drenched in blood, upon her dead husband's corpse:

> When she thought how the pain which had previously opened such a gulf between herself and her dying husband was now to become a part of her own experience, she saw before her only the joy of herself entering a realm her husband had already made his own . . . Reiko sensed that at last she would be able to taste the true bitterness and sweetness of the great moral principle in which her husband believed. (Mishima 1966: 117)

Keiko's suicide brings the story to a close, but her role in the narrative also introduces a difficultly for Mishima's logic. The lieutenant's seppuku requires an eyewitness in order for its nature to be grasped, appreciated, and for its full Beauty to be realised. The ritual needs to be seen from the outside and its memory preserved from the perspective of a consciousness that can behold its entire, 'beautiful' arc. The problem with any deed ending in death is that the actor in such a drama can never appreciate the whole performance, since its conclusion entails the actor's own non-existence. It is Keiko's responsibility, thus, to play the part of an observer to the lieutenant's act, and this is why she must die only after he has disembowelled himself. Yet Keiko herself will also die as part of the ritual, and so the memory of her husband's suicide will still be lost when she expires. Additionally, she herself has no witness. In order for her own suicide to attain the same aesthetic fullness as her husband's death, and for the entire ritual to survive as an idea, she also would need someone to observe the process – including her own suicide – from beginning to end. Perhaps it is those who discover the lovers' corpses, or even the readers of the story, who Mishima intends as these third-party witnesses. Nevertheless, even those potential onlookers must themselves eventually die, leaving us on the

Figure 9.2 Lt Takeyama (Yukio Mishima) commits seppuku in *Patriotism* (1966).

horns of a nihilistic dilemma: if everyone dies, the memories evaporate; but if even one spectator remains, those idealised memories continue to be tainted by the finitude of physical embodiment.

Patriotism describes the process of turning destructive, nihilistic energies inwards, against one's own body, instead of directing them outwards against the bodies of others. It is a story of active nihilism; but unlike the active nihilism of *The Temple of the Golden Pavilion* or of *Sailor Who Fell From Grace With the Sea*, what occurs here is not depicted as at all perverse, wicked or aberrant. Instead, the active urge for destruction here realises its appropriate terminus by being aimed toward its correct target: the self who is the origin of superlative ideals. Both the vandalism perpetrated by Mizoguchi (in *Temple*) and the murder carried out by Norburo (in *Sailor*) ultimately had to fail in their aims insofar as they left untouched the true source of nihilistic despair and discontent, which is the incongruity spawned by the characters' own frustrated idealism. In *Patriotism*, on the other hand, Lieutenant Takeyama and Reiko correctly turn their energies inward, toward the destruction of the self who generates the very ideals that are in conflict with actual reality. In this, they succeed in their rebellion against the order of things, dismantling the gap that separates the real from the ideal at its birthplace. As a consequence, the gruesome suicides described in this tale are depicted as positive acts leading toward personal purification and perfection. In suicide, there is the dissolution of the finite, physical tether holding the characters to the fallen and defective state of existence that separates them from their highest ideals. Therefore, what is imagined here does not culminate in despair, but represents an optimistic shift in the direction of completion and excellence. In fact, Mishima writes, 'This is neither a comedy nor a tragedy but simply a story of happiness' (Scott-Stokes 1974: 234). In particular, the happiness expressed in *Patriotism* is the happiness that comes from no longer being tied to a world that chafes against one's own infinite aspirations.

The only remaining problem concerns the witness. In order for nihilistic suicide to be successful, and for nihilism to be overcome, there must remain an awareness keeping alive the ideals to which the finite body has been sacrificed. In this perfect 'super consciousness', the ideal becomes solidified, whole and immutable. It becomes an eternal form, as Plato had imagined. But in order for this kind of ideal to be conceived, the conscious witness must remain disembodied, for if it does possess a body, that would perpetuate the incongruity spawning the problem of nihilism all over again. While being hinted at in *Patriotism*, this final conundrum in Mishima's logic never seems to have fully been worked out, but it was a theme he returns to once again in his final work, *The Sea of Fertility Tetralogy*, completed on the day he himself committed suicide before the watchful eyes of some of his own students.

THE SEA OF FERTILITY

Mishima's life came to an end on 25 November 1970 after he and four students from his private army, the Tatenokai, barricaded themselves in the office of General Mashida, commander of the Eastern Army. Mishima read a manifesto to the troops assembled outside the office, hoping to rouse them to revolution. They were not at all moved, and he was driven back into the General's office by their jeers. Inside, he sat on the floor and committed seppuku, drawing his short sword left to right across his belly:

> The wound Mishima made by disembowelment started 1.6 inches below his navel, 5.5 inches long from left to right, and 1.6 to 2 inches deep. Twenty inches of his intestines came out. (Inose 2012: 729)

Naoki Inose, the vice governor of Tokyo, declares, 'It was a magnificent seppuku' (Inose 2012: 729). The actual details of the ritual, however, were botched, failing to embody the sort of perfect ideal that Mishima had earlier imagined in his story *Patriotism*. For one thing, his student Morita, who had been tasked with beheading Mishima, missed his mark, wounding his mentor in the back, intensifying and prolonging Mishima's suffering. Another student, Furu-Koga, stepped in to decapitate Mishima with one stroke, and then also decapitated Morita, who had botched his own disembowelment. The serene joy and perfection that Mishima had imagined in his literary fantasy, thus, appears not to have been reflected in the actual flesh and blood suicide.

On the morning of his death Mishima left the final volume of *The Sea of Fertility Tetralogy* with his maid, giving instructions for its delivery to the publisher. This final volume was the culmination of a four-book cycle of novels consisting of *Spring Snow*, *Runaway Horses*, *The Temple of Dawn* and *The Decay of the Angel*. This series tells the story of the (apparent) reincarnation of a single soul in four different people who are fated to die tragic, youthful deaths. The various incarnations of this soul are witnessed by Honda, a Japanese lawyer who is the story's central character.

Honda is the embodiment of the witness, in some ways repeating the role played by Keiko in *Patriotism*. As the one whose duty it is to behold the beautifully tragic ends of the young men and the young woman appearing over the course of the cycle, Honda is positioned aesthetically to appreciate the cycles of life and death unfolding before his eyes. In the third novel we learn that Honda has literally developed into a voyeur who not only spies on young lovers at outdoor parks, but also on the female guests at his own home. The scenes of voyeurism in this novel recall scenes from *The Sailor Who Fell From Grace With the Sea*, in which young Noburo watches through a peephole as his mother masturbates and then later has sex with a visiting sailor. In the case of the earlier novel, the boy's youth at least partially excuses his indiscretion, while in this later novel Honda's advanced age merely makes the impropriety seem more perverse and inexcusably aberrant. Regardless of this moral difference, the logic played out in both stories charts a similar, death-bound trajectory. In *The Sailor Who Fell From Grace With the Sea*, the young boy's voyeuristic pleasure leads to the idealisation of the sailor, who must ultimately die so that he does not contravene the image of perfection he inspired in the boy's mind. In *The Temple of Dawn*, Honda similarly comes to the realisation that the pleasure he achieves through voyeurism is related to a desire to disappear completely, to see without being seen, and thus to die to the world around him:

> Honda's ultimate desire, what he really, really wanted to see could exist only in a world where he did not. In order to see what he truly wished to, he must die. When a voyeur recognises that he can realise his ends only by eliminating the basic act of watching, this means his death as such. (Mishima 1973b: 277)

But Honda does not die, and this is what makes him imperfect, ugly and flawed. His role throughout the *Sea of Fertility* is to be the one who remains embedded in the world of physical existence, watching others who are more beautiful and pure than himself shatter into puffs of nothingness.

In his own life, Mishima, in the end, made the decision not to live like Honda, but to follow a destructive path to perfection. This is why in Schrader's film *Mishima: A Life in Four Chapters*, it is suggested that Mishima's true self is most clearly reflected in the young character Isao, who commits seppuku in *Runaway Horses*, the second novel in *The Sea of Fertility Tetraology*. However, I suspect that we also get to see a deep part of Mishima's psychology – one that he was vigorously fighting against – reflected in the character of Honda. While the physically disciplined and ideological Isao perhaps represents the positive ideal that Mishima aspired to, with Honda I think we find the actual reality Mishima feared he was descending into as he grew older; a negative ideal that he wanted to avoid. The descriptions of Honda's perverse lust in *The Temple of Dawn* are very detailed and convincing, leading readers to imagine that the author himself may have been in the grips of precisely these same feelings. The book is filled with detailed, erotic descriptions of young lovers groping at one another lustily, of Honda's voyeuristic joy at watching, through a peephole, as three of his guests engage in a threesome, and of Honda's lascivious responses to the budding sexuality of a young Thai princess. All of this culminates in an extremely graphic description of the Thai princess's lesbian encounter with Keiko, Honda's neighbour, as Honda secretly watches. At the same time that it seems as if Mishima takes a great deal of pleasure in describing these erotic scenarios, there is also an atmosphere of abjection and misery that accompanies them. This wretchedness is connected to the fact that it is through the perspective of Honda, an old man, that we get these accounts. His own aging flesh possesses none of the erotic attraction that he finds in the flesh of those he lusts after, and his voyeurism thus becomes something 'disgusting' and 'repugnant' (Mishima 1974: 271).

Honda's reality, as well as Mishima's, is a wounded one in which pleasure and self-disgust intermingle, opening a gash in the fabric of Being. To look at the suppleness and innocence of youth – to long for it, but to be separated from it by one's own aging body – symbolises the nihilistic fissure characterising all of existence. Our bodies are impermanent but our minds wish for infinity; or as Mishima himself wrote in his final note before committing suicide: 'Human life is limited, but I want to live forever' (Flanagan 2014: 236). It is this nihilistic sentiment that strikes me as the central theme in *The Sea of Fertility*.

Mishima's final work may represent an attempt to steel himself for the fate that awaited upon disembowelment. When facing the finality of death, we could imagine that Mishima's resolve might waver. Why not live a bit longer and write a few more books? Mishima's answer to this seems to be that he does not want to end up like Honda. This one concrete example of a decaying old pervert may have been enough of an aesthetic offence to Mishima that it buttressed his confidence that a beautiful, tragic death was preferable to lingering on into old age as a mere spectator.

CONCLUSION

Mishima's writing, acting, directing, bodybuilding and political activity came to a permanent end with his death. This is an obvious enough observation, but it is worthwhile reinforcing the point in order to draw attention to one of the major consequences implied by his defeat of nihilism. In death, not only did Mishima's body die, but so did his creativity. While it may be the case that his demise evaporated the gap between aspiration and actuality, it also permanently evaporated the potential for the expression of vital, ongoing artistry. In Mishima, Apollo finally triumphed over Dionysus. For the man himself, perhaps the mental and spiritual conviction he achieved was worthwhile, bringing a sense of completion and climax to his life story; a conclusion that helped to shape and make sense of everything he had experienced up to that point. After all, this is why the overcoming of nihilism has consistently been declared a spiritual benefit throughout the history of human thinking. Nihilism undermines the very conditions allowing for confidence, certitude, stability and the achievement of superlative goals, and thus it has – almost without exception – been treated as an unequivocal evil to be overcome and defeated in the name of human success and happiness. In defeating nihilism, it may be that Mishima triumphed over a world that compelled him to pollute his principles.

Indeed, many of us admire Mishima's resolve to die on his own terms in the same way that we admire Socrates' decision to go to his death in defiance of those who would have had him compromise his ideals and beliefs. There is a brave and heroic resolve in these figures who chose to accept the destruction of their own finite bodies in order to guard the integrity of their ideals; ideals, which as it turns out, still survive and influence people today (for better or for worse). Religions and ideologies have been founded on these sorts of sacrifices, offering guidance and comfort to followers. If the point of human existence is final contentment and happiness, then perhaps we need look no further than these sorts of self-confident martyrs for direction on how to live life. All we need to do, perhaps, is to follow the leader.

But this is to overlook the fact that what is really interesting and extraordinary about a man like Mishima (as well as Socrates) is not the conclusions he came to, but the process he went through in order to arrive at those conclusions. Mishima's creative career is a complicated, ambiguous and confused search for identity that started with his early attempts to articulate the distress of the nihilistic experience, and leading through his increasingly focused ideas about how this experience might be overcome. The body of literature, the films and the other artworks he created in the process of thinking through this issue comprise an astounding and sublime record of his spiritual journey and his deep degree of reflection. In fact, Mishima's seppuku itself only becomes really interesting when understood against this background of creative activity. On its own, his suicide is merely a bizarre curiosity. His artwork, however, would still retain its power and importance independent of his strange death; and this precisely because of the way that it authentically struggles to articulate and understand a basic human truth: all humans, even great humans, live in a state of finitude, incompleteness and relative incomprehension. The ongoing aspiration to resolve this state of perplexity is what makes life philosophically full. Once this aspiration is brought to an end – either out of spiritual exhaustion or the premature claim to final wisdom – the philosophical life ceases.

The nihilistic gap existing between the 'real' Mishima and his works is a void that is profound precisely because it can never be filled. It invites an endless stream of interpretation and commentary, and in so doing encourages us to remain philosophically active and lively in our understanding of this great Japanese artist's work, life and death. But there is an omnipresent danger in any encounter with Mishima that also threatens to lead in the opposite direction. Because he was such a skilful artist and powerful spokesperson for issues of universal human significance, we are constantly vulnerable to being seduced by his words, imagery and logic too quickly and thus of too passively following him down a single road of nihilistic logic from which there is no return. In both his literary and cinematic creations, Mishima's idiosyncratic way of leading us through the maze of Truth is at times so intoxicating that we may be tempted to abandon our own critical faculties in order to embrace the aesthetic vision of a man who, in our more sober moments, we must remember was, like the rest of us, trying to resolve his own confused and broken identity.

Mishima's writings, and the films he is associated with, are important as touchstones that remind us of the long, difficult and always unfolding path that leads in the direction of self-understanding. Just as Yukio Mishima was, until the moment of his death, 'bound toward Mishima', so too are the rest of us bound toward our own unique identities. Perfect self-understanding, the kind that requires no further struggle, suffering or effort, is a useful ideal that encourages us to pursue progress in life. But it is, I think, the process of movement itself, rather than actually reaching the final goal that is most important.

Bibliography

Agamben, Giorgio (2002), *Remnants of Auschwitz: The Witness and the Archive*, New York: Zone Books.

Ambrose, Darren (2013), *Film, Nihilism and the Restoration of Belief*, Winchester: Zero Books.

Arendt, Hannah [1950] (1976), *The Origins of Totalitarianism*, New York: Harcourt.

Aristotle [335 BC] (1941), *Poetics*, in Richard McKeon (ed.), *The Basic Works of Aristotle*, New York: Random House, pp. 1455–87.

Armstrong, Karen (2001), *Buddha*, New York: Penguin Books.

Balkind, Nicola (2013), 'Glasgow: Hollywood Film Set', in Nicola Balkind (ed.), *World Film Locations: Glasgow*, Chicago: University of Chicago Press, pp. 92–3.

Beauvoir, Simone de [1949] (1989), *The Second Sex*, H. M. Parshley (trans.), New York: Vintage Books.

Bordo, Susan (1993), *Unbearable Weight: Feminism, Western Culture, and the Body*, Berkeley: University of California Press.

Bordo, Susan (1999), *The Male Body: A New Look at Men in Public and in Private*, New York: Farrar, Straus and Giroux.

Bradshaw, Peter (2010), '*The Human Centipede (First Sequence)*', *The Guardian*, 19 August, <http://www.theguardian.com/film/2010/aug/19/the-human centipede-first-sequence-review> (last accessed 7 December 2014).

Brown, Simon (2011), '"Anywhere but Scotland?" Transnationalism and New Scottish Cinema', *International Journal of Scottish Theatre and Screen*, Vol. 4, No.1, <http://journals.qmu.ac.uk/index.php/IJOSTS/article/view/109> (last accessed 17 January 2014).

Brunner, Elizabeth A (2003), 'Impotence, Nostalgia and Objectification: Patriarchal Visual Rhetoric to Contain Women', *Visual Culture and Gender* Vol. 8, 2003, pp. 28–45.

Buber, Martin [1923] (1999), *I and Thou*, Walter Kaufman (trans.), New York: Book-of-the-Month-Club.

Campbell, Alex (2006), 'The Search for Authenticity: An Exploration of an Online Skinhead Newsgroup', *New Media & Society* 8.2, pp. 269–94.

Campbell, Joseph [1949] (2008), *The Hero With a Thousand Faces*. Novato: New World Library.

Camus, Albert [1942] (1955), 'The Myth of Sisyphus', in *The Myth of Sisyphus and Other Essays*, Justin O'Brien (trans.), New York: Vintage Books, pp. 88–91.

Carr, Karen L. (1992), *The Banalization of Nihilism*, Albany: State University of New York Press.

Carroll, Noël (1990), *The Philosophy of Horror: Or Paradoxes of the Heart*, New York: Routledge.

Carroll, Noël (2003), *Engaging the Moving Image*, New Haven and London: Yale University Press.

Chen, David (2009), 'The/Filmcast Interview: James Cameron, Director of *Avatar*', /*Filmcast*, 18 December, <http://www.slashfilm.com/2009/12/18/the-filmcast-inter view-james-cameron-director-of-avatar/> (last accessed 28 January 2010).

Cho, Stephen Wagner (1995), 'Before Nietzsche: Nihilism as a Critique of German Idealism', *Graduate Faculty Philosophy Journal*, Vol. 18, No. 1, pp. 205–32.

Clark, Cathy (2011), 'Peter Mullan: The Swot Who Lost the Plot', *The Guardian*. Wednesday, 19 January 2011. <http://www.guardian.co.uk/film/2011/jan/19/peter-mullan-neds-interview> (last accessed 19 June 2012).

CNN Politics (2008), 'Obama: New Dog could be "mutt like me"', 7 November, <http:// politicalticker.blogs.cnn.com/2008/11/07/obama-new-dog-could-be-mutt-like-me/> (last accessed 7 November 2008).

Cogan, Brian (2008), *The Encyclopedia of Punk*, New York: Sterling.

Cohen, Stanley [1972] (1980), *Folk Devils and Moral Panics*, New York: St. Martin's.

Cortez, Daniel (2005–9), *Skinhead Revolt*, 4 September 2009,<skinheadrevolt.com>.

Craig, Cairns (1982), 'Myths Against History: Tartantry and Kailyard in 19th-Century Scottish Literature', in *Scotch Reels: Scotland in Cinema and Television*, Colin McArthur (ed.), London: BFI, pp. 7–15.

Derrida, Jacques (1996), *The Gift of Death*, Walter Kaufman (trans.), Chicago: University of Chicago Press.

Ebert, Roger (1996), '*Breaking the Waves*', *Chicago Sun Times,* 29 November 1996. <http:// rogerebert.suntimes.com/apps/pbcs.dll/article?AID=/19961129/REVIEWS/611290302/ 1023> (last accessed 13 June 2012).

Ebert, Roger (2004), '*Night of the Living Dead*', *RogerEbert.com*, 2004. <http://www. rogerebert.com/reviews/the-night-of-the-living-dead-1968>, (last accessed 14 March 2015).

Ebert, Roger (2010), '*The Human Centipede*', <http://www.rogerebert.com/reviews/the-human-centipede-2010> (last accessed 7 December 2104).

Faber, Michel (2000), *Under the Skin*, Orlando: Harvest Books.

Flanagan, Damian (2014), *Yukio Mishima*, London: Reaktion Books.

Franks, Benjamin (2005), 'Demotic Possession: The Hierarchic and Anarchic in *The Wicker Man*', in *Constructing the Wicker Man: Film and Cultural Studies Perspectives*, Jonathan Murray, Lesley Stevenson, Stephen Harper and Benjamin Franks (eds), Glasgow: University of Glasgow, Crichton Publications, pp. 63–77.

Freud, Sigmund [1930] (1961), *Civilization and Its Discontents*, James Strachey (trans. and ed.), New York: W. W. Norton & Company.

Freud, Sigmund [1920] (1990), *Beyond the Pleasure Principle*, James Strachey (trans.) New York: W. W. Norton.

Gillespie, Michael Allen (1995), *Nihilism Before Nietzsche*, Chicago: University of Chicago Press.

Gonen, Jay (2000), *The Roots of Nazi Psychology*, Lexington: University Press of Kentucky.

Goode, Ian (2007), 'Different Trajectories: Europe and Scotland in Recent Scottish Cinema', *PORTAL Journal of Multidisciplinary International Studies*, Vol. 4, No. 2, July 2007. <http://epress.lib.uts.edu.au/journals/index.php/portal/article/view/420/448> (last accessed 30 July 2012).

Goudsblom, Johan (1980), *Nihilism and Culture*, Lanham, MD: Rowman & Littlefield.

Hardy, Forsyth (1990), *Scotland in Film*, Edinburgh: Edinburgh University Press.

Harrison, William (1975), *Rollerball Murder*, New York: Warner Books.

Hebdige, Dick [1979] (1981), *Subculture: The Meaning of Style*, New York: Methuen.

Hegel, G. W. F. [1807] (1977), *Phenomenology of Spirit*, A. V. Miller (trans.), Oxford: Oxford University Press.

Heidegger, Martin (1991), *Nietzsche: Volumes Three and Four*, David Farrell Krell (ed.), San Francisco: HarperSanFrancisco.

Heidegger, Martin (1993a), 'The Origin of the Work of Art', in David Farrell Krell (ed.), *Martin Heidegger: Basic Writings*, San Francisco: HarperCollins, pp. 139–206.

Heidegger, Martin (1993b), 'Building Dwelling Thinking', in David Farrell Krell (ed.), *Martin Heidegger: Basic Writings*, San Francisco: HarperCollins, pp. 343–63.

Heidegger, Martin [1927] (1996), *Being and Time*, Joan Stambaugh (trans.), Albany: State University of New York Press.

Hibbs, Thomas S. [1999] (2012), *Shows About Nothing: Nihilism in Popular Culture*, Waco: Baylor University Press.

Hitler, Adolf [1925] (1971), *Mein Kampf*, Ralph Manheim (trans.), Boston: Houghton Mifflin.

Hunter, Stephen (1998), 'History X: Hate With a Passion', *Washington Post*, 30 October 1998, <www.washingtonpost.com/wpsrv/style/longterm/movies/videos/americanhistoryxhunter.htm>, (last accessed 3 May 2006).

Hubert, Henri and Mauss, Marcel [1964] (1981), *Sacrifice: Its Nature and Function*, W. D. Halls (trans.), Chicago: University of Chicago Press.

Indie London (2010), '*The Human Centipede*: Tom Six Interview', <http://www.indielondon.co.uk/Film-Review/the-human-centipede-tom-six interview> (last accessed 7 December 2014).

Inose, Naoki and Hiroaki Sato (2012), *Persona: A Biography of Yukio Mishima*, Berkeley: Stone Bridge Press.

Kant, Immanuel [1781] (1965), *Critique of Pure Reason*, Norman Kemp Smith (trans.), New York: St. Martin's Press.

Kaplan, E. Ann (1983), *Women and Film: Both Sides of the Camera*, New York: Routledge.

Keenan, Dennis King (2005), *The Question of Sacrifice*, Bloomington and Indianapolis: Indiana University Press.

Khan, Huma (2010), 'The Politics of "Avatar:" Conservatives Attack Film's Political Message', *abcnews.go.com*, 6 January, <http://abcnews.go.com/Politics/politics-avatar-conservatives-attack-movies-political-messaging/story?id=9484885> (last accessed 28 January 2010).

Knight, Nick (1982), *Skinhead*, London: Omnibus.

Kristeva, Julia (1982), *Powers of Horror: An Essay on Abjection*, Leon S. Roudiez (trans.), New York: Columbia University Press.

Lyotard, Jean-Francios [1979] (1997), *The Postmodern Condition: A Report on Knowledge*, Geoff Bennington and Brian Massumi (trans.), Minneapolis: University of Minnesota Press.

McArthur, Colin (1982), 'Scotland and Cinema: The Iniquity of the Fathers', in Colin McArthur (ed.), *Scotch Reels: Scotland in Cinema and Television*, London: BFI, pp. 40–69.

Marmysz, John (2003), *Laughing at Nothing: Humor as a Response to Nihilism*, Albany: State University of New York Press.

Marshall, George (1994), *Spirit of '69: A Skinhead Bible*, Lockerbie: STP Publishing.

Marshall, George (2003), *Skinhead Nation*, <http://web.archive.org/web/20040131091612/http://skinheadnation.com/>, (last accessed 4 September 2009).

Martin-Jones, David (2010), *Scotland: Global Cinema*, Edinburgh: Edinburgh University Press.

Mishima, Yukio (1958), *Confessions of a Mask*, Meredith Weatherby (trans.), New York: New Directions.

Mishima, Yukio (1959), *The Temple of the Golden Pavilion*, Ivan Morris (trans.), New York: Perigee Books.

Mishima, Yukio (1965), *The Sailor Who Fell From Grace With the Sea*, John Nathan (trans.), New York: Perigee Books.

Mishima, Yukio (1966), *Death in Midsummer and Other Stories*, New York: New Directions.

Mishima, Yukio (1972), *Spring Snow*, Michael Gallagher (trans.), New York: Washington Square Press.

Mishima, Yukio (1973a), *Runaway Horses*, Michael Gallagher (trans.), New York: Washington Square Press.

Mishima, Yukio (1973b), *The Temple of Dawn*, E. Dale Saunders and Cecilia Segawa Seigle (eds), New York: Washington Square Press.

Mishima, Yukio (1974), *The Decay of the Angel*, Edward G. Seidensticker (trans.), New York: Washington Square Press.

Mishima, Yukio (1982), *Sun and Steel*, John Bester (trans.) Tokyo: Kodansha International.

Moreall, John (1983), *Taking Laughter Seriously*, Albany: State University of New York Press.

Mullan, Peter (2011), 'Peter Mullan and the true story behind Neds – Video', *The Guardian*, Wednesday, 19 January 2011, <http://www.guardian.co.uk/film/video/2011/jan/19/peter-mullan-neds-interview-real%20(accessed%206/19/12)> (last accessed 30 July 2012).

Mulvey, Laura (2009), 'Visual Pleasure and Narrative Cinema', in *Film Theory and Criticism: Introductory Readings*, Leo Braudy and Marshall Cohen (eds), New York: Oxford University Press, pp. 711–22.

Mussolini, Benito (1932), 'The Doctrine of Fascism', *World Future Fund*, <http://www.worldfuturefund.org/wffmaster/Reading/Germany/mussolini.htm> (last accessed 8 January 2017).

Neely, Sarah (2008), 'Contemporary Scottish Cinema', in Neil Blain and David Hutchison (eds), *The Media in Scotland*, Edinburgh: Edinburgh University Press, pp. 151–65.

Nenon, Thomas (2010), 'Immanuel Kant's Turn to Transcendental Philosophy', in Thomas Nenon (ed.), *The History of Continental Philosophy: Volume 1*, Chicago: University of Chicago Press, pp. 15–47.

Nietzsche, Friedrich (1968a), *The Will to Power*, Walter Kaufman and R. J. Hollingdale (trans.), New York: Vintage Books.

Nietzsche, Friedrich [1886] (1968b), *Beyond Good and Evil*, in *Basic Writings of Nietzsche*, Walter Kaufman (trans.), New York: The Modern Library, pp. 181–331.

Nietzsche, Friedrich [1887] (1968c), *Genealogy of Morals*, in *Basic Writings of Nietzsche*, Walter Kaufman (trans.), New York: Vintage Books, pp. 439–599.

Nietzsche, Friedrich [1872] (1968d), *The Birth of Tragedy*, in *Basic Writings of Nietzsche*, Walter Kaufmann (trans.), New York: Modern Library, pp. 3–144.

Nietzsche, Friedrich [1882] (1974), *The Gay Science*, Walter Kaufman (trans.), New York: Vintage Books.

Nietzsche, Friedrich [1883–1891] (1976a), *Thus Spoke Zarathustra*, in *The Portable Nietzsche*, Walter Kaufman (trans.), New York: Penguin Books, pp. 103–439.

Nietzsche, Friedrich [1889] (1976b), *Twilight of the Idols*, in *The Portable Nietzsche*, Walter Kaufman (trans.), New York: Penguin Books, pp. 463–564.

Nietzsche, Friedrich [1895] (1976c) *The Antichrist* in *The Portable Nietzsche*, Walter Kaufman (trans.), New York: Penguin Books, pp. 565–656.

Nietzsche, Friedrich [1874] (1988), 'On the Uses and Disadvantages of History for Life', in *Untimely Meditations*, R. J. Hollingdale (trans.), Cambridge: Cambridge University Press, pp. 57–123.

Novak, Michael (1970), *The Experience of Nothingness*, New York: Harper Torchbooks.

Oria Gomez, Beatriz (2008), 'Imagining Scotland: Local Hero (1983) and Kailyardism', *Barcelona English Language and Literature Studies*, No. 17, Autumn, <http://www.publicacions.ub.edu/revistes/bells17/>, (last accessed 18 January 2014).

Palahniuk, Chuck (1996), *Fight Club*, New York: Owl Books.

Petrie, Duncan (2000), *Screening Scotland*, London: BFI.

Piazza, Jo (2010), 'Audiences experience "Avatar" blues', CNN.com, 11 January 2010, <http://www.cnn.com/2010/SHOWBIZ/Movies/01/11/avatar.movies.blues/index.html> (last accessed 28 January 2010).

Plato (1997a), *Apology*, in *Plato: Complete Works*, John M. Cooper (ed.), Indianapolis: Hackett Publishing Company, pp. 17–36.

Plato (1997b), *Republic*, in *Plato: Complete Works*, John M. Cooper (ed.), Indianapolis: Hackett Publishing Company, pp. 971–1223.

Plato (1997c), *Phaedo*, in *Plato: Complete Works*, John M. Cooper (ed.), Indianapolis: Hackett Publishing Company, pp. 49–100.

Rancid (1994), 'The Ballad of Jimmy and Johnny', *Let's Go*, Epitaph.

Reich, Wilhelm (1946), *The Mass Psychology of Fascism*, Theodore P. Wolfe (ed.), New York: Orgone Institute Press.

Rogers, Kara (2009), 'Beyond Darwin: Eugenics, Social Darwinism, and the Social Theory of the Natural Selection of Humans', 9 February, <http://www.britannica.com/blogs/2009/02/beyond-darwin-eugenics-social-darwinism-and-the-social-theory-of-the-natural-selection-of-humans/> (last accessed 28 January 2010).

Romero, George (1979a), 'George Romero: Cinema's Dark Dreamer Steps into the Light', *Questar*, number 4, August.

Romero, George (1979b), Personal correspondence.

Romero, George (2008), 'For the Record: The Making of Diary of the Dead', (DVD).

Rorty, Richard (1989), *Contingency, Irony and Solidarity*, Cambridge: Cambridge University Press.

Samuels, Stuart (1983), *Midnight Movies*, New York: Collier Books.

Sartre, Jean-Paul [1943] (1992), *Being and Nothingness*, Hazel Barnes (trans.), New York: Washington Square Press.

Schatz, Thomas (2004), *Hollywood: Crit Concepts V4*, New York: Routledge.

Schorer, Mark (1968), 'The Necessity of Myth', in Henry Murray (ed.), *Myth and Mythmaking*, Boston: Beacon Press, pp. 354–8.

Scott-Stokes, Henry (1974), *The Life and Death of Yukio Mishima*, New York: Dell Publishing.

Shirer, William (1960), *The Rise and Fall of the Third Reich*, New York: Simon and Schuster.

Slocombe, Will (2006), *Nihilism and the Sublime Postmodern*, New York & London: Routledge.

Sontag, Susan (1975), 'Fascinating Fascism', *The New York Review of Books*, Vol. 22, No. 1, 6 February, <http://www.nybooks.com/articles/9280> (last accessed 28 January 2010).

Starrs, Roy (1994), *Deadly Dialectics: Sex, Violence and Nihilism in the World of Yukio Mishima*, Honolulu: University of Hawaii Press.

Stoehr, Kevin L. (2006), *Nihilism in Film and Television: A Critical Overview from Citizen Kane to The Sopranos*, Jefferson, NC: McFarland and Company.

Street, Sarah (2009), 'New Scottish Cinema as Trans-national Cinema', in Jonathan Murray,

Fidelma Farley and Rod Stoneman (eds), *Scottish Cinema Now*, Newcastle: Cambridge Scholars, pp. 139–52.

Tasker, Yvonne (1993), *Spectacular Bodies: Gender, Genre and the Action Cinema*, New York: Routledge.

Van Gogh, Vincent (1886), *A Pair of Shoes* [oil on canvas] held at Van Gogh Museum, Amsterdam.

Williams, Linda (1999), *Hardcore: Power, Pleasure, and the Frenzy of the Visible*, Berkeley: University of California Press.

Wood, Robert (2006), *Straightedge Youth: Complexities and Contradictions of a Subculture*, Syracuse, NY: Syracuse University Press.

Yancy, George (2008), *Black Bodies, White Gazes: The Continuing Significance of Race.* Lanham, MD: Rowman & Littlefield.

Yourcenar, Marguerite (1987), *Mishima: A Vision of the Void*, Alberto Manguel (trans.), Toronto: Collins Publishers.

Filmography

16 Years of Alcohol (UK, Richard Jobson, 2003)
American History X (US, Tony Kaye, 1998)
Avatar (US, James Cameron, 2009)
Basketball Diaries, The (US, Scott Kalvert, 1995)
Believer, The (US, Henry Beam, 2001)
Braveheart (US, Mel Gibson, 1995)
Breaking the Waves (Denmark, Lars von Trier, 1996)
Brigadoon (US, Vincent Minnelli, 1954)
Cloud Atlas (US, Lana Wachowski, and Tom Tykwer and Andy Wachowski, 2013)
Crying Game, The (US, Neil Jordan, 1992)
Dark Knight Rises, The (US, Christopher Nolan, 2012)
Dawn of the Dead (US, George Romero, 1978)
Day of the Dead (US, George Romero, 1985)
Diary of the Dead (US, George Romero, 2007)
Eyes Wide Shut (US, Stanley Kubrick, 1999)
Fight Club (US, David Fincher, 1999)
Flight 93 (US, Peter Markle, 2006)
Green Room, The (US, Jeremy Saulnier, 2015)
Harry Potter (US, Chris Columbus, 2001)
House of Mirth, The (UK, Terence Davies, 2000)
Human Centipede, The (First Sequence) (US, Tom Six, 2009)
Human Centipede II, The (Full Sequence) (Australia, Tom Six, 2011)
Human Centipede III, The (Final Sequence) (Netherlands, Tom Six, 2015)
Imperium (US, Daniel Ragussis, 2016)
Land of the Dead (US, George Romero, 2005)
Local Hero (UK, Bill Forsyth, 1983)
Lord of the Rings, The (New Zealand/US, Peter Jackson, 2001)
Made in Britain (UK, Alan Clarke, 1982)
Meantime (UK, Mike Leigh, 1984)
Mishima: A Life in Four Chapters (US/Japan, Paul Schrader, 1985)
Natural Born Killers (US, Oliver Stone, 1994)
NEDs (UK, Peter Mullan, 2010)
Night of the Living Dead (US, George Romero, 1968)

No Skin Off My Ass (US, Bruce La Bruce, 1991)
Nymphomaniac: Vol. I (US, Lars von Trier, 2013)
Nymphomaniac: Vol. II (US, Lars von Trier, 2013)
Pariah (US, Randolph Kret, 1998)
Patriotism (Japan, Yukio Mishima and Masaki Domoto, 1966)
Perfect Sense (UK, David Mackenzie, 2011)
Prometheus (US, Ridley Scott, 2012)
Ratcatcher (UK, Lynne Ramsay, 1999)
Rob Roy (US, Michael Caton-Jones, 1995)
Rollerball (US, Norman Jewison, 1975)
Rollerball (US, John McTiernan, 2002)
Romper Stomper (Australia, Geoffrey Wright, 1992)
Sailor Who Fell From Grace With the Sea, The (UK, Lewis John Carlino, 1976)
Simpsons, The (TV Show, US, James Brooks, 1989–)
Skinheads: The Second Coming of Hate (US, Greydon Clark, 1989)
Small Faces (UK, Gillies Mackinnon, 1996)
Star Wars (US, George Lucas, 1977)
Survival of the Dead (US, George Romero, 2009)
This is England (UK, Shane Meadows, 2006)
Trainspotting (UK, Danny Boyle, 1996)
Under the Skin (UK, Jonathan Glazer, 2013)
Videodrome (US, David Cronenberg, 1983)
Wicker Man, The (UK, Robin Hardy, 1973)
World War Z (US, Marc Forster, 2013)

Index